VOICES and VISIONS

VOICES and VISIONS

Essays on
New Orleans's
Literary History

Edited by Nancy Dixon
and Leslie Petty

University Press of Mississippi / Jackson

The University Press of Mississippi is the scholarly publishing agency of the Mississippi Institutions of Higher Learning: Alcorn State University, Delta State University, Jackson State University, Mississippi State University, Mississippi University for Women, Mississippi Valley State University, University of Mississippi, and University of Southern Mississippi.

www.upress.state.ms.us

The University Press of Mississippi is a member of the Association of University Presses.

Any discriminatory or derogatory language or hate speech regarding race, ethnicity, religion, sex, gender, class, national origin, age, or disability that has been retained or appears in elided form is in no way an endorsement of the use of such language outside a scholarly context.

Copyright © 2025 by University Press of Mississippi
All rights reserved
Manufactured in the United States of America
∞

Library of Congress Cataloging-in-Publication Data

Names: Dixon, Nancy, 1955– editor. | Petty, Leslie, 1970– editor.
Title: Voices and visions : essays on New Orleans's literary history / edited by Nancy Dixon and Leslie Petty.
Description: Jackson : University Press of Mississippi, 2025. | Includes bibliographical references and index.
Identifiers: LCCN 2024043599 (print) | LCCN 2024043600 (ebook) | ISBN 9781496853639 (hardback) | ISBN 9781496853646 (trade paperback) | ISBN 9781496853653 (epub) | ISBN 9781496853660 (epub) | ISBN 9781496853677 (pdf) | ISBN 9781496853684 (pdf)
Subjects: LCSH: American literature—Louisiana—New Orleans—History and criticism. | New Orleans (La.)—Intellectual life. | New Orleans (La.)—In literature. | LCGFT: Essays.
Classification: LCC PS267.N49 V65 2025 (print) | LCC PS267.N49 (ebook) | DDC 810.9/976335—dc23
LC record available at https://lccn.loc.gov/2024043599
LC ebook record available at https://lccn.loc.gov/2024043600

British Library Cataloging-in-Publication Data available

CONTENTS

Introduction 3
Nancy Dixon and Leslie Petty

PART 1: PROSE

1. *Blake* in the Crescent City
   Martin R. Delany Reimagines Antebellum Radicalism 13
   Paul Fess

2. Moral Contagion
   Yellow Fever and the Moral Character of New Orleans 38
   Kathleen Downes

3. "The Voice of the Sea"
   The Specter of Transatlantic Slavery in *The Awakening* 56
   Carina Evans Hoffpauir

4. "Moving from the Inside Out"
   Malwida von Meysenbug and the Portrayal of a New Feminine
   Experience in *The Awakening* 72
   Heidi Podlasli-Labrenz

5. "The Unjust Spirit of Caste" in Charles W. Chesnutt's
   and George Washington Cable's New Orleans Novels 90
   Matthew Teutsch

6. More than One City of New Orleans
   Eudora Welty and Zora Neale Hurston's Crescent City 105
   Ruth R. Caillouet

7. New Orleans in Walker Percy's Works
   Place, Placement, Nonplacement, and Misplacement 119
   Edward J. Dupuy

PART 2: POETRY

8. *Les Cenelles* and Censorship 137
   Nancy Dixon

9. (Re)mapping the Colonial City
   Joy Harjo's Composite Poetic in "New Orleans" 146
   Tierney S. Powell

10. A Cabdriver Sings the Blues
    Mem Shannon's Articulation of Urban Life and Working-Class
    Resistance in Late Twentieth-Century New Orleans 160
    Marcus Charles Tribbett

11. Slave-Bricked Streets and Women's Work
    The Practiced Place of Brenda Marie Osbey's New Orleans 180
    Shari Evans

12. Demythologizing the New Orleans "Octoroon"
    Natasha Trethewey's *Bellocq's Ophelia* 198
    Mary C. Carruth

13. "Because We Need to Hurt in Public"
    Embodying the Spectacle of Hurricane Katrina's Black Suffering in
    Patricia Smith's *Blood Dazzler* 213
    Shanna M. Salinas

About the Contributors 231

Index 235

VOICES and VISIONS

INTRODUCTION

Nancy Dixon and Leslie Petty

This collection of essays began as a call for papers for the American Literature Association Symposium, "The City in American Literature," which was held at the Hotel Monteleone in New Orleans. While the symposium theme was broad, the submissions—and thus the final program—were heavily weighted towards literature of and about the American South, and in particular, New Orleans. This concentration is perhaps not surprising, given the destination of the conference. Location, however, cannot solely account for this evidence of an enduring scholarly preoccupation with New Orleans. The city was, after all, built on the kind of contradictions that animate academic discourse. Tennessee Williams understood the two sides of the French Quarter, with St. Louis Cathedral looming large over the city center, while hookers, drag queens, and "big-ass beers" crowd the streets. In fact, he said that such contradictions provided the creative tension necessary for his writing. So it seems only apt that the majority of the essays we received focus on New Orleans, a Catholic town whose slogan reads: *Laissez les bon temps rouler!* Nonetheless, the city's liberal attitude cannot mask its darker side, and scholarly interest has always focused on the enduring dissonances of the city's more complex and often unappealing reality: slavery and its legacy, race and racial oppression, and sexism, all of which were laid bare in the twenty-first century by the devastating flood following Hurricane Katrina, a storm that also shed light on the economic and geographical fragility of the city and state.

In recent years, however, scholars have expanded the questions they are asking about not only the history of New Orleans, but its literary and cultural representations as well. New inquiries into transatlantic connections, as well as the inclusion of marginalized voices and experiences that do not fit neatly into the binary of white and Black have begun to animate scholarly conversations across disciplines, causing reassessments of canonical texts and bringing new texts to the fore. *Voices and Visions: Essays on New Orleans's Literary History* builds on this growing body of scholarship that treats the city in this global, heterogeneous context. Expanding the conversation begun in recent works of history such as *Louisiana: Crossroads of the Atlantic World* (2014), *Hispanic and Latino New Orleans: Immigration and Identity since the Eighteenth Century* (2015), *New Orleans & the World, 1718–2018* (2018), this collection turns its focus specifically to literary representations of the city, its place (local, national and international), and its people (Creole, Cajun, Indigenous, white, Black, Latino, Asian). Our aim is to be both comprehensive and diverse in this collection, which spans over two hundred years and includes canonical, contemporary, and experimental writers. Placing this wide array of voices in conversation demonstrates the myriad ways New Orleans's storied past has affected its present day as seen in over two centuries of writing. The thirteen essays, organized generically and chronologically, treat enduring themes—race, gender, religion, disease, art—but do so in the context of emerging conversations: New Orleans as part of the Global South and the Black diaspora, the transformation of New Orleans after Hurricane Katrina, and the recovery of previously lost voices, including those of Native Americans and immigrants, the legacy of pandemics and racial violence that in more recent years has been manifest in the COVID-19 outbreak and the Black Lives Matter movement.

Perhaps not surprisingly, one of the dominant themes here is the transatlantic slave trade and its presence (or its present absence) for those writing in or about New Orleans. The "Prose" section of the volume begins with Paul Fess's essay on Martin R. Delany's antebellum novel about a fugitive slave hero, *Blake; or the Huts of America* (1859). Fess points out that, although New Orleans only makes a brief appearance in the novel, its influence looms large. Not only does it exist as an "unfree" place where "quotidian and revolutionary struggles for freedom" nevertheless take place, but it also becomes the point of connection between the American slave trade and the "circum-Caribbean world" that Blake (and by extension, Delany) hopes to revolutionize. Thus, Fess argues, Delany resituates New Orleans in an international context, not only as a significant site of enslavement but also as a seat from which to launch a global resistance. Like Fess, Kathleen Downes is interested in the imprint slavery and racism made on antebellum and reconstruction New Orleans. For Downes, however, racial oppression is one of a litany of vices that are imaginatively connected to the yellow fever epidemic in this global, cosmopolitan city. Downes situates the German immigrant Baron Ludwig von Reizenstein's *The Mysteries of New Orleans* (1854), originally written in German and published in *Louisiana Staats-Zeitung*, alongside two novels written by native-born Americans: George Washington Cable's *The Grandissimes* (1880) and M. E. M. Davis's *The Queen's Garden* (1900). Because the source of yellow fever was unknown until around 1900, Downes argues that it serves in these novels as a "floating signifier" to critique the city's moral and social ills. In other words, the writers posit that, at least metaphorically speaking, immorality—in the various forms of xenophobia, racial oppression, sexual licentiousness, and aristocratic callousness—figures as the "source" of yellow fever. In each case, this "moral contagion" means that the "city is doomed" unless its inhabitants are willing to eradicate its festering abuses.

Two essays in this collection analyze perhaps the best-known novel about nineteenth-century New Orleans, Kate Chopin's *The Awakening* (1899); each helps us see the novel in new ways by reading it alongside twenty-first century music and German literature respectively. Carina Evans Hoffpauir draws an intriguing comparison between the video for Beyoncé's song, "Formation," with its "call to action for Gulf Coast black women" and the end of *The Awakening*, when Edna swims into the sea. Hoffpauir observes that in each case, it is difficult to tell if the female's submersion in water is "re-birthing or drowning self-sacrifice." The comparison underscores Hoffpauir's larger point: the troubling paradox that Chopin's novel presents a serene racial hierarchy that belies the intense racial tension of 1890s Louisiana even as it simultaneously employs the tropes of bondage and human property to represent Edna's "soul slavery" and her quest for freedom. Such a construction, Hoffpauir argues, emphasizes sexist oppression experienced by white women while it erases altogether the prejudice and bigotry faced by women of color.

Heidi Podlasli-Labrenz also analyzes *The Awakening* in a comparative way, demonstrating that the German writer, Malwida von Meysenbug, as well as Kate Chopin's own experiences in Germany and throughout Europe, inspired the American writer to depict heroines who roam the streets of New Orleans, most notably, Edna Pontellier. Podlasli-Labrenz notes that the freedom to "move around alone within and from city to city," gained during the German Revolution of 1848, radicalized Meysenbug's worldview and influenced the way she described women as autonomous, self-reliant beings. Podlasli-Labrenz argues that Chopin experienced a similar giddiness and freedom when she escaped American social mores and toured Europe in the 1870s. The essay makes a convincing case that not only would Chopin have known Meysenbug's work but that it would have struck a sympathetic chord, given Chopin's own physical exertions not only in Europe but back home in New Orleans, when she continued to explore the city by herself. The German writer's influence can thus be seen in Chopin's depiction of Edna Pontellier's increasingly bold excursions, which lead not only to physical freedom but to the realization and preservation of an "inner dignity" that Podlasli-Lebrenz argues is kept intact by Edna's final walk into the sea.

Matthew Teutsch looks back at the antebellum setting of *The Grandissimes* but pairs it with another novel set in pre–Civil War New Orleans that was nevertheless written decades later, Charles Chesnutt's *Paul Marchand, F.M.C.* (1921). In both cases, Teutsch argues, the complex social and racial landscape of an older New Orleans, one that wasn't quite as Americanized, was useful terrain for exploring—and debunking—essentialist notions of race. Specifically, the recognized category of "free people of color" in antebellum Louisiana allows for a complex rendering of race relations that undermines simple binaries. Likewise, the use of the term "caste" instead of "race" by Cable and Chesnutt (a friend and mentee of Cable) foregrounds the constructed nature of race, suggesting that the category is human-made and socially enforced and therefore open to interrogation, transformation, and perhaps eventually eradication.

The final essays in the "Prose" section demonstrate the influence New Orleans had on mid-twentieth century American literature. Ruth R. Caillouet, for example, argues that the lives and works of two writers not often associated with New Orleans or with each other—Zora Neale Hurston and Eudora Welty—were profoundly influenced by their respective experiences in the famed city. While at first glance this may seem an unlikely pairing, Caillouet points out that both were worldly women who nevertheless returned to their childhood homes in the South, both documented the lives of rural communities, one through anthropology and one through photography, and most pertinently, both gleaned a great deal from their experiences in New Orleans. However, Caillouet rightly points out that Hurston's New Orleans was nothing like Welty's. Hurston immersed herself in the city's Hoodoo/Voodoo culture, becoming so adept at its practices that she was asked to take over a leading witch doctor's practice. Welty, by contrast, spent her youthful New Orleans excursions having dinner at Galatoire's, an establishment of the city's elite, and her later years documenting the parades and revelries of Mardi Gras. In each case, Caillouet persuasively argues that these experiences permeated (often covertly) the authors' respective writings, once again highlighting the richness of a city that resonates equally in Hurston's folkloric tales and Welty's modernist stories of manners.

Edward J. Dupuy's essay examines another American author inspired by New Orleans, Walker Percy, who spent his career searching for a "middle way and interstitial place" that would heal the "bifurcation of the self." Binx Bolling, *The Moviegoer*'s protagonist, is emblematic of this search, as he finds himself displaced in the old South of his ancestors and yet unsure of his place—his "self"—in the modern South. New Orleans, described by another Percy character as "neither damned nor saved," is, according to Dupuy, the ideal backdrop for Binx's search. Later, when Percy writes about his move to Covington, an hour north of New Orleans, he addresses the racial turmoil of the late 1960s in a series of essays, but instead of seeking a resolution, he simply focuses on a way forward during a moment of deep divisions. Dupuy argues that, taken together, these works narrate Percy's quest for a place of productive "inbetween-ness" for himself, his characters, and his community to confront the nihilism, violence, and racism of his historical moment.

Section Two of the volume, "Poetry," begins with Nancy Dixon's essay about a rarely discussed group of antebellum writers, who were Catholic, free Creole men of color: *Les Cenelles*, or *The Mayhaws*. This name honors the springtime tradition of gathering sweet mayhaw berries to give to one's love interest, her mother, and other women in her family. These men wrote poetry and offered it to readers just as young men would offer mayhaws, as we see in the collection's dedicatory poem, "Fair Sex of Louisiana." Also addressed in that poem, and several others in the collection, is the virtuousness of Creole women of color, as well as the growing racism in the city in the years leading up to the Civil War, when New Orleans Creoles of Color, many of whom fought in the Confederate Army and even some of these writers, would lose the status and freedom they once enjoyed.

In the next essay, Tierney Powell reads Joy Harjo's 1983 poem, "New Orleans" as a text that respatializes and remaps the city by exploring the history of "settler-colonialism and its modern corollaries," which has seemingly erased the presence of the indigenous Creek peoples. Powell argues that Harjo's main concern is the way the speaker is "traumatized by the evident erasure of indigeneity" that is a legacy of New Orleans's history of privileged occupation and material consumption. The equestrian statue in Jackson Square, the most prominent remaining tribute to a white slaveowner, becomes a symbol of the repetition of occupation and colonization: it could be DeSoto's as easily as Andrew Jackson's, and its current status as the image of the city center cements this erasure even more. But, Powell argues, Harjo's poem subverts this domination by "giving voice to the indigenous historical perspective." According to Powell, Harjo's speaker recounts her walk through the city, and in doing so, reanimates the past and "(re)create[s] the knowledge of the formation of the United States through the shared perspective of the Creeks."

Like Powell's essay on Harjo, Marcus Tribbett's essay reads Mem Shannon's debut album, *A Cabdriver's Blues* (1995), as resonating with the (sometimes hidden) multiplicity and heterogeneity that define New Orleans. By juxtaposing spoken *audio verité* recordings from his cab with blues songs, Shannon represents the contradictory voices of New Orleans inhabitants, including prostitutes, cabdrivers, and other "urban workers," by placing them in a conversation with those of wealthy tourists who often exploit the inhabitants for pleasure, sexual and otherwise. In this way, the album contradicts a monolithic vision of the city that some outsiders may have and instead offers, according to Tribbett, "an urban scene that is complicated enough to both repel and attract cabbie, resident, tourist and listeners alike." At its heart, though, the album is a critique of consumer culture and neoliberalism, along with the gendered, racial, and class hierarchies that sustain (and are sustained by) them. Tribbett ultimately argues that the lessons of *A Cabdriver's Blues* are even more urgent in post-Katrina New Orleans, as the city is "an even meaner one with an even glitzier tourist economy."

Reading Shari Evans's essay, "Slave-Bricked Streets and Women's Works: The Practiced Place of Brenda Marie Osbey's New Orleans," alongside Powell's and Tribbett's reveals a surprising affinity between the three writers. Like Harjo and Shannon, Osbey is equally concerned with the erasure of the marginalized voices and lives of New Orleans inhabitants. Osbey is focused particularly on New Orleanians of color, and her poetry is a textual monument to them. In particular, Evans argues that Osbey's collection, *All Saints* (1998), almost literally "call[s] [a community] into being" through the poetic rendering of the past and present of women's lives. In the poem "Faubourg," Osbey recounts the daily routines, rituals and labor of the women of color from the old part of the city. Everything from cooking to shopping at the market becomes memorialized and implicated in the way the women preserve the past and honor the dead in the very act of existing. More personally, Osbey writes about her grandmother's early life in "Alberta." Set in a garment factory, much like the Haspel Brothers factory where so many Creoles of color worked, Alberta and her colleagues sew steadily without so much as a "thank you" from the "white mannequins" who stand in for the "larger society that is largely unaware of and ungrateful for their labor." Nevertheless, the poem itself is a testament to the garment workers' diligence and effort. Evans notes that the material world in Osbey's works is steeped in historical meaning, such as the "slave-bricked streets" and the "blackened wood" in Alberta's factory. Such attention to the lived environment, along with the inclusion of a glossary, gives readers—especially outsiders to New Orleans's culture—a choice of entering into the multilayered meaning of the poetry by understanding the specific historical connotations of Osbey's New Orleans's vocabulary and brings the city to life in profound ways. Ultimately, Evans argues that the poetry turns New Orleans into a space that is both temporal and spatial and animates the "intricacies of [the city's] traumatic and multi-layered past."

According to Mary C. Carruth, Natasha Tretheway's poetry collection, *Bellocq's Ophelia* (2002), also brings New Orleans women of the past into the present by giving voice and agency to a mixed-race prostitute whose image was captured in the early 1900s by the photographer, E. J. Bellocq, in a series of portraits of sex-workers in Storyville, New Orleans's red-light district. In "Demythologizing the New Orleans 'Octoroon': Natasha Tretheway's *Bellocq's Ophelia*," Carruth notes that Tretheway, who grew up in New Orleans and on the Mississippi Gulf Coast, was introduced to Bellocq's photographs in graduate school but initially assumed the women in the pictures were white. When she learned that at least some of them had been photographed at a brothel of mixed-race workers, she saw them as a vehicle for exploring her own biracialism. In adopting this "poetic persona," Tretheway imagines the lives of the women that cannot be captured in a photograph: their desires, their intellect, their agency, their ability to control the image that others see. In doing so, Carruth argues that Tretheway is able to "illuminat[e] the present" by "animat[ing] the still bodies in photographs," exploring what it means to be a mixed-race woman in the twenty-first century by giving voice to past generations of multiracial New Orleans women.

Fittingly, the final essay in the collection was inspired by the horrific disaster of Hurricane Katrina and its aftermath. Shanna M. Salinas analyzes Patricia Smith's comprehensive and contradictory representation of Hurricane Katrina and its aftermath, undermining the prevailing narrative of the Hurricane as a "media weather event." Salinas suggests that Smith's poetry "compels [those who experienced the storm secondhand through media] to interrogate what we have seen." *Blood Dazzler* does so by drawing attention to the ways Black bodies are put on display as signs and symbols of suffering, ironically because they are disposable, marginalized. Smith's acclaimed poetry collection exposes the way the spectacle of Black suffering was exploited by news outlets and government officials, the very institutions that disembodied and dehumanized the those who suffered the most from Katrina and the debacle of its aftermath. However, Salinas concludes that Smith's poems not only expose this exploitation but ultimately, in some measure, "give a voice and an identity back to the unheard and unseen." In so doing, they make readers recognize their own complicity in this silencing and also "disrupt the gaze that fixes suffering and reifies black disposability."

Over and over, these essays situate New Orleans comparatively in its global context but also interrogate its status as a unique American city. New Orleans, after all, was one of America's first major port cities, thanks in large part to the cotton and slave trades, linking it commercially and culturally to the rest of the world from its very inception, and the themes that animate literature about New Orleans—race, class, sexuality, agency, responsibility—are fundamental to the human experience, regardless of location. And yet, at the same time, several essays in the collection remind us of New Orleans's singularity, its history, and its reputation for being a world unto itself. Taken as a whole, the authors included here provide a complex, contradictory, hopeful, devastating, yet honest rendering of the city of New Orleans and its literary history for over two hundred years.

Part 1

PROSE

BLAKE IN THE CRESCENT CITY
Martin R. Delany Reimagines Antebellum Radicalism

Paul Fess

After traveling extensively throughout the deep South, going from "plantation to plantation, sowing seeds of future devastation and ruin to the master and redemption to the slave," Henry Blake, the fugitive slave hero of Martin R. Delany's *Blake; or, the Huts of America* (1859; 1861–62), enters the city of New Orleans, a move that takes the novel's representation of US enslavement, and Henry's plan to undo it, off of the plantations along the Mississippi and Red Rivers and into one of the most important urban centers in the nineteenth-century circum-Caribbean world.[1] The novel's New Orleans section is brief—just two short chapters—yet it conveys Delany's nuanced understanding of his text's antislavery political position and the place New Orleans held within antislavery discourse, especially for African American activists. Henry's travel to this city is one of the many episodes in which the novel departs from the antislavery literature of the day, particularly the widely popular slave narratives and sentimentalist abolitionist novels. Rather than creating a figure whose main struggle is to flee enslavement, Delany gives us the story of an ex-enslaved character who maneuvers with relative ease throughout a landscape that includes the American South and North, Canada, and Cuba, organizing a revolutionary spirit among the enslaved, often in the very midst of their enslavers. This "general insurrection" precipitates from events early in the novel when Henry leaves the plantation to which he's attached in Natchez, Mississippi, after learning that his wife has been sold to a slave trader.[2] As the novel progresses from this tragedy, his larger project becomes one of organizing freedom fighters within spaces of *un*freedom, with the ultimate goal of overthrowing Spanish Cuba and forming a Black republic there.

While it would be difficult to assert the preeminence of a singular place within the range of *Blake*'s far-reaching geography, "the portentous city of New Orleans"—as the narrator describes it before Henry arrives—stands out as an odd but suggestive location for a fugitive slave to linger.[3] Just what, exactly, does the very seat of the slave system *portend* for our hero? Not only is this move one of the many ways that the novel flouts the conventions of antislavery literature, but this section also recasts New Orleans itself as a place where the practices of enslavement confront the quotidian and revolutionary struggles for freedom undertaken by enslaved and free people of color during the decade before the Civil War. New Orleans's portentousness echoes through other sections of the text as well. It is the place from which Henry mulls over "the portentious [*sic*] purpose of a final decision on the hour to strike the first blow" against the likes of the white power brokers we meet in the novel's first pages.[4] It is this experience with "the rebel blacks" that gives Henry the impetus to form his own insurrectionary group over the course of the rest of the novel.[5] Here, Henry witnesses an activist organization in a scene that has its source in the rumors of an uprising that gained currency in the city in 1853, an allusion to the events of Delany's time that has, until now, gone undiscovered. In the novel's imagining of this event, Henry finds himself at a meeting of a group of enslaved and free people of color secretly plotting a rebellion under the cover of the distractions of Mardi Gras. The portent of Henry's experience in New Orleans also looms large when he begins organizing in Cuba. We learn in Part II of the novel that the city's connections to Havana enable Henry's first encounter with the work of the revolutionary poet Placido, who appears as a fictionalized representation of the historical Cuban dissident poet, and martyr Plácido, an association Delany only attempts to obscure by removing the accent mark from this figure's *nom de plume*.[6] From Placido's poetry, Henry discovers, "the fire of liberty blazed as from the altar of a freeman's heart."[7] In his nuanced representation of the Americas of the nineteenth century, Delany continually insists that due to the connections formed from New Orleans along with the capitalist networks that depended upon and supported slavery, Henry was allowed some freedom of movement and thereby, the circulation of print material, like antislavery poetry, was still bound to the slave system.

New Orleans, then, appears in the novel as an intriguing example of the way Delany depicts revolutionary activity from within spaces structured by enslavement, and Henry's time in this city deserves closer inspection because this seemingly counterintuitive sojourn into the deepest of the deep antebellum South conveys important aspects of the state of Black politics and shows how the Crescent City shaped those politics. When one takes a closer look at such paradoxical representations—at the strangeness of the narrative choice to move his protagonist into New Orleans rather than further away from it—the questions become how does this city shape Delany's complex vision for antislavery and Black radical activism in the tumultuous decade before the War and how does *Blake* offer up a distinct representation of this city in the nineteenth century?

Reshaping the conversation about antislavery activism was, of course, central to Delany's project. In this essay, I focus on two ways the novel's New Orleans section advances Delany's intervention: on the one hand, he uses New Orleans as a place from which to theorize the inadequacy of United States sectional politics by using the city to prefigure the international scope of the novel's later episodes; on the other, he ponders the possibilities for African American political action within unfree spaces. In his introduction to the first serialization of the novel in the *Anglo-African Magazine*, Delany lays out this dual focus succinctly: "[*Blake*] not only shows the combined political and commercial interests that unite the north and south, but gives in the most familiar manner the formidable understanding among the slaves throughout the United States and Cuba."[8] New Orleans was an important microcosm for both of these structural elements of the novel. Geographically within, but still in many ways culturally outside, the United States, nineteenth-century New Orleans straddled the line between the US and the circum-Caribbean region. The diversity of its African American citizenry, too, made it a difficult example for abolitionists to deploy without leaving out this complex component of city life.

As the most northern Caribbean city—a descriptor many still use today—New Orleans is an apt coordinate in Henry's remapping of abolitionist discourse, as he imagines a Black radicalism that exceeded US domestic politics, unlike, for instance, Frederick Douglass, with whom Delany split over the effectiveness of domestic reforms.[9] As Andy Doolen has argued, operating "from within the national model" of reforming domestic politics around slavery tended to "reinscribe the normativities of white nationalism that it was attempting to negate."[10] In *Blake*, Delany attempts to avoid this tendency by aiming his narrative scrutiny at the power structures that supported the slave system and imagining connections between black political actors across the circum-Caribbean world. As a city divided by its allegiances, Delany saw in the New Orleans of the 1850s a city that was concurrently emblematic of American trade practices and Afro-Caribbean and European cultural forms.

Additionally, with his representation of the diversity of African American culture within the city and the political organization that existed there, Delany raises questions about the relationships between politics, activism, organization, and everyday life. New Orleans was ripe for this kind of thinking because, as Matt Sandler argues, the city "produced slavery and freedom simultaneously."[11] Unlike other cities in the South, New Orleans comprised one of the largest populations of free persons of color alongside a thriving slave market that continually brought enslaved people to the city. Delany understood the political environment such complexity created as free persons of color actively sought to exert liberal influence on the city's racial policies while proslavery forces lobbied to strengthen laws regulating this group as well as enslaved Africans.

Within this milieu, Delany represents the "dialectically inter-related" concepts of revolutionary and everyday resistance that the development of New Orleans made possible.[12] In this section of the novel, Delany displays the value of the everyday resistant acts performed by enslaved people, such as ignoring curfew and lampooning popular songs, in comparison to the open rebellion Henry finds brewing in the "Lower Faubourg."[13] In this way, Delany juxtaposes what French philosopher Michel de Certeau would call the everyday "tactics" employed by enslaved and free New Orleanians of color with the revolutionary "strategy" Henry attempts to realize throughout the novel in response to the dominant power structure.[14] De Certeau defines "tactics" as momentary, calculated actions undertaken by weak and oppressed people who seize opportunities and "make use of the cracks" within a given social order.[15] By contrast, "strategies" seek to manipulate this social order. The enslaved people Henry observes ignoring the curfew call at the beginning of the New Orleans section are using tactics to briefly subvert laws without necessarily seeking changes to these laws, and Henry's developing plan to form a Black republic employs strategies to shape a new social order, one led by Afro-Caribbean people so as to undo the disciplinary strategies of the slave system. In New Orleans and the novel as a whole, Henry implicitly puzzles over this distinction in his efforts to figure out the relationship between the revolutionary and the everyday, raising questions about the nature of Black agency, a longstanding concern for scholars.

Even though *Blake* isn't usually grouped with other examples of nineteenth-century New Orleans literature, the novel's representation of this city distills many of the complexities surrounding the relationship between freedom and enslavement exuded by nineteenth-century New Orleans itself. Within a few short pages, Delany gives us a panorama of the city's African American population alongside its carnival celebrations, musical traditions, and religious practices, all cultural ground from which New Orleanians negotiated the terms of freedom and enslavement throughout the 1850s and the nineteenth century more generally. Through Henry's ambitions in Cuba, Delany links his story to the filibustering expeditions launched from New Orleans during the decade. These adventures sought to grab land in order to extend slavery and signaled the beginning of the US imperialism in Latin America that would take full shape toward the end of the century. *Blake* imagines a protagonist who, in his mission to form a Black republic, turns these desires to perpetuate the slave system upside down. Rather than writing from the perspective of an insider within New Orleans's African American culture, he theorizes what this culture signifies for circum-Caribbean African American culture writ large, shaping a literary representation that shows New Orleans to be a typical place, in the sense of its participation in what Clyde Woods calls the "plantation bloc," as well as a paradoxical one, in its range of responses to this diverse population.[16]

This literary representation of New Orleans is distinct from most other American antislavery literature that features the city. One need look no further than Harriet Beecher Stowe, one of Delany's imagined interlocutors in *Blake*, and her novel *Uncle Tom's Cabin*, for a typical example of how abolitionists characterized the city as signifying the worst abuses of the slave system, standing as an emblem for sectional differences in the United States.[17] With its auction blocks, economic ties to the cotton trade, and association with the systematized concubinage of *plaçage*, the New Orleans slave market came to stand as a potent symbol for the antislavery movement in the 1850s, reinforcing the divide in most antislavery literature between the free North and benighted South.[18] Stowe's depiction of the city provides an apt counterexample to Delany's because she uses Tom's sale to a slave trader headed to the New Orleans market in order to contradict claims about the benignity of this system in places like Kentucky, where we are told Tom led a life of relative ease. Tom's sale is a virtual death sentence in the world of the novel. In the scenes featuring New Orleans, *Uncle Tom's Cabin* focuses on the decay of the St. Clare household and the slave market when Tom is sold to Simon Legree, trading on commonplace midcentury tropes that characterized the city as an immoral, unproductive place made the worse by the stranglehold of slavery. Frederick Douglass strikes a similar chord in *My Bondage and My Freedom* (1855) when he imagines the workings of the internal trade and its endpoint, New Orleans. "Follow this drove to New Orleans," he directs his reader.[19] "Attend the auction; see men examined like horses; see the forms of women rudely and brutally exposed to the shocking gaze of American slave-buyers. See this drove sold and separated forever; and never forget the deep, sad sobs that arose from that scattered multitude."[20] To be sure, these and similar descriptions of New Orleans held sway because they reflected actual practices. These citations of Stowe and Douglass, of course, bring to mind the shifts in abolitionist political discourse of the 1840s and 1850s, about which there is little space to discuss in detail here; however, both Stowe's and Douglass's politics, like many other abolitionist writers, mostly looked inward, focusing on the domestic trade and its effects, a trend in antislavery literature that was encouraged by the official closing of the international trade in 1807 and the passage of the Fugitive Slave Act in 1850.[21] Though Stowe's endorsement of the Liberian colonization movement at the end of *Uncle Tom's Cabin* suggests an internationalist antislavery agenda, unlike Delany's depiction in *Blake* it rested on the paternalist assumption that, for the scheme to work, liberal white Americans needed to prepare and educate freedmen for self-governance. Over the course of the 1850s Stowe's depiction of the end of slavery shifted its focus from African colonization to the formation of ex-enslaved communities in the northern United States, as evidenced in her 1857 novel *Dred*. Frederick Douglass began his turn toward domestic antislavery political reform with the rise of the Liberty Party in the 1840s, splitting with William Lloyd Garrison's belief in changing hearts and minds through moral suasion. More to the point of my argument here, Douglass also split with Delany over the issue of emigration from the United States, preferring to build antislavery platforms in order to end the slave system. Within the milieu of abolitionism during the 1850s, then, New Orleans presents a much more complex case. It certainly became the center of the interstate slave trade by midcentury; however, while these markets were pernicious, ever-present specters for enslaved people in the US and readymade symbols for many abolitionists, concentrating on the domestic trade tended to downplay slavery's global reach and the ways enslaved people themselves and free African Americans negotiated their instability within unfree spaces like New Orleans.

Many African American writers who experienced the city expressed fear of the unpredictability and brutality presented by the market and simultaneously showed how the city enabled them to manipulate the conditions of their enslavement. As Lisa Ze Winters points out, "for enslaved and free(d) African Americans [. . .] antebellum New Orleans epitomized the slave South and provoked visceral terror," and "the passage of black captives through the city signified inevitably tragic and often horrific endings inextricably linked to the specter of New Orleans over the US landscape."[22] At the same time, however, "antebellum New Orleans was [. . .] a place that witnessed extraordinary examples of black authority and self-determination in the face of the racial and sexual economies of slavery."[23] Many ex-enslaved writers registered these countervailing aspects of the city through a sense of ambivalence about their time there. For these writers, being enslaved in New Orleans meant learning to negotiate what moving through the system meant. Henry Bibb, for instance, writes about being tasked with finding his own buyer when his master takes him to the New Orleans market, an opportunity that he uses to seek out a customer from a border state, which would put him closer to Canada. In an ironic turn of events, this would-be buyer mistakes Bibb for a slave *owner*.[24] Solomon Northup, who was taken to New Orleans after being kidnapped into slavery in Washington, DC, attempted to use his ability to play the violin to attract an owner who dwelt in New Orleans so that he would be in a better position to escape.[25]

This keen awareness of the opportunities and pitfalls of New Orleans resonates with other ex-enslaved literature about antebellum cityscapes more generally. When fugitive slaves moved to northern cities they simultaneously rejoiced at their status as free persons as well as lamented their fears that they would be forced to return to their former plantations. After the passage of the Fugitive Slave Act (1850), New York, for example, was swarming with slave catchers on the lookout for escaped slaves, a situation that caused Douglass to remark, "Mason and Dixon's line has been obliterated."[26] When Douglass first got to New York he was elated: "A free state around me, and a free earth under my feet!"[27] However, after meeting a fellow fugitive who reminded him of the possibility that they would both be captured Douglass felt himself "alone again, an easy prey to the kidnappers, if any should happen to be on my track."[28] Harriet Jacobs, too, expressed similar misgivings. Of her experience after escaping enslavement she writes:

> All that winter I lived in a state of anxiety. When I took the children out to breathe the air, I closely observed the countenances of all I met. I dreaded the approach of summer, when snakes and slaveholders make their appearance. I was, in fact, a slave in New York, as subject to slave laws as I had been in a Slave State. Strange incongruity in a State called free![29]

Her anxiety was only relieved when her employer purchased her from her southern owner, prompting her condemnation: "A human being sold in the free city of New York!"[30] To be sure, the legality of slavery and the slave trade in New Orleans made it a much more onerous place than New York, and New Orleans became even more restrictive in the 1850s. Yet, these writers, much like Delany himself, focused on the power relations that underwrote the slave system and generally exposed the irrationality of regional politics, which tended to obscure the moral significance of ending the system. In this light, *Blake*'s New Orleans section simultaneously connects the city to the circum-Caribbean world and accounts for the diversity of the city's African American population in order to convey a more complex understanding of the politics of slavery.

While it has been widely noted by scholars that *Blake* looks beyond the frame of the United States and the regionalist views of slavery that constituted so much of the conversation about the institution, little has been said about New Orleans's place within the novel's geography. Since its recovery in 1970 by Floyd J. Miller, who characterized Delany's position as "nationalist and emigrationist," scholarship about *Blake* has focused on the ways the novel depicts African-American antislavery activism as a transnational project.[31] Within this line of criticism, Paul Gilroy has influentially argued that "the topography of the black Atlantic world is directly incorporated into Delany's tale" and that as such, "the novel makes the African-American experience visible within a hemispheric order of racial oppression."[32] Gilroy's observation that Delany, by midcentury, had "outgrown the boundaries of North America" bears out in the *Proceedings* of the 1854 National Emigration Convention, a meeting that Delany helped organize when he broke with Frederick Douglass over Douglass's adherence to US nationalism.[33] In this

Blake in the Crescent City: Antebellum Radicalism

document, the convention body published resolutions condemning the government for the passage of the Fugitive Slave Act (1850), which "dispelled the lingering patriotism in our bosoms," and an essay advocating immigration to the West Indies.[34] Delany's activism during the 1850s sought alternative models of association to those offered by the United States, advocating the abandonment of the nation entirely, and in this sense, the novel that would be born from this position, as Eric Sundquist assesses it, became "a virtual chronicle of the black revolutionary moment of the Americas."[35]

Yet, this line of criticism pays little attention to the problems and opportunities Delany works through in depicting New Orleans, which was, after all, one of the most important stepping stones from the United States to the circum-Caribbean world he would revolutionize. As Kirsten Silva Gruesz notes, New Orleans in the 1850s was "fundamentally a *Caribbean* city, strategically positioned within the transportation and communications system of the Gulf of Mexico's half-moon, linked to Cuba, Puerto Rico, Santo Domingo, and Mexico's Gulf Coast and Yucatán."[36] Silva Gruesz's work specifically ties nineteenth-century New Orleans to Havana, a feature of early New Orleans history that other scholars continue to underscore. Ned Sublette, for example, argues that the cultural ties between New Orleans and Cuba were some of the most important features of African American life during the late eighteenth and early nineteenth centuries.[37] Delany clearly picks up on this connection with *Blake*. The city itself also remained divided between its French, American, and Spanish cultural identities even a half century after the Louisiana Purchase (1803). New Orleans, then, was a "conduit point," a node in a network that "defied a fixed location in the geographical imaginary."[38]

The New Orleans of the 1850s was a rich place from which to speculate about other kinds of collectivities beyond the bounds of the US. As Katy Chiles has asserted, Delany's representation of Black radicalism in the novel "presents a nation-state in which local, regional, national, and transnational figurations overlap and permeate each other."[39] It is in the "Caribbean city" of New Orleans that Delany begins to represent the overlapping of these formations in his vision of Black nationalism during a time when the US was developing a unilateral imperialism that sought the annexation of Cuba, among other territories, in order to extend the slave trade. Delany uses New Orleans, then, as symbolic, not just for the interstate slave trade—as other antislavery activists might—but as a place deeply enmeshed in international slavery during the nineteenth century. In doing this, Delany ties what were often characterized as sectional antislavery politics to the full scope of circum-Caribbean freedom struggles.

Paul Gilroy rightly notes that ships "occupy a primary symbolic and political place" in *Blake*, and as Henry observes the Mississippi slave-boatmen working the New Orleans docks and singing songs, we are reminded that the novel, even when it settles in a particular place, focuses on the networks formed by and resistant to the slave system throughout the American South and Caribbean.[40] Delany never specifies this, but these sailors are likely enslaved people who facilitate the trade of goods along the Mississippi River; however, this scene also signals Henry's move to include the Gulf of Mexico within his geographic scope. When he encounters the boatmen, Henry resolves to dispel the false consciousness enslaved people might cleave to. Instead, he wishes "to make them sensible that liberty was legitimately and essentially theirs," anticipating his later discussions with Placido about his own revolutionary activity in Cuba.[41] As mentioned above, Henry emphasizes the connection between New Orleans and Cuba by noting that he first becomes aware of Placido's poetry in New Orleans, but the connection between the two cities also resonates with Henry's mock-filibuster-turned-radical-revolution in Cuba and Delany's own activism around the persistence of the international slave trade between this island and the US through New Orleans.

It would be difficult to discuss New Orleans's place in this novel or in the 1850s more generally without also discussing the filibusterers who attempted to take possession of various parcels of land in Latin America during this decade. Nineteenth-century New Orleans was a place torn between international business interests and southern mores, and the contentious debates that erupted over the prospects of annexing places in the Caribbean stand as stark examples of this tension. As historian William Freehling puts it, many antebellum southerners' "most exotic fantasy was that proslavery expansionists would land several dozen or several hundred American freedom fighters on Central or South American shores."[42] New Orleans's merchant community attempted to materialize this fantasy by providing a "disproportionate share of filibustering buccaneers with money, recruits, publicity, spirit, and rationale." However, rural Louisiana planters worried about the influx of Caribbean sugar, specifically from Cuba, which produced four times as much as the tariff-protected Americans.[43] Others in the South worried about the "africanization" of Cuba, which saw a relaxing of laws regarding enslaved and ex-enslaved Africans during the 1850s. These tensions manifested as concerns for southern propriety, evident in the "newspaper wars" between the fast and loose New Orleans and the tradition-bound Charleston.[44] In *Blake*, Delany exploits these anxieties by having Henry travel to Charleston just after the New Orleans scene. Here, Henry finds that "to impress the Negro with a sense of his own inferiority is a leading precept of their social system."[45] In his juxtaposition of these two cities, Delany highlights the ways New Orleans's relatively liberal society fostered both revolutionary, freebooting organization—the kind that could lead to the opposing tendencies of Black action and white filibustering—as well as forms of social control more diffuse than the disciplinary character of Charleston.

Two of the most famous filibustering expeditions that launched from New Orleans were those of Narciso López, who, in 1850, invaded and was promptly expelled from Cárdenas, Cuba, and William Walker, who declared himself president of Nicaragua in 1856. Even though filibustering was an illegal practice, López's and Walker's actions reflected positions that were circulating amongst politicians and businessmen interested in securing the South's prominence during this period. One of the most notorious outgrowths of these developments was the prospect of officially annexing Cuba as a US territory, which became a real possibility in the 1850s. Following López's attempted takeover of Cuba, the secretive Ostend Manifesto (1854), written by, among others, future president James Buchanan, laid out the case for annexation and brought into relief the ways the North and South were jockeying for power over the slave system on the international stage. In a speech at New Orleans, the year after the Ostend Manifesto was published, John Quitman, governor of Mississippi and supporter of López, put this connection plainly, arguing that Cuba was integral for the "salvation of southern institutions" and any resistance to its annexation was a result of "the antislavery sentiment" gaining traction in Congress.[46] William Walker's invasion of Nicaragua took on a similar valence: one of his first acts as "president" was the reinstitution of slavery in the area.[47] Interestingly, Delany was elected mayor of San Juan Del Norte, an important trading post in Nicaragua, in 1852, an event that resulted from his efforts to organize against the proslavery "Cotton" Americans, who were streaming into the area. Delany's electoral victory took place without him setting foot in the town, but, as Jake Mattox discusses, the election speaks to Delany's focus on the importance of geographical representation in his antislavery appeals.

Blake's Cuba narrative responds to these developments and reappropriates the ways enslavement structured historical filibusters by imagining a nation-building project undertaken by enslaved Africans. In doing so, the novel revises the geographical and sectional divides that animate López's and Walker's activities in order to conceive of the circum-Caribbean world as one where freedom was possible despite a history of enslavement. Delany's eye is on international politics from the novel's first page, but New Orleans appears as an important link between the historical activities of people in power and the mobilization of Black people Henry tries to foment. The filibusters of the 1850s that launched from the port of New Orleans speak to the ways that the city traded social stability for commercial gains, but Delany shows how this social situation made New Orleans a place ripe for black radical action as well.

To Delany's mind, these fantasies of adding Cuba as a slave territory had their genesis in the persistence of the illegal slave trade between Havana and New Orleans.[48] He expressed these suspicions in both *Blake* and his political writing during the decade. In the novel, for instance, the narrator declares, "It is confidently believed upon good authority that the American steamers plying between Havana and New Orleans, as a profitable part of the enterprise, are actively engaged in the slave trade between the two places."[49] Delany made the same point in a piece that appeared in the *North Star* in 1849, the year Narciso López began organizing his US operation. Here, he made plain his views that annexation meant the extension of slavery and anticipated the tenor of his novel's engagement with the island. Anticipating Henry's efforts to revolutionize Cuba, Delany issues a call to his *North Star* readers that asks for Black-led resistance to annexation:

> The cause is ours—we are the interested party, and every colored man should make common cause of it, uniting in mind, heart, sentiment, and action, sending up one united voice of solemn indignation against this and every such scheme, and by every means in his power enlighten his brethren in slavery upon the subject of their inalienable God-given rights: this we conceive to be, as freemen, our heaven-required duty, and should use every possible means to accomplish it.[50]

The solidarity he advocated here is similar to what Henry struggles for throughout *Blake*, which begins with the New Orleans section. How will

Blake in the Crescent City: Antebellum Radicalism

he get such a diverse range of people as existed within the Afro-Caribbean world facing in the same direction? And, further, how will he bring them to a state of "readiness"? These questions come to the fore in New Orleans as Henry sees the problems with organizing radical activity when faced with the diversity of the people he encounters on the city streets and the infighting among the insurrectionaries, particularly with respect to the incendiary character Tibs, whose impatience leads to a diffusion of the group, stifling the project of slave revolt in the city. The concept of "readiness," too, resonates throughout *Blake* as part of these questions of political organization and makes a significant appearance in the New Orleans section when Henry tells the agitated Tibs, "You are not yet ready for a strike; you are not yet ready to do anything effective."[51]

In the second part of the novel, Delany continually links Henry's experiences in Cuba directly to his time in New Orleans. In addition to the direct, material connection between Henry and Placido through the latter's poetry, the novel represents the less material circulation of performance and festival culture through its depiction of the Kings Day celebration on the island, which the narrator describes as "being identical, but more systematic, grand and imposing, [than] the 'Congo Dance.'"[52] Delany also implies another connection to New Orleans, here, since Kings Day takes place on the Epiphany, the first day of Carnival season, and Henry's time in New Orleans takes place over Mardi Gras, the last day of the season. Despite this obvious connection with New Orleans city life, however, Delany explicitly aligns Kings Day with the Afrocentric culture of Congo Square, an important shift because Mardi Gras, rather than an unequivocal loosening of laws and norms, served the counterintuitive function of reasserting social order. Particularly in the second half of the nineteenth century, Mardi Gras became an event that, in purporting to invert the power structure, ultimately reified it through courtly rituals enacted by leading citizens. In this light Congo Square, like the Kings Day celebration he describes, signals Black-led cultural formations as necessary for Henry's revolution. Mardi Gras, though, *is* like Delany's depiction of Kings Day in one regard: both appear as occasions for stoking white fears of Black insurrection. Martial law reigns when the rebels are discovered in New Orleans. After the meeting is uncovered, "the place," we are told, "was at once thrown into an intense excitement, the military called into requisition, dragoons flying in every direction, cannon from the old fort sending forth hourly through the night, thundering peals to give assurance of their sufficiency, and the infantry on duty traversing the street."[53] A similar scene plays out in Cuba after rumors spread that white Americans are agitating enslaved people in order to overthrow the Spanish government. These fears are quelled, but the episode ultimately signifies the weaknesses of the ruling class, a revelation apparent in the narrator's assessment of the events: "A dreamy existence of the most fearful apprehensions, of dread, horror and dismay; suspicion and distrust, jealousy and envy continually pervade the community; and Havana, New Orleans, Charleston or Richmond may be thrown into consternation by an idle expression of the most trifling or ordinary ignorant black. A sleeping wake or waking sleep, a living death or tormented life is that of the Cuban and American slaveholder."[54] Once again Delany turns conventional thinking about nineteenth-century slavery on its head, this time by highlighting the precarity of slave masters rather than the people they enslave. Here, it is not the slave population who experiences social death, to evoke Orlando Patterson's influential formulation; rather, the master class undergoes a kind of living death that stems from their fears of the Africans they have enslaved.

I want to underscore the importance of the narrator's mention of New Orleans here because the New Orleans section of the novel is framed by similar fears. It is in these moments that *Blake* shows how ideas about freedom can become intimately tied to the processes of enslavement. As we see in the Cuba section, relaxing laws as part of Kings Day creates the conditions of possibility for stricter enforcement of these laws under the rubric of security, a structural dynamic of the novel that has its genesis in the section that finds Henry walking the streets of New Orleans during Mardi Gras. *Blake* certainly asks us to think about slavery beyond the borders of the United States, but it is the Americanizing, rather than wholly American, New Orleans of the 1850s that helps him develop this international perspective and its implications for African American agency within the institution. In the New Orleans section, Henry gains new critical purchase on the US system of enslavement that is different from standard sectional politics, and rather than conceiving the problem as regional, Henry becomes attuned to the relations of power that governed African American life in the nineteenth century. While I've been focusing on how the novel trains our gaze outward from New Orleans to Cuba, in the last section of this essay I turn to the New Orleans section itself. This section is key for Henry's sense of African American agency within the context of

Blake in the Crescent City: Antebellum Radicalism

enslavement, which develops from his implicit awareness of the distinction between what de Certeau terms "tactics" and "strategies."

When he arrives in New Orleans the first aspect of the city Henry acknowledges is the seeming ease with which its African American citizens negotiate the landscape:

> Though the cannon at the old fort in the Lower Faubourg had fired the significant warning, admonishing the slaves as well as free blacks to limit their movement, still there were passing to and fro with seeming indifference Negroes, both free and slaves, as well as the whites and Creole quadroons, fearlessly along the public highways, in seeming defiance of the established usage of Negro limitation.[55]

This short paragraph serves as a thumbnail sketch of the events of the broader New Orleans section. The cannon that announces curfew here is the same one that will be used to sound the alarm after the rebels are disarmed at the end of the chapter. Here, Delany conveys the uneasy discrepancy between the disciplinary practices of the canon with the ways that New Orleanians actually conducted themselves. The panorama view Delany gives at the beginning of this scene moves along the city streets, to the shops on "Chartier Street"—probably Chartres Street—to St. Louis Cathedral, where he hears the sometime "reverential prayers of many a Creole, male or female, black, white or mixed race," and closes when he hears the boatmen along the Mississippi River.[56] The narrative arc of Henry's stroll through the city develops the ideas of this paragraph in that the "unlimited privileges" of New Orleans's enslaved and free people of color are undercut by the workings of the slave system—the "iron cable of despotism"—that Henry is reminded of at the close of this panoramic view.[57] In this first part of his time in the city, then, Henry attempts to capture a sense of the liberal New Orleans society that enabled momentary tactical freedoms to exist in tandem with civic strategies to control the population that, in turn, always threatened to undermine the supposed relaxed nature of city life.

Given this dynamic, New Orleans was an intriguing place from which to theorize belonging, especially in light of the changes experienced by its African American population, a historical feature that Henry registers in this scene. African American New Orleanians during this decade saw significant shifts in their numbers and legal statuses. Between 1850 and 1865 there were about 10,000 free people of color, down from 20,000 a decade earlier, and there were about 15,000 enslaved Africans.[58] Free people of color held a wide range of jobs—both skilled and unskilled, some even engaged in banking and real estate—and participated in much of the cultural life of the city. Enslaved Africans worked in such positions as draymen, blacksmiths, and carpenters, among others. Antislavery periodicals from this decade continually drew inspiration in their attempts to assess the lives of African Americans in the city. In a letter to the editor, for instance, the *National Era* lauded the peculiar, exceptional status of free people of color, declaring "The legal condition of the free negro of Louisiana, contrasted with this legal condition in the Northern States, is largely in his favor. The free negro in Louisiana is governed by the same laws which govern the free blanc, or white man; and, what is more, they are administered with exact justice to both."[59] *Frederick Douglass's Paper* published a long piece detailing the "liberalizing tendency" brought about by African American-led educational institutions in the city, and the *New York Daily Times* described the relative ease with which an enslaved person could be emancipated in the state. Taking the implications of these conditions further, both the *North Star* and *The Liberator* published articles intimating that New Orleans was a place where abolitionism could thrive. *The Liberator*, for instance, published a piece in 1853, the year of the rumored slave revolt that inspired *Blake*'s New Orleans section, describing the city as a "hotbed of abolitionism."[60]

New Orleans newspapers, however, were much less sanguine about this situation, and managing the different populations of enslaved and free people of color was a constant theme in their pages. In his account of New Orleans, Frederick Law Olmsted reprints some of these complaints such as this one from the *New Orleans Crescent*:

GUINEA-LIKE.—Passing along Baronne street, between Perdido and Poydras streets, any Sunday afternoon, the white passer-by might easily suppose himself in Guinea, Caffraria, or any other thickly-peopled region in the land of Ham. Where the darkies all come from, what they do there, or where they go to, constitute a problem somewhat beyond our algebra. It seems to be a sort of nigger exchange. We know there are in that vicinity a colored church, colored ice-cream saloon, colored restaurant, colored coffee-houses, and a colored barbershop, which, we have heard say, has a back communication with one of the groggeries, for the benefit of slaves; but as the police haven't found it out yet, we suppose it ain't so.[61]

Such objections to the activities of African Americans created the political climate for enacting stricter laws regulating the lives of enslaved and free people of color in the second half of the decade. This culminated in a series of regulations regarding black New Orleanians of all social statuses. Enslaved persons were much more heavily regulated under *The laws and general ordinances of the city of New Orleans* that passed in 1857. There are two types of regulations in this document that resonate with *Blake* in particular. Fearing organized revolt, several changes strengthened laws against the assembly of slaves, and one prohibited slaves from singing of songs while working on the docks; both of these activities are featured in the New Orleans section of the novel. This same year the state legislature also passed laws curtailing the emancipation of slaves. Free people of color, too, felt the stings of similar crackdowns as their civic rights continually eroded throughout the decade. An 1859 law extended these restrictions to all free people of color entering the city, requiring that they either spend their time in the city jail or be confined to the boat on which they arrived until it left port. These changes to the city laws, while certainly repressive, created an environment readymade for a literary representation of the kind of Black radicalism seen in *Blake*. Caryn Cossé Bell and Joseph Logsdon argue that the coercion of these stricter laws "helped to develop a young leadership class that resisted Americanization and stood poised to create a new order based not merely on French ideas but also on recent applications of those ideas in other areas of the New World."[62]

Before Henry arrives at the meeting of these types of rebellious New Orleanians, he focuses on the ways various types of African Americans in the city deployed tactics to get by. The most significant of these representations comes in his account of the songs of the city. Delany's turn to music as a means of representing enslaved humanity works because the parodic songs he writes for his enslaved characters carefully walk the line between participating in the dominant white culture and acting as subversive attempts to undo this culture. He sets this up by including a lyric from the song "Hunters of Kentucky":

I suppose you've heard how New Orleans
Is famed for wealth and beauty;
There's girls of every hue, it seems,
From snowy white to sooty.[63]

This was a popular song used by Andrew Jackson in his 1828 campaign for President against John Quincy Adams, and it commemorates the people of Kentucky who fought in the Battle of New Orleans (1815). More could be said about how this battle resonates with Delany's antislavery writing and its significance for African Americans in New Orleans more generally; however, what is important here is that this song champions Kentucky fighters, instead of the enslaved and free people of color who derived much pride from their participation in this conflict, and it characterizes New Orleans as a city of licentiousness, a town of large fortunes and easy sex. In citing this particular verse, Delany sets up the popular representation of New Orleans that this section complicates as well as signals the divisions within the city's culture between French creoles and "Kaintucks," as they came to be known. This song was also—by virtue of its association with Jackson's campaign—aligned with proslavery ideology. Yet, while these associations are true, the phrase "from snowy white to sooty" had a strange double currency in the nineteenth century. As a result of the song's popularity, it became a cliché phrase, used by proslavery and antislavery writers to discuss what was known as amalgamation—the mixing of races—and its effects on the institution.

Tuning one's ear to these countervailing purposes apparent in Delany's use of this lyric gets to the heart of how parody works, and significantly, Delany evokes these multiple valences of "The Hunters of Kentucky" just before introducing the Mississippi River boatmen, whose song takes this satirical tendency further by reworking "Old Folks at Home," one of Stephen Foster's most popular tunes.[64] Henry hears the boatmen sing,

Way down upon the Mobile river,
Close to Mobile bay;
There's where my thoughts is running ever,
All through the livelong day:
There I've a good and fond old mother,
Though she is a slave;
There I've a sister and a brother,
Lying in their peaceful graves.[65]

Foster's original imagines an enslaved person pining for his former plantation home. In *Blake*, Delany invokes Foster's familiar melody and changes the lyrics to convey a sense of how enslavement brutalized families. In this way, Delany makes what Eric Lott has called "guerrilla appropriations" of the blackface minstrel tradition, writing "black agency back into history through blackface songs taken 'back' from those who had plundered black cultural practices."[66] These uses of blackface culture ultimately show the slippages and inadequacies embedded within the fictions of the power structure on which the slave system was predicated; though, as Henry recognizes, they fall short of setting an agenda to overthrow the slave system. A similar moment occurs later in this chapter during the clandestine meeting when one of the enslaved Africans celebrates in song the death of a master, clearly a reversal of Foster songs such as "Massa's in de Cold Ground" and "Uncle Ned." New Orleans was fitting for this kind of scene because, as a port city, it was a place of exchange, a feature that extended to the circulation of musical practices that entered the city from across the circum-Caribbean world. Additionally, New Orleans was—and still remains—a place that nurtured parody and satire, and Delany picks up on this tradition in this section of *Blake*.

The boatmen's parody of Foster's song, though, remains squarely in the momentary, elusive tactics of coping with slavery. In this way, the scene conveys a sense of enslaved humanity that enacts its politics in tandem with the cultural formations of everyday life. In *Blake* this becomes apparent through the paradoxical terms by which the narrator describes the boatmen. "The glee of these men of sorrow was touchingly appropriate and impressive," we are told.[67] The narrator continues in this line: "Men of sorrow they are in reality; for if there be a class of men anywhere to be found, whose sentiments of song and words of lament are made to reach the sympathies of others, the black slave-boatmen of the Mississippi river is that class."[68] For Henry, the dissonance displayed by these boatmen—in chronicling the abuses of slavery while doing so inconspicuously and without organized resistance—only serves to highlight their condition as slaves, and he resolves to enlighten them by organizing a revolutionary strategy that will dispel what he sees as the false consciousness on display in New Orleans. Rather than continuing to represent the tactical practices of enslaved New Orleanians, then, he seeks out the "rebel blacks" in the next part of the New Orleans section.

After witnessing the boatmen's song, Henry begins to think of himself as "a messenger of light and destruction," turning to his strategy of overthrowing the slave system.[69] He soon finds himself at a meeting of enslaved and free people of color who are debating an uprising. In this scene, Henry observes how the often-chaotic atmosphere of New Orleans during Mardi

Gras could create the conditions for a strategic, rather than tactical, response to enslavement, but he stops short of fully embracing the rebels he meets here. He worries over the group's reliance on religion—a constant theme when he meets new groups of enslaved people throughout the book. In the New Orleans section he declares at one moment, "my warfare is earthly, not Heavenly," suggesting that focusing on the hereafter might dismantle the logic of the political struggles with which he's engaged.[70] He also is troubled by the Samson-like, eager revolutionary Tibs, whom Henry judges not to be ready. Tibs refuses to continue with the careful plotting of the group and becomes increasingly irate. His rowdiness alerts the gendarmes, causing the meeting to disperse, and Tibs flees the scene shouting, "Insurrection! Insurrection! Death to every white!"[71]

This problem of readiness is raised throughout the novel and Delany finally leaves it unresolved by the novel's end. What's important, though, is that Afro-Caribbean "readiness" is the concept on which the novel's depiction of revolution turns, and New Orleans is the place from which Henry begins to puzzle over how to channel the nascent rebelliousness he sees animating the Afro-Caribbean world into a usable readiness. In New Orleans, as in Cuba, it becomes the difference between actions that lead to successful movements and those that more deeply entrench the status quo. Over the course of this scene, then, Henry witnesses a would-be revolution become fodder for tighter controls on the New Orleans population, prefiguring similar events that happen as part of the Kings Day celebration in Cuba. The New Orleans section thus ends with a depiction of how the relatively loose organization of the city could paradoxically lead to a strengthening of laws that would limit freedoms for Afro-New Orleanians aimed at providing white citizens with security.

This is in fact what happened as reports circulated about an actual uprising in June of 1853. In my work on *Blake* I have yet to find mention of this source in the scholarship on the novel, yet the details of how this event unfolded in the mainstream press prefigure how Delany worked out questions of revolution in the New Orleans section and his novel as a whole. As in *Blake*, this uprising was thought to have been the result of the plotting of a white schoolteacher and led to a citywide panic that fed into the changes to laws later in the decade.

In the first accounts of this rumored uprising, an unnamed free person of color confesses to knowledge of a widespread insurrection to be set off

Blake in the Crescent City: Antebellum Radicalism

around the city involving "2500 organized negroes."[72] This informant also told the police that the city was to be set on fire, "the flames to be the signal for revolt among the slaves on the neighboring plantations."[73] In the initial reports, this seems to be the kind of rebellion that Henry continually strives for in *Blake*, a coordinated attack that would devastate the opposition. However, the event was quickly deemed a false alarm, and within days it was widely reported that the information came from Albert, "a drunken negro" attached to a physician in the city.[74] Still, even in debunking the reality of this event papers registered the fears that these rumors called forth. The *New York Daily Times*, for instance, in the days surrounding the rebellion's discovery reported, "It has . . . been ascertained that quite a number of negroes have disappeared from their masters' residences, and that armed negroes in considerable bands have been seen in the neighborhood of Carrollton."[75] Delany puts such fears on display, as I discuss above, in both the New Orleans and Cuba sections. His novel also transforms Albert from his debunked status as "drunken," and therefore unreliable, informant into Tibs, who appears as an enraged Nat Turneresque character. Albert, too, may have been more like Tibs than most accounts of this event suggest. In its assessment of the events, the *New York Daily Times* recounted, "The wild stories of this very negro are proof, too, that his mind has been disturbed by influences that never suggest themselves spontaneously to a slave—and gross as the imposture is which they create, it is evidence of an unseen agency of mischief. . . ."[76] Delany alludes to this largely now forgotten historical event in order to show the precariousness with which his would-be revolutionary hero must conduct himself within a society predicated on the rationalization of enslavement. What constitutes "readiness" in such a situation, and when should one strike given the inevitability of the fearful backlash that will ensue? In this light, *Blake* could be seen as an extended attempt to clarify the relationships between activism, organization, everyday life, and political action.

The chaos and tightening of controls that animate the end of the New Orleans section also appear at the end of the novel, and since Delany never finished it, *Blake* never resolves the problems that these scenes raise. When Delany began serializing an expanded version of his novel in the *Weekly Anglo-African* in 1861, the Civil War was already underway and the national conversation about slavery was rapidly changing. 1862, the year that sections of the novel stopped appearing, New Orleans itself underwent great change with respect to its cultural, ethnic, and national alignments: the beginning of this year, for instance, saw the rise of the Louisiana Native Guard, a Confederate troop formed from the free Black community of the city, and by April the city fell to Union forces. Delany, too, adopted a different orientation to the project of racial uplift as he successfully lobbied Abraham Lincoln for a position in the Union Army and, after the war, as an administrator of the Freedmen's Bureau. However, in leaving the problems of revolutionizing enslaved Africans open-ended, *Blake* provides a heuristic for scholars of nineteenth-century slavery to assess the philosophical problems of Black agency within the confinements of this institution. As Delany suggests in his novel, New Orleans is a key component of this reassessment because, in the 1850s, the organization of the city walked a line between permissiveness and disciplinary control. On this score, more needs to be said about the function of *Blake*'s representation of religion in its New Orleans section since the African Methodist Episcopal church was a vibrant political force in the 1850s; in fact, the New Orleans delegates to Delany's 1854 convention in Cleveland came from this organization. In this light, the novel's dismissal of the New Orleans revolutionaries' religious sensibilities neglects the complexities of how this organization functioned for black New Orleanians. Even in light of this oversight, however, *Blake*'s New Orleans section importantly points to ways the city shaped Black political action and abolitionism more generally in the years before the War.

Notes

1. Martin R. Delany, *Blake; or, the Huts of America*, ed. Floyd J. Miller (Boston: Beacon Press, 1970), 83. *Blake* was first serialized in the *Anglo-African Magazine* from January through July of 1859. What would become chapters 29–31 in Miller's edition of the novel were first published in January 1859. The next month, the *Anglo-African* began publishing the novel sequentially from chapter 1, stopping in July with chapter 23, the New Orleans section of the novel. Two years later, the *Weekly Anglo-African* began serializing the novel, publishing chapters 1–74. The last installment known to exist appeared in April 1862, leaving the novel incomplete. It is believed that the novel's final chapters were published in the May 1862 edition of the magazine, but this has since been lost; Joseph Roach, *Cities of the Dead: Circum-Atlantic Performance* (New York: Columbia University Press, 1996), 179–80. Here, I follow Roach's description of New Orleans as a city that, by 1859, "had become America's fourth largest city and one of its busiest ports, a circum-Caribbean cosmopolis." Roach's characterization of the city purposefully turns away from a formulation of New Orleans as an "American" city in order to place it in the broader international context of cultural exchange.

2. Delany, *Blake; or, the Huts of America*, 39.

3. Delany, *Blake; or, the Huts of America*, 98.

Blake in the Crescent City: Antebellum Radicalism

4. Delany, *Blake; or, the Huts of America*, 102.

5. Delany, *Blake; or, the Huts of America*, 107.

6. Rodrigo Lazo, *Writing to Cuba: Filibustering and Cuban Exiles in the United States*, (Chapel Hill: UNC University Press, 2005), 142–43. Lazo explains the details of Delany's character Placido and the Cuban poet Gabriel de la Concepción Valdés, better known as Plácido. Lazo asserts that this poet, killed during a Spanish purge of enslaved revolutionaries in the 1840s, gave Delany an occasion to explore the effectiveness of writers during revolutionary upheavals. But Lazo's comments also note important political differences between the two figures.

7. Delany, *Blake; or, the Huts of America* 195.

8. Martin R. Delany, "Blake: or the Huts of America: A Tale of the Mississippi Valley, the Southern United States, and Cuba," *Anglo-African Magazine*, January 1, 1859, 20.

9. Robert Levine, *Martin Delany, Frederick Douglass, and the Politics of Representative Identity* (Chapel Hill: UNC University Press, 1997), 87–88.

10. Andy Doolen, "'Be Cautious of the Word 'Rebel': Race, Revolution, and Transnational History in Martin Delany's 'Blake; or, The Huts of America,'" *American Literature* 81, no. 1 (2009): 156.

11. Matt Sandler, "Kindred Darkness: Whitman in New Orleans," in *Whitman Noir: Black America and the Good Grey Poet*, ed. Ivy Wilson (Des Moines: University of Iowa Press, 2014), 66.

12. Walter Johnson, "On Agency," *Journal of Social History* 37, no. 1 (2003): 118.

13. Delany, *Blake; or, the Huts of America*, 98.

14. Michel de Certeau, *The Practice of Everyday Life*, trans. Steven F. Rendall (Berkley: University of California Press, 1988), 36–37.

15. Certeau, *The Practice of Everyday Life*, 37.

16. Clyde Woods, *Development Arrested: The Blues and Plantation Power in the Mississippi Delta* (London: Verso, 1998), 2.

17. Levine, 92. Levine details Stowe's novel as a key factor in the political divide between Delany and Frederick Douglass, which revolved around the book's representations of geography. This split led to rival conventions: one in 1853 held in Rochester, NY led by Douglass and featuring heavily the ideas on display in Stowe's novel and one in 1854 in Cleveland led by Delany that advocated West Indian emigration.

18. See, for example, Lydia Maria Child, *An Appeal in Favor of that Class of Americans Called Africans* (Boston: Allen and Ticknor, 1833); Fredrika Bremer, *America of the Fifties: Letters of Fredrika Bremer*, ed. Adolph Benson (New York: The American Scandinavian Society, 1924); Frederick Law Olmsted, *A Journey in the Seaboard Slave States; With Remarks on Their Economy* (New York: Negro Universities Press, 1968); Theodore Dwight Weld, *American Slavery As It Is: Testimony of a Thousand Witnesses* (New York: American Anti-Slavery Society, 1839); Harriet Beecher Stowe, *A Key to Uncle Tom's Cabin* (Boston: John P. Jewett and Co., 1853).

19. Frederick Douglass, *My Bondage and My Freedom*, ed. Henry Louis Gates (New York: Library of America, 1994), 437.

20. Douglass, *My Bondage and My Freedom*, 437.

21. Walter Johnson, *Soul by Soul: Life in the Antebellum Slave Market* (Cambridge: Harvard University Press, 1999), 22

22. Lisa Ze Winters, *The Mulatta Concubine: Terror, Intimacy, Freedom, and Desire in the Black Transatlantic* (Athens: University of Georgia Press, 2016), 161.

23. Winters, *The Mulatta Concubine*, 162.

24. Henry Bibb, *Narrative of the Life and Adventures of Henry Bibb: An American Slave* (1849) (New York: Dover, 2005), 106–7.

25. Walter Johnson, *Soul by Soul*, 171.

26. Douglass, *My Bondage and My Freedom*, 324.

27. Douglass, *My Bondage and My Freedom*, 326.

28. Douglass, *My Bondage and My Freedom*, 328.

29. Harriet Jacobs, *Incidents in the Life of a Slave Girl* (1861) (New York: Dover, 2001), 157.

30. Jacobs, *Incidents in the Life of a Slave Girl*, 163.

31. Floyd J. Miller, "Introduction," *Blake; or, the Huts of America*, ed. Floyd J. Miller (Boston: Beacon Press, 1970), xii.

32. Paul Gilroy, *The Black Atlantic: Modernity and Double-Consciousness* (Cambridge, MA: Harvard University Press, 1993), 27.

33. Gilroy, *The Black Atlantic*, 28.; National Emigration Convention of Colored People Cleveland (1854). *Proceedings of the National Emigration Convention of Colored People, held at Cleveland, Ohio, Thursday, Friday and Saturday, the 24th, 25th and 26th of August 1854.* [s.l.: s.n.].

34. National Emigration Convention of Colored People Cleveland, 20.

35. Eric Sundquist, *To Wake the Nations: Race in the Making of American Literature* (Cambridge: Harvard University Press, 1998), 188.

36. Kirsten Silva Gruesz, "Delta 'Desterrados': Antebellum New Orleans and New World Print Culture," *Look Away: The U.S. South in New World Studies* (Durham: Duke University Press, 2004), 55.

37. Ned Sublette, *The World that Made New Orleans: From Spanish Silver to Congo Square* (Chicago: Lawrence Hill Books, 2008), 104–5.

38. Silva Gruesz, "Delta 'Desterrados,'" 53–54.

39. Katy Chiles, "Within and Without Raced Nations: Intratextuality, Martin Delany, and 'Blake; or, the Huts of America,'" *American Literature* 80, no. 2 (2008): 325.

40. Gilroy, *The Black Atlantic*, 27.

41. Delany, *Blake; or, the Huts of America*, 101.

42. William W. Freehling, *The Road to Disunion, Volume II: Segregationists Triumphant: 1854–1861* (Oxford: Oxford University Press, 2007), 145.

43. Freehling, *The Road to Disunion*, 157.

44. Freehling, *The Road to Disunion*, 158–59.

45. Delany, *Blake; or, the Huts of America*, 109.

46. "Democratic Mass Meeting at New Orleans—Speech of Vernal John A. Quitman," *New York Daily Times* (New York, NY), August 25, 1855.

47. Jake Mattox, "The Mayor of San Juan Del Norte: Nicaragua, Martin Delany, and the 'Cotton' Americans," *American Literature* 81, no. 3 (2009).

48. See Arthur T. Downey, *The Creole Affair: The Slave Rebellion that Led the U.S. and Great Britain the Brink of War* (New York: Rowman and Littlefield Publishers, 2014) and Miller, 321 n.41. Downey gives an account of the changes in the piratical slave trade and US-British politics. Miller provides a comprehensive historiography of diverse scholars who have written about the illegal slave trade in the nineteenth century.

49. Delany, *Blake; or, the Huts of America*, 295.

50. Martin Delany, "Annexation of Cuba," *North Star* (Rochester, NY), April 27, 1849.

51. Delany, *Blake; or, the Huts of America*, 105.

52. Delany, *Blake; or, the Huts of America*, 299.

53. Delany, *Blake; or, the Huts of America*, 106–7

54. Delany, *Blake; or, the Huts of America*, 305.

55. Delany, *Blake; or, the Huts of America*, 98.

56. Delany, *Blake; or, the Huts of America*, 99–100.

57. Delany, *Blake; or, the Huts of America*, 100.

58. John Blassingame, *Black New Orleans, 1860–1880* (Chicago: University of Chicago Press, 1976), 2; Shirley Elizabeth Thompson, *Exiles at Home: The Struggle to Become American in Creole New Orleans* (Cambridge: Harvard University Press, 2009), 14

59. "The Condition of the Free Negro in Louisiana," *National Era* (Washington DC), June 29, 1848.

60. "From the Anti-Slavery Bugle: Abolitionism in New Orleans," *The Liberator*, (Boston, MA), September 16, 1853.

61. Olmsted, *A Journey in the Seaboard Slave States*, 592.

62. Joseph Logsdon and Caryn Cossé Bell, "The Americization of Black New Orleans: 1850–1900," *Creole New Orleans: Race and Americanization* (Baton Rouge: LSU Press, 1992), 208.

63. Delany, *Blake; or, the Huts of America*, 99.

64. Ken Emerson, *Doo-dah!: Stephen Foster and the Rise of American Popular Culture*, (New York: Simon and Schuster, 1997). In his biography of Stephen Foster, Ken Emerson explores the ways Foster's and Delany's paths crossed in Pittsburgh.

65. Delany, *Blake; or, the Huts of America*, 100–101.

66. Eric Lott, *Love and Theft: Blackface Minstrelsy and the American Working Class* (Oxford: Oxford University Press, 1995), 236.

67. Delany, *Blake; or, the Huts of America*, 100.

68. Delany, *Blake; or, the Huts of America*, 100.

69. Delany, *Blake; or, the Huts of America*, 101.

70. Delany, *Blake; or, the Huts of America*, 101.

71. Delany, *Blake; or, the Huts of America*, 106.

72. "Important from New Orleans—Projected Insurrection Among the Slaves—Preparations to Attack the City, etc." *Hartford Daily Courant* (Hartford, CT), June 16, 1853.

73. "Important from New Orleans."

74. "Important from New Orleans."

75. "The Negro Alarm in New Orleans—Language of the Press" (New York, NY), June 22, 1853.

76. "The Negro Alarm."

2

MORAL CONTAGION
Yellow Fever and the Moral Character of New Orleans[1]

Kathleen Downes

No discussion of yellow fever in New Orleans can begin without first examining its role in the Haitian Revolution. In October of 1801, Toussaint L'Ouverture, after a successful slave revolt against France, introduced a new constitution that abolished slavery. This constitution prompted Napoleon Bonaparte, in November of that year, to send General Victor-Emmanuel Charles Leclerc and forty-three thousand troops to Haiti to regain control from L'Ouverture and reestablish slavery. The French did not fare well against the revolutionary forces; as Ned Sublette recounts in *The World that Made New Orleans*, "the resistance of the black Domingans [*sic*] was ferocious," but "French soldiers and sailors died of yellow fever even faster than they could be killed."[2] General Leclerc himself died of yellow fever in November of 1802. By the end of the bloody conflict, of the forty-three thousand men that went, only eight thousand survived. To cut his losses, Bonaparte sold New Orleans and the Louisiana territory to the United States on May 2, 1803.

Not only was yellow fever a crucial role in how New Orleans became a part of the continental United States, but its endemic presence in the region played a key role in narratives of identity that generated from the cultural clash that New Orleans experienced after the Louisiana Purchase and throughout most of the nineteenth century. Due to the fact that yellow fever's etiology was unknown, authors employed the disease to criticize the practices and beliefs of their current society. Priscilla Wald, in her book *Contagious: Cultures, Carriers, and the Outbreak Narrative*, explains that

[l]iterary depictions of plague-ridden societies evince the complex vocabulary through which members of a ravaged population both respond to epidemics and experience the social connections that make them a community. The word *contagion* means literally "to touch together," and one of its earliest usages in the fourteenth century referred to the circulation of ideas and attitudes.... The circulation of disease and the circulation of ideas were material and experiential, even if not visible. Both displayed the power and danger of bodies in contact and demonstrated the simultaneous fragility and tenacity of social bonds.[3]

Yellow fever's presence signified for nineteenth-century New Orleanians a cultural sickness that was contagious, even if the disease itself was not. Imbedded in the literature of New Orleans are yellow fever acclimatization narratives that reveal the complex cultural clash that existed after the Louisiana Purchase. To resist Americanization, native New Orleanians subscribed to a yellow fever acclimatization narrative that the populations immigrating and migrating to New Orleans were susceptible to yellow fever because they were physically and morally unfit, and thus the cause of the continual presence of the disease. To combat these the nativist narratives, yellow fever in *The Mysteries of New Orleans* by Baron Ludwig von Reizenstein, *The Grandissimes* by George Washington Cable, and *The Queen's Garden* by M. E. M. Davis signifies a pervasive illness that stems from systemic inequalities that are upheld by white creole New Orleans society. Through the setting of New Orleans, these authors not only criticize white creole society, but use their novels to hold a mirror up to the nation and reveal that the systemic injustices upheld by white creole society are also sustained in larger nineteenth-century American society.

Today we know that yellow fever is an acute viral hemorrhagic fever. The virus has two phases of infection. After the initial incubation period of three to six days, the patient enters the first phase of infection which causes symptoms similar to that of influenza. The patient may experience fever, headache, muscle aches (primarily backache), shivers, nausea, and vomiting. Most patients recover after this phase and are immune to future infections. However, in some cases, the patient enters into the second and toxic phase of the disease. After a brief remission in which the patient appears to have recovered, the patient experiences organ failure and develops jaundice which causes the yellow skin color that gives the disease its name. The patient may have bleeding in the eyes, mouth, and stomach. Blood also appears in vomit and feces. The Spanish called this illness "Vomito Negro" because of the partially digested blood from stomach bleeding that colors the patient's vomit black. Fifty percent of the patients that enter this phase will die within ten to fourteen days.

Walter Reed's discovery in 1900 of yellow fever's transmission by the female *Aedes aegypti* mosquito led to mosquito control measures that eliminated the species and thus the virus from North America. However, yellow fever is not a disease of the past. It is estimated that every year 200,000 people are infected and 30,000 will die of the virus. Ninety percent of these cases are in Africa with the remainder appearing in Latin America. Due to urbanization, deforestation, and limited access to vaccination, it is believed that these numbers are climbing.

Yellow fever, or its carrier, the *Aedes aegypti* mosquito, is thought to have been introduced into the Western Hemisphere by slave ships coming from Africa. The Caribbean or West Indies provided a perfect climate for the incubation of the virus. In the southern United States, the first frost usually wiped out the mosquito population, thus causing the disease to disappear until the following summer, when the slave and trade ships coming from the West Indies would reintroduce the virus and the mosquito population would have regained healthy numbers. The disease was and is particularly deadly in urbanized regions. During the nineteenth century, most households in New Orleans relied on cisterns as a source of clean water, which was the prime breeding ground for mosquitos. Many people would leave urban areas for the summer months, favoring cooler and less swampy climates, thus lessening their exposure to mosquitos.

Yellow fever's transmission and the issues surrounding immunity to the disease greatly complicated the social structures in New Orleans after the Louisiana Purchase. Many nineteenth-century theories of the cause of yellow fever pointed to sanitation and poverty, the major cause of most other epidemics, like cholera. However, the actual transmission of the virus made these theories suspect because the illness was not confined to the poorer neighborhoods of New Orleans where sewage, livestock, and other refuse filled the streets. A brimming cistern in the back of a wealthy home could just as easily house the mosquito that spread yellow fever.

During the four decades that preceded the Louisiana Purchase, New Orleans had changed governmental hands four times. Originally colonized by France, New Orleans was given to Spain under the Treaty of Fontainebleau in 1762. In 1802, under the Third Treaty of San Ildefonso, Spain returned Louisiana to France. And a year later, the French sold the territory to the United States. The shift from French to Spanish rule in 1762 was less disruptive culturally than the shift to American rule after the 1803 Louisiana Purchase. Joseph Tregle Jr. explains in his essay "Creoles and Americans" that "[l]ike France, Spain was monarchic, her culture Latin, grounded in Roman law and Catholicism."[4] The Americans, however, were predominantly Protestant democratic republicans. In other words, the nation now controlling New Orleans stood in direct opposition to their entire way of life: culturally, religiously, and politically. By the same token, migrant and immigrant populations had to negotiate Latin culture, politics, and religion. In his book *Sword of Pestilence: The New Orleans Yellow Fever Epidemic of 1853*, John Duffy points specifically to the role of French Catholicism, which newcomers believed to be "exceedingly liberal and understanding of human frailties." The asceticism of Irish Catholicism and American Protestantism found these liberalities to be the root cause of the vice and sin in which "much of New Orleans's reputation for wickedness arose," and this reputation was perpetuated by "the jaundiced reports of sturdy New Englanders desperately fighting losing battles with their consciences."[5] Compounding these "jaundiced reports" was the fact that the demographics hardest hit by yellow fever were the immigrating Europeans and migrating Americans after the Louisiana Purchase. Native-born New Orleanians had a greater chance of contracting the disease in their youth during which survival rate is highest.

Because of the clear distinction that the disease's immunity draws between newcomer and native, nativist narratives circulated that painted the fever as a "stranger's disease" and cast the populations of immigrating Europeans and Americans as sickly and unfit for life in the city. Many narratives highlighted the inhospitable climate of heat and humidity to which the newcomer was unacclimated and argued that working under such conditions only weakened the newcomer's constitution, making them more susceptible to disease. Lafcadio Hearn, who immigrated to America in 1869 from Ireland and arrived in New Orleans by way of Cincinnati in 1877, describes a process in which a newly arrived individual must physically acclimate to the climate of this region. Hearn warns in his sketch "The Creole Doctor: Some Curiosities of Medicine in Louisiana" that the newly arrived individual in New Orleans must take extra caution until the process of acclimatization is complete. He explains that "[d]uring this process of enervation the stranger is particularly liable to fever. . . . The acclimated citizen rarely suffers from these maladies; but woe to the incautious and energetic stranger who attempts to live in this subtropical and pyrogenic region, indifferent to the danger of excessive fatigue, or the perils of self-exposure to sudden changes of temperature."[6] Hearn's warning underscores the nativist argument that newcomers were less physically fit than native New Orleanians. While Hearn focuses on the physical susceptibility to the disease, the nativist acclimatization narrative also included concerns about the moral fitness of the newcomers. Benjamin Trask, in his book *Fearful Ravages: Yellow Fever in New Orleans, 1796–1905*, refers to another yellow fever narrative called the "Seaman's Fate." New Orleans, as a port city, attracted a large transient population who left their families behind in pursuit of wealth. These populations, freed from social responsibility, were believed to live a life of excessive physical indulgences, taking part in gambling, prostitution, and drunkenness. Trask explains that "[t]o avoid the seaman's fate, according to nineteenth-century thought, a person needed to demonstrate self-control. Excesses drained individuals of their strength and natural ability to fight infections."[7] The nineteenth-century nativist acclimatization narrative argued that yellow fever susceptibility was indicative of the physical and moral unfitness of newcomers. Additionally, surviving infection with yellow fever became known as the "'city Creolism' process," signifying the entanglement of health as both a physiological and cultural experience.[8] This narrative of yellow fever views the endemic presence not as a symptom of a failing public health system but as further evidence of the physical and moral superiority of the native New Orleanians over the migrating and immigrating populations.

While the migrant and immigrant yellow fever narratives cannot dismiss the susceptibility of migrant and immigrant populations to the disease, they refocus the continual presence of yellow fever in New Orleans onto the larger systemic inequalities upheld by white Creole society. Each of these texts interrogate the nativist narrative by arguing that the endemic presence of yellow fever is due, not to the physical and moral unfitness of migrating and immigrating populations, but to white creole society's support for slavery and adherence to a racial and aristocratic class system. Through their criticisms of a unique and regional culture, these writers work to hold a mirror up for the rest of the nation to see their complacency in these institutions that are also present in the larger American society.

Baron Ludwig von Reizenstein, a German immigrant, published the *Mysteries of New Orleans* as a serial publication in the German newspaper *Louisiana Staats-Zeitung* in 1854. As part of the city mysteries genre, Reizenstein's novel explores the seamy underbelly of New Orleans and sets out to reveal the hypocrisy and greed inherent in a culture that supports the institution of slavery. Reizenstein, who emigrated from Germany to the US in 1848, wrote his novel during and after the 1853 yellow fever epidemic. This epidemic was particularly devastating, and as Duffy explains, "[w]ithin four and a half months, a tenth of the population died and over 40 percent sickened."[9] Reizenstein's own demographic—German immigrants—were particularly devastated during this epidemic.

Reizenstein repurposes the acclimatization narrative to reveal the injustices committed by the native citizens of New Orleans and those immigrants who have acclimated. In Reizenstein's text, yellow fever exists in New Orleans as a scourge for slavery. However, this sickness doesn't affect those who are complicit in the sins of capitalistic greed and slavery but finds its victims in the innocent. Much like the nativist narrative, survival is predicated on adapting to the culture, which, in Reizenstein's argument is the relinquishing of one's morality. Affliction with the disease is a sign of one's moral purity. Reizenstein is not offering a solution for the ills of Creole and American society. His vision for the future is apocalyptic at best. Through the spread of yellow fever, Reizenstein highlights the immoral institutions and practices of New Orleans and, by extension, American society and the chaotic retribution that can be expected. Infection with the disease is the sign of one's purity. To survive the disease is to not just acclimate physically but to forfeit one's moral purity and become compliant in a hypocritical system of government that touts freedom but continues to enslave human beings.

To expose New Orleans's adherence to an exploitative economic system, Reizenstein focuses his narrative on the experiences of a German aristocratic family emigrating to New Orleans. Emil's and Lajo's acclimatization to the culture and politics of American society leads Emil's parents and siblings into precarious conditions in which they are exposed to the disease, left without medical care, and ultimately become victims of the disease.

Emil, despite his German aristocratic background and an aborted attempt to return home, quickly falls prey to the allure of the American way of life. That fall is clear after Emil finds out that his slave Tiberius has been sold. Reizenstein's narrator explains that "[t]his news delivered a painful blow, not so much to his heart as to his pride. One must know about certain practices among the Creoles, to which Emil had accustomed his German character immediately after arriving in New Orleans and which he bore on the whole in quite a proper manner."[10] The narrator concludes that Emil's pride being hurt above his heart is evidence that Emil has adapted to New Orleans culture because his morality has been compromised. Another indication of Emil's acclimatization is his wavering remorse for leaving his wife, Jenny. In a tirade he asks himself how he could ever leave Jenny and places the blame on his mistress, Lucy, whom he describes as "this money-loving whore, this slippery snake!"[11] Hiram, an apocalyptic figure who uses Emil to bring about revolution, quickly calms Emil by offering money. Emil at "the sight of money, which was in good notes drawn on the Citizens' Bank . . . was greatly relieved . . . Jenny and her sister-in-law were forgotten, as were his dear parents."[12] Emil, like a "money-loving whore," is quick to forget his marital loyalty at the sight of money. Reizenstein characterizes Emil's acclimatization to New Orleans culture as an acceptance of exploitative capitalism that encourages him to abandon his wife and family. The narrator prophesizes that Emil's "disobedience, his poor fulfillment of his duty after he and Lucy left the upper chambers of the Atchafalaya Bank—O dreadful fate, for this disobedience his dear parents and his innocent siblings were to be punished."[13] While Emil never contracts yellow fever, his acclimatization to exploitative capitalism leaves his family exposed to circumstances that will eventually lead to their deaths by yellow fever.

Lajos, Frida's husband, has similarly acclimated to the American system. Upon reaching America, Lajos has become a murderer and arsonist. He has set himself up in fraudulent business with a French priest named Dubreuil and an Italian merchant, who hire themselves out as arsonists so that their clients can collect insurance money. Unfortunately, Emil's family resides in one of the buildings that Lajos is contracted to burn down. During the fire, Emil's mother braves the flames to save a portrait of Emil, only to have all the family's money ripped from her hands by Lajos. This act leaves the family destitute and forced to live in a filthy tenement which previously "had been held by a black washerwoman who also practiced a horizontal profession."[14] It is in this tenement housing that his family contracts yellow fever and dies. Lajos's greed leaves the family destitute without any means to properly care for themselves. Reizenstein, in this scene, explores the popular belief that sanitation and poverty are to blame for the spread of fever. However, Reizenstein reveals that poverty is not always linked to individual vice, but through the experiences of an aristocratic German family, he is able to reveal the role that exploitative capitalism plays in the spread of disease.

Those who have acclimated themselves to the degenerate mores of the city are not the only ones implicated in the death of innocents in Reizenstein's novel. The author also critiques those who should have been responsible for the alleviation of the suffering caused by yellow fever. Reizenstein describes a scene in which Gertrude, Emil's sister, is searching for a doctor to save her family. Reizenstein addresses readers directly in his attempt to pull at their hearts: "[t]he intelligent little face, which appears already to have seen things beyond the ken of children, has to capture the heart at the first glance, and when you see the child pale and suffering, you are driven to ask from the innermost part of your being: 'Child, what's the matter? And if I can help you, will you trust me?'"[15] Sadly for Gertrude, she meets no such sympathetic, trustworthy person who can help her. When she finally finds a doctor, he refuses to help her because she can't provide payment up front. In the novel, American doctors are embroiled in capitalistic greed and have little compassion for their patients unless a large sum of money is offered first. If not, they are quick to let them die.

Reizenstein also depicts American philanthropists as highly suspect. He writes, "[t]hese philanthropists from the 'upper-ten' class were often such base persons, despite their great donations to charitable institutions that whatever they gave with one hand they sought to win back again with the other, double or triple."[16] He describes a wealthy housing proprietor who donates to the Howard Association, an organization that was much heralded as a saving force during yellow fever epidemics, but a man who cares little for those suffering in his own tenements. Due to the epidemic, his wealthier tenants have fled the city, leaving much of the proprietor's better housing empty. Despite his seemingly gracious donation, this gentleman makes no move to assist his tenants by offering them empty housing to nurse their sick. Thus, his pitiful donation could hardly compensate for his avaricious housing business. Further illustrating this horror, we find Emil's family suffering from the fever in a similar tenement. Reizenstein's depiction of doctors and philanthropists of the novel reveals that the greed inherent in exploitative capitalism further exacerbates the conditions that lead to increased exposure to yellow fever and inhibit proper medical care.

Finally, Reizenstein attempts to subvert the nativist argument that surviving yellow fever is in some way indicative of one's physical and moral fitness. Instead, Reizenstein describes some of his most despicable characters as physically displaying a kind of rot from within that often resembles the symptoms of yellow fever. He reveals these characters to be carriers of a kind of moral sickness. For example, he describes Dubreuil, a French priest who actively takes part in sexual slavery, as a man whose "entire manner, his slack facial features, his unsteady, unclean gaze, continually leering at the rows of the girls, testified to his identity as a man who had plunged to the depths. . . . His face had that indeterminate color between that of one recovering from yellow fever and that of a drunken decadent."[17] Another such character whose greed transforms into a sickly appearance is an Italian travelling merchant, rumored to have taken advantage of an immigrant heiress by promising to marry her in exchange for money, but instead he murders her. He is described as one whose "continuous excesses in all sorts of debauchery managed to give him that paunchy, yellowed appearance that elicits no admiration and fills any healthy, strongman with contempt and disgust."[18] Despite these characters' sickly appearances and excessive and immoral lifestyles, they do not die of yellow fever. Much like Emil and Lajos, their immorality has secured their survival.

In contrast to the sickly appearances of the acclimated citizens are the innocent victims of the fever. The first victim, Miss Dudley Evans, is described as "the perfect image of a saint, and if she had lived a hundred years earlier, she would certainly have been canonized."[19] Dudley Evans's death signifies her purity and incorruptibility. Another such pure character is a young girl named Gertrude whom Reizenstein describes as having forget-me-not blue eyes that "gazed out at the world so true-heartedly."[20] After a heroic effort to find aid for her ailing family she succumbs to the disease.

Reizenstein uses the yellow fever epidemic to critique the hypocritical nature of American democracy. The actions of the acclimatized immigrants and the native-born citizens of New Orleans bring about the destruction of innocents. If Emil had not chosen money over his family, if the philanthropist had the compassion to open the better tenements to his suffering tenants, if the doctors could see past their need for payment to offer aid in a time of great need, Emil's family might have lived or the suffering been minimized. Ultimately, however, if American greed could be restrained and the institution of slavery abolished, the threat of yellow fever would become a distant memory. Reizenstein's ultimate goal for his novel was to expose the hypocrisy of American capitalistic democracy. Yellow fever in Reizenstein's text plays a critical role in revealing the exploitative greed inherent in American capitalism that cares little about the well-being of the poor and sick and is willing to enslave others for the sake of a dollar.

Similar to Reizenstein, yellow fever in George Washington Cable's novel *The Grandissimes* is indicative of the injustices brought about by the institution of slavery and by extension the injustices still being committed by a society unwilling to relinquish the way of life under the plantation system in post–Civil War America. George Washington Cable's perspective on yellow fever and New Orleans is unique because he, unlike Reizenstein and M. E. M. Davis, was born and raised in the city. His parents, however, were from the North: his mother from Indiana and his father from Pennsylvania. Because of his parentage, Cable was considered an American and not part of the Creole society. In fact, his writings about Creoles in Louisiana were often reviled by Creole society. While Cable's reception was mixed, his works still exposed the complex nature of life in New Orleans. Cable's works focused on the experiences of immigrants, the struggles of Americanization, the complicated issue of race, all the while painting a portrait of Creole society as un-American and backwards. As a reformed secessionist, who had fought for the Confederate side in the Civil War, Cable dedicated much of his work to social reform. Many of his texts dealt with issues of race and class facing New Orleans and the American South after Reconstruction.

Cable's novel, *The Grandissimes*, was published in 1879, shortly after the devastating yellow fever epidemic of 1878, the worst in American history. Cable, himself, lost a son and brother-in-law during this epidemic. Cable's novel is the story of a Creole family and their struggle to retain their political and economic dominance in the face of invading Americans after the Louisiana Purchase. The Creoles in Cable's novel are resistant to the change that the Louisiana Purchase has caused and the issues needing to be faced surrounding racial equality. Cable's novel was intended to stand as a mirror to his own contemporary society who faced similar issues during the post–Civil War and Reconstruction era. Yellow fever in Cable's novel is a sickness that stems from an inability to rise to the correct action to accept change in these significant moments of transition and move towards racial equality. Setting the novel in antebellum Louisiana, where slavery was still an active practice, allows Cable to criticize his own postbellum society in which slavery had been abolished, and use yellow fever's endemic presence in the South to argue that abolishing slavery is by no means the end of the race issue.

Cable's novel features two protagonists: one is a progressive Creole named Honoré Grandissime[21] who believes that the institution of slavery is wrong but is unable to act due to the pressure of familial responsibility; the second is an American migrant named Joseph Frowenfeld whose resistance to wholly acclimatize to Creole society allows him to inspire Honoré into progressive action and work towards racial equality.

In a chapter titled "The Fate of the Immigrant," Cable explores the nativist narratives of yellow fever that emphasize the immigrant's susceptibility to both the disease and death. Upon arrival in New Orleans, he, his parents, and two young sisters contract the disease and all but Frowenfeld die. In a graveyard, mourning the loss of his family, Frowenfeld meets and befriends Honoré Grandissime, who further explains the acclimatization process, of which yellow fever is only the beginning. Honoré explains that adaptation is

> not in body only, that you have done; but in mind—in taste—in conversation—in convictions too, yes, ha, ha! They all do it—all who come. They hold out a little while—a very little, then they open their stores on Sunday, they import cargoes of Africans, they bribe the officials, they smuggle goods, they have colored housekeepers. My-de'-seh, the water must expect to take the shape of the bucket; eh?[22]

In this passage, Cable makes a most scathing criticism of Creole society. Honoré clearly views Creole society's adherence to slavery and illegal business practices as wrong, but he also believes that everyone that enters New Orleans is susceptible to immoral business practices. For Cable, the Creoles live a hedonistic lifestyle above both law and God. Full acclimatization includes the acquisition of a physical constitution that can withstand fevers and the blazing sun as well as flexible moral principles that allow for slavery and illegal business practices.

While Frowenfeld has acclimated physically, he questions Creole society mores and resists adopting them. Honoré admits that the institution of slavery is wrong; however, he argues that "one man walks where he sees another's track; that is what makes a path; but you want a man, instead of passing around this prickly bush, to lay hold of it with his naked hands and pull it up by the roots."[23] Frowenfeld counters Honoré's argument by saying, "[b]ut a man armed with the truth is far from being barehanded."[24] The Creoles immersed in the social mores of their own culture cannot see a way out of that culture's ethically immoral practices. By resisting cultural acclimatization and by questioning Honoré, Frowenfeld becomes the mirror in which Honoré, a progressive Creole, is able to fully understand the actions that need to be taken so that his family and his society can move forward.

Honoré too experiences a kind of residual fever stemming from his inability to move past his loyalty to his family and society and towards a more equal future. Honoré explains to Frowenfeld that "there is a kind of tree not dreamed of in botany, that lets fall its fruit every day in the year—you know? We call it—with—reverence—'our dead father's mistakes.' I have had to eat much of that fruit; a man who has to do that must expect to have now and then a little fever."[25] Yellow fever in Cable's novel represents a pervasive cultural sickness, comprising both the immoral practices that perpetuate racial inequality and the festering resistance to change these immoral practices. The American Frowenfeld's resistance to the cultural acclimatization allows Honoré to see a way in which he can move beyond the responsibility to his family and help to alleviate racial inequality and end the South's affliction by yellow fever. In effect, Honoré begins to acclimate to the newcomer.

In his exploration of the process of acclimatization, Cable is suggesting that if newcomers consistently acclimate socially and morally, the city is doomed. Yellow fever's endemic presence, both in antebellum and postbellum American South is a festering illness stemming from a society unwilling to face the issues of racial inequality and take action to correct these issues.

Like Cable, Mollie Evelyn Moore Davis also suggests that a brighter future for New Orleans is only possible with the assistance of the newcomer. M. E. M. Davis, as she was known, was born in Benton County, Alabama, in 1844, and in 1855 she moved to West Texas, where her father practiced medicine. In 1874, she married Thomas E. Davis, who lost his tobacco fortune in 1875. Four years later, the couple moved to New Orleans. There Thomas Davis found work as an editorial writer with *The Picayune*, which later became the *Times-Picayune* when it merged with the *New Orleans Times* in 1914.

Davis's novel, *The Queen's Garden*, was published in 1900 just as the cause of the disease was being discovered. However, yellow fever remained endemic in the southern United States till 1905. Davis's yellow fever narrative explores the tensions between a Creole aristocratic class system that excludes the migrating and immigrating populations. Davis's novel is distinct from the other two in that it explores the process of acclimatization from the perspective of a woman. The sensuous setting of New Orleans not only allows for Davis to criticize an immovable class system, but it gives her the space to explore female sexuality and agency in the United States at the turn of the century.

Noel Lepeyre, the protagonist in *The Queen's Garden*, is thin, plain, and exceedingly innocent. Orphaned at a young age, Noel has lived an austere life depending on her mother's family for support. The novel opens with Noel travelling to New Orleans to be chaperoned by her father's sister, Tante Marguerite. In contrast to Noel's innocent and austere, and arguably American appearance, are the exotic descriptions of the landscape and people of her new home. On the train Noel finds that "[t]he landscape, poetic, semi-tropical, unfamiliar, harmonized, to . . . [her] dreaming fancy, with the foreign speech of a group of girls."[26] Noel concludes that "[a]pparently there was nothing foreign about herself except her name. Her fluttering neighbors were dark-haired, velvet-eyed, plump, bewitching. Noel was tall and slim—much too meagre, indeed, for beauty."[27] Noel finds herself enchanted, but behind the bewitching, exotic imagery is something ominous. The Mississippi River, as Noel crosses it, is "motionless under the darkening sky. Only a bit of drift-wood swirling by, here and there betrayed the treacherous undercurrent at that moment gnawing away the very point upon which the ferry-landing was constructed."[28] While the landscape may be poetic, harmonious, and placid, beneath it something gnaws at the very ground Noel walks on, waiting to consume her. Noel longs to become a part of her new home, but the narrator foreshadows that there is something treacherous about her new home.

In contrast to the river, the French Quarter very visibly reveals the filth and debauched nature of the city. The streets are filled with nauseating sewage and street urchins. Just a "half square away" from her aunt's home is a house of ill repute.[29] The description of New Orleans emphasizes the narrative of yellow fever that connects the disease to sanitation issues, poverty, and moral looseness. Yet, yellow fever exists within the safety of her aunt's house. Upon arrival, Noel learns that her aunt has fallen ill with the fever, and due to the laws surrounding the illness, both are to be quarantined from the city as well as from each other.

Deprived of her only chaperone. She spends most of her time in her aunt's garden, which reminds her of "far-off islands of citron and spice, of lithe brown lads and slender, large-hipped girls,—the land of the pomegranate and the nightingale, the land of the Thousand and One Nights."[30] The garden is full of the exotic, poetic imagery of the landscape described during Noel's train ride. Davis writes that Noel is like "[t]he dragon-fly just escaped from the chrysalis . . . trying its wings for the first time, giddy with a sense of freedom, and loath to alight!"[31] Her newfound freedom, the sensuous and exotic nature of the garden and, by extension, New Orleans, encourage Noel to psychologically and physically awaken. She relinquishes her austere garments of black for white muslin. Within the garden, "[a]ll the repressed girlhood within Noel Lepeyre, with its instinctive love for pretty and dainty things, bubbled to the surface. She danced across the bare polished floor,—which reflected her figure like a still mountain lake,—to the swinging cheval glass."[32] Noel, released for the strict supervision of her mother's family, is free in New Orleans to express and enjoy herself.

It is also within this garden that Noel begins to sexually awaken. Next door to her aunt's is a young journalist. The suitor leaves Noel red roses on the balcony, and in the innocent mind of Noel, she imagines that "'[i]t must have been the Beast!'"[33] Noel finds "herself suddenly alone; a desire for companionship possessed her; a sick longing seized her which seemed to turn all her body, now hot, now cold."[34] Davis mirrors the symptoms of yellow fever with that of love and physical desire.

Her courtship and transformation climax as she meets her lover, Richard, one night in the garden. While pledging their love to each other, the two witness the blossoming of a night-blooming cactus. The *Epiphyllum oxypetalum* is a container plant that has been grown by generations of New Orleanians and is commonly referred to as "Queen of the Night."[35] In each other's arms, Noel and Richard witness "[s]now-white and lovely, like a bride awaiting her bridegroom, the exquisite blossom, wide open,—a radiant wheel,—swayed as if to spirit music on the up-curbed bracket-like stem; the slender petals whispered to some invisible Presence; the golden heart quivered as if under the caress of an unseen lover."[36] This highly coded night scene of quivering buds and love pledges is arguably Noel and Richard physically pledging their love to each other. Upon parting, Richard warns Noel of the terrible illness that is spreading through New Orleans. She is to be especially careful since she is not a native—and possibly because she has just committed an act of indulgence.

The next morning Noel finds herself feeling heavy and slow-moving, and she looks on the garden with "bloodshot eyes, whose luminous gray was faded to a wan yellow."[37] Like Noel, the flower is in a state of ruin: "[a]n unsightly semblance of a refolded bud drooped upon an inert discolored stem. A few limp, yellowish white petals straggled from the inclosing sheath; a sickly odor exhaled from them. It was like a corpse from which even the still beauty of death had departed."[38] The garden that was once beautiful is transformed into a scene of death and ruination. The garden and Noel's ruinous state after her sexual awakening with Richard seems to align with the acclimatization narrative that excess leaves the body susceptible to disease.

However, yellow fever was already present in the household when Noel arrived. Noel's aunt's affliction with yellow fever, and arguably the endemic presence of the disease in New Orleans, symbolizes the decaying values and mores of Creole society. Davis is critical of Creole society for its adherence to an aristocratic caste system. Much of Noel's aunt's house is described as decadent and very much in the fashion of the Old World. Her own bedroom is described as having a "[p]syche dressing-table draped with dotted muslin; and cheval glass, much spotted and discolored within its heavy frame. A bronze clock, silent and somber on the mantel, bore the date of the first French Empire."[39] Time has stopped in her aunt's house, emphasizing the white Creole society's inability to change and move forward. The home plays a crucial role also in Davis's criticism of the Creole's adherence to European ways. Davis describes the drawing room from Noel's naïve perspective:

> A funereal atmosphere pervaded the dim vastness. The antique furniture, cumbrous, obsolete, and handsome. . . . The priceless pictures on the walls were wellnigh [sic] meaningless to her uneducated eyes; great dark forest landscapes, peopled with fleeing nymphs and pursuing gods; Greek temples once white, now fallen yellow and cracked on their wooded heights; sallow martyres [sic], blue-mantled virgins, somber crucifixions.[40]

The funereal atmosphere simultaneously emphasizes the decaying and backwards nature of New Orleans aristocracy while foreshadowing Noel's aunt's eventual demise. Subverting the cultural acclimatization narrative of yellow fever, Noel survives the disease while her aunt succumbs to yellow fever.

While Noel's contraction of yellow fever seems to hinge on Noel's sexual awakening, Davis complicates this reading through a fairytale that Noel's father told her as a child, a tale called "The Queen's Garden." In the story, a queen, who is locked in a garden, is visited by a prince who travels a secret passage called "Claude's Way."[41] Noel learns, while in the garden, that the queen was actually her aunt and the lover was Dr. Grafton, who was also a close friend of her father's. Her aunt's choice of family and class over her lover caused Noel's father to sever ties with his family. Additionally, even though

Dr. Grafton attends Aunt Marguerite after she contracts yellow fever, he is unable to save her. Nevertheless, when Noel chooses to traverse "Claude's Way" to administer to her ill lover next door, Dr. Grafton, who was called to administer to Richard, is made aware of her need for treatment and is able to save both Richard and Noel. Noel was forced to make a choice similar to that of her aunt. However, Noel's salvation lies in her choosing love over class which ultimately saved her life.

In her novel, Davis explores two possible narratives about the spread of yellow fever. While Noel sickens after acting upon her sexual desires, the far graver sin is to deny one's heart for the sake of class status. The funereal images pervasive throughout Noel's aunt's house and the eventual death of her aunt remind us of Cable's critique of an immovable Creole society unwilling to change and move towards a more just, progressive future. While Davis stealthily couches Noel's sexual awakening by suggesting her contraction of yellow fever is linked to her sexual act with Richard, it is just as arguable that her contraction of yellow fever is linked to Creole society's adherence to their aristocratic class system. In *The Queen's Garden*, Davis is able to explore female sexuality and agency without overtly condoning Noel's sexual awakening. Noel's experience in New Orleans and with yellow fever transforms her into a woman capable of making decisions of social and even political consequences. Like Frowenfeld, in *The Grandissimes*, Noel's refusal to fully acclimate to her new home reveals a path to a more equal society and a vision for a more American New Orleans.

Yellow fever narratives set in New Orleans in the nineteenth century reveal more about the struggles of a southern city in America than about the nature of the disease. These narratives use yellow fever acclimatization narratives in New Orleans to hold a mirror up to the nation to reveal how larger systemic inequalities are to blame for the endemic presence of "disease" in the southern United States.

Notes

1. A version of this work appears in Downes's master's thesis. Kathleen Downes, "Contagious Deadly Sins: Yellow Fever in Nineteenth-Century New Orleans Literature" (master's thesis, University of New Orleans, 2015).

2. Ned Sublette, *The World that Made New Orleans: From Spanish Silver to Congo Square*, (Chicago: Chicago Review Press, 2009), 196.

3. Priscilla Wald, *Contagious: Cultures, Carriers, and the Outbreak Narrative* (Durham: Duke University Press, 2008), 12–13.

4. Joseph Tregle Jr., "Creoles and Americans," in *Creole New Orleans: Race and Americanization*, ed. Arnold R. Hirsch and Joseph Logsdon (Baton Rouge: LSU Press, 1992), 134.

5. John Duffy, *Sword of Pestilence: The New Orleans Yellow Fever Epidemic of 1853* (Baton Rouge: LSU Press, 1966), 3.

6. Lafcadio Hearn, *Inventing New Orleans* (Jackson: University Press of Mississippi, 2001), 65–66.

7. Benjamin Trask, *Fearful Ravages: Yellow Fever in New Orleans 1796–1905* (Lafayette: University of Louisiana Press, 2005), 51.

8. Trask, *Fearful Ravages*, 8.

9. Duffy, *Sword of Pestilence*, vii.

10. Baron Ludwig von Reizenstein, *The Mysteries of New Orleans* (Baltimore: Johns Hopkins University Press, 2002), 456.

11. Reizenstein, *The Mysteries of New Orleans*, 463.

12. Reizenstein, *The Mysteries of New Orleans*, 467.

13. Reizenstein, *The Mysteries of New Orleans*, 503.

14. Reizenstein, *The Mysteries of New Orleans*, 431.

15. Reizenstein, *The Mysteries of New Orleans*, 421.

16. Reizenstein, *The Mysteries of New Orleans*, 428.

17. Reizenstein, *The Mysteries of New Orleans*, 52.

18. Reizenstein, *The Mysteries of New Orleans*, 257.

19. Reizenstein, *The Mysteries of New Orleans*, 56.

20. Reizenstein, *The Mysteries of New Orleans*, 192.

21. It is important to note that there are three characters named Honoré Grandissime. The novel opens with a brief history of the Grandissime family in which the first Honoré Grandissime is in a love relationship with a woman of mixed race. This relationship procures the second Honoré Grandissime known as a free man of color (f. m. c.). Due to familial pressures, the first Honoré Grandissime marries a white woman of whom the third Honoré Grandissime is born. It is the legitimate son who is featured as a protagonist.

22. George Washington Cable, *The Grandissimes* (New York: Penguin Books, 1988), 38.

23. Cable, *The Grandissimes*, 39.

24. Cable, *The Grandissimes*, 39

25. Cable, *The Grandissimes*, 219.

26. Mollie E. M. Davis, *The Queen's Garden* (Cambridge, MA: The Riverside Press, 1900), 2.

27. Davis, *The Queen's Garden*, 2.

28. Davis, *The Queen's Garden*, 12.

29. Davis, *The Queen's Garden*, 19.

30. Davis, *The Queen's Garden*, 73.

31. Davis, *The Queen's Garden*, 58.

32. Davis, *The Queen's Garden*, 47.

33. Davis, *The Queen's Garden*, 66.

34. Davis, *The Queen's Garden*, 66.

35. Dan Gill, "Tips for growing night blooming cereus: Dan Gill's mailbag," Nola.com, September 5, 2014, http://www.nola.come/homegarden/index.ssf/2014/09/tips_for _growing_night_bloomin.html.

36. Davis, *The Queen's Garden*, 103.
37. Davis, *The Queen's Garden*, 116.
38. Davis, *The Queen's Garden*, 109–10.
39. Davis, *The Queen's Garden*, 46.
40. Davis, *The Queen's Garden*, 60.
41. Davis, *The Queen's Garden*, 133.

3

"THE VOICE OF THE SEA"
The Specter of Transatlantic Slavery in *The Awakening*

Carina Evans Hoffpauir

When the video for Beyoncé's "Formation" was released in early 2016, a spotlight was once again cast on New Orleans as a vibrant site of US historical and cultural significance. While we need only to look to early jazz to know there's nothing new about popular music celebrating the vitality of New Orleans, Beyoncé's explicit call to action for Gulf Coast Black women emerged as a feminist intervention in this tradition. The song's lyrics and visuals—indicated by the chorus, "Okay, ladies, now let's get in formation"—serve as a paean to Black female survival in the old and new South, attempting to make visible the generations of those who have been oppressed, overlooked, and silenced in the region. Throughout the video, rising water is used as a visual metaphor for the Gulf Coast Black female experience; Beyoncé is shown astride a New Orleans police cruiser while floodwater threatens to engulf the vehicle. The water is simultaneously a threat and a placeholder for potential forms of liberation. As Wesley Morris explains in the *New York Times* explication of the video, "The image of Beyoncé in that dress atop the cruiser has some Toni Morrison poetry. You don't know whether the shots constitute a baptism or a drowning."[1] Morris is wise here to treat "Formation" as text and merge its criticism with existing literary conversations about Black female survival in the South. I draw upon these metaphors in "Formation" as an opportunity to focus on related forms of aquatic and regional imagery in Kate Chopin's *The Awakening*. While set apart by more than a century, Chopin's 1899 novel shares the same regional space and it similarly uses Gulf Coast imagery to explore themes of feminist empowerment; the difference is that

The Specter of Transatlantic Slavery in *The Awakening*   57

while one text makes visible the experience of Black women, the other ironically subverts this narrative to instead feed burgeoning forms of privileged white feminist consciousness. *The Awakening* serves as an example of what would compel response from Beyoncé and her literary predecessors.

Metaphors of the sea and slavery abound in *The Awakening*, and readers are encouraged to contemplate these forces calling to the protagonist, Edna Pontellier. While vacationing on Grand Isle, Edna experiences a transformation, an unmooring from her responsibilities as a dutiful wife and mother: "Sailing across the bay [. . .], Edna felt as if she were being borne away from some anchorage which had held her fast, whose chains had been loosening. [. . .]"[2] This scene referencing Edna's "loosened" chains suggests subtle parallels between the "indescribable oppression"[3] of patriarchy and the specter of transatlantic slavery. Elsewhere in the novel, there are additional reminders of enslavement in the largely silent cast of Black servants who labor as nannies, maids, cooks, and other paid assistants. This essay examines the traces of transatlantic slavery in *The Awakening*, comparing Edna's marital enslavement with antebellum and postbellum forms of Black labor; her position as her husband's "valuable piece of personal property" is reinforced by implicit comparison with the nameless Black servants responsible for the upkeep of Creole households.[4] With slavery looming in its shadows, *The Awakening* situates New Orleans specifically as a crossroads for the exchange of bodies, culture, and ideas. The transatlantic "voice of the sea"[5] Edna hears ironically urges her to contemplate and resist her own objectification while leaving intact her privilege. In exploration of this idea, my essay analyzes the novel's representation of mistress-maid dynamics and its erasure of slavery and racial history. It is because of slavery and New Orleans's history that Edna finally sees herself as a "slave," even as she is unable to empathize with the novel's Black characters.

The centrality of *The Awakening* within the American canon is significant to a number of possible readings. First, it functions as an important rendering of the turn-of-the-century New Woman and a foretelling of contemporary feminist concerns such as gender equality and sexual freedom. Second, it offers a rich portrait of affluent creole life in New Orleans, a representation of the interlocking class, ethnic/racial, and regional identities that define Creole culture. By extension, it also presents a glimpse of the South in the 1890s, a world still contending with the ghosts of the Civil War and slavery's remnants in the form of Jim Crow. In the rich and varied body of Chopin criticism, the novel is largely read as a feminist and/or regionalist text, with some consideration of the intersecting possibilities of these categories.

While dominant approaches to *The Awakening* have given extensive consideration to questions about gender and regionalism, an emergent conversation about Kate Chopin's representations of race has gained traction in the last twenty-five years. Elizabeth Ammons's 1991 *Conflicting Stories: American Women Writers at the Turn into the Twentieth Century* ushered in a wave of critical responses to the novel's treatment (or lack thereof) of race and racism. In this work, Ammons makes the foundational claim that Edna's freedom is purchased at the expense of Black women.[6] After Ammons, other important contributions include Michelle Birnbaum's "'Alien Hands': Kate Chopin and the Colonization of Race" (1994) in which Birnbaum argues: "Edna locates in racial and ethnic others a territory necessary for a liberating alterity: in their difference, she finds herself."[7] A year later, Sandra Gunning's "Kate Chopin's Local Color Fiction and the Politics of White Supremacy" (1995) traced the Chopin family's own encounter with slavery and white supremacy. Gunning argues, "Kate Chopin engages with turn-of-the-century white-supremacist ideologies that drew their popularity from an urgent need to reconfigure the social, political, and economic landscape after national and regional moves from black slavery to freedom."[8] In 2002, Joyce Dyer reflected upon these representative arguments in her essay "Reading *The Awakening* with Toni Morrison," in which she credits Toni Morrison with urging Chopin critics to turn their attention to race: "It seems to me, having read Morrison as well as other Chopin critics who have read her too, that race only appears to be insignificant to Kate Chopin, a privileged white woman. In fact, it is on her mind always and has a lasting effect on her art and her life. It is an inevitable source of anxiety."[9] The assertion of race as "an inevitable source of anxiety" for Chopin draws attention to all of the ways that she simultaneously signifies and erases race in her work. While *The Awakening* is seemingly not about race, the novel cannot escape its historical and regional positionality: race is present in every scene of the novel.

This genealogy of criticism exploring representations of race in *The Awakening* is particularly indebted to Toni Morrison's "Unspeakable Things Unspoken: The Afro-American Presence in American Literature." In this work, Morrison asks a powerful question about the silencing and erasure of Black perspectives in canonical American texts:

The Specter of Transatlantic Slavery in *The Awakening*   59

Looking at the scope of American literature, I can't help thinking that the question should never have been "Why am I, an Afro-American, absent from it?" It is not a particularly interesting query anyway. The spectacularly interesting question is "What intellectual feats had to be performed by the author or his critic to erase me from a society seething with my presence, and what effect has that performance had on the work?" What are the strategies of escape from knowledge? Of willful oblivion?[10]

This essay is an attempt to answer Morrison's questions by narrowing her discussion of race to consideration of the erasure of slavery in *The Awakening*, even though the novel is set in the late nineteenth-early twentieth centuries. While for obvious reasons I would not call *The Awakening* a neoslave narrative, I affirm the importance of the legacy of slavery in the work even with its meaningful silences that resist such identification. To extend Morrison's questions to my reading, what intellectual feats had to be performed to erase slavery from *The Awakening*? What is the effect of slavery's erasure, and what insights arise from reinserting this history into the text—contextualizing the novel in spite of its own efforts to push away the past? My intent is not to refute or challenge other Chopin critics, but rather to extend what has already been so helpfully established by Ammons et al. in pursuit of Morrison's methodology, other critics have given extensive attention to the "intellectual feats [that] had to be performed" to erase Blackness;[11] I seek to further reinscribe the buried traces of slavery in *The Awakening* by demonstrating that, in spite of the novel's affirmation of the importance of place in its descriptions of Grand Isle and New Orleans, there is an ironic erasure of a regional and transatlantic past and present seething with racial tensions.

Just three years before publication of *The Awakening*, the 1896 *Plessy v. Ferguson* decision gave rise to *de jure* segregation in the South. The case holds particular relevance for reading Chopin since it was in Louisiana that Homer Plessy, an active member of the New Orleans civil rights organization the *Comité de Citoyens*, unsuccessfully challenged the 1890 Louisiana law creating segregated passage on railways, a Jim Crow law arising out of racial tensions in Louisiana following the end of the Civil War and Reconstruction. Plessy, who was seven-eighths white and one-eighth Black, was first jailed and brought to trial in New Orleans for sitting in a whites-only railway car; his case was then heard by the Supreme Court igniting both local and national dialogue about race and segregation. Following the *Plessy* decision, segregation in most other aspects of southern public life became standard, and efforts to disenfranchise and intimidate Black citizens took hold. Speaking specifically to the consequences of Jim Crow in fin de siècle New Orleans, Dale A. Somers explains,

> [. . .] the color line became increasingly visible and rigid after the late 1880s, primarily because a majority of the whites in New Orleans and elsewhere became committed to white supremacy and a caste system identified with the southern way of life. By the end of the century racial segregation had become the established policy of the white population; black citizens, deprived of the vote, intimidated by violence, and often betrayed by white allies, had little choice but to submit. Evidence of this change in the city's racial practices abounded. Separation of the races in public institutions and accommodations, widespread throughout the postwar period, became complete toward the end of the century.[12]

It is against this tense backdrop that *The Awakening* reflects life on one side of the color line. Cases like *Plessy*, however, also illustrate how very blurry the color line was in a multiethnic region. As further example, the 1890s also saw the horrific mass lynching of eleven Italian immigrants—one of the largest in American history—in the streets of New Orleans, largely because of fears about ethnic immigrants and crime. Worries about these ethnic "others" were expressed by the city's business community and daily newspapers, which publicly supported the lynching. As reported by the *Times-Picayune* newspaper, "A survey showed that 42 of the nation's newspapers approved of the action, while 58 disapproved. A grand jury indicated that if there was guilt, it was shared by the entire mob, estimated at between 6,000 and 8,000 people."[13] The shocking level of mob complicity in the Sicilian Lynchings of 1891 and the Plessy decision just a few years later demonstrate the violent state of race relations in turn-of-the-century New Orleans.

These incidents and others like them reflect Louisianan anxieties about racial and ethnic identity. In a region with such a complex hierarchy of class and race, determining who lays claim to whiteness and its social privileges becomes imperative to the regional project. The position of Louisiana Creoles, which includes Chopin's imaginary Pontellier family, reflects this ongoing negotiation of who is white, as articulated by Andrew J. Jolivétte in his 2007 study of the Creoles as a "group that has historically self-constructed

The Specter of Transatlantic Slavery in *The Awakening*   61

a community identity based in part on social and economic circumstances and simultaneously from a shared history, culture, and geography."[14] Within the complex landscape of Chopin's Louisiana, the Creoles are merely one group among many others sharing the cultural and geographical spaces of Grand Isle and New Orleans; this narrative of multiculturalism, however, also exists alongside efforts to define and reinforce the color line, to determine with precise clarity the distinction between Black and white, and to police these boundaries through the deployment of various measures ensuring white supremacy. Robert Young's *Colonial Desire: Hybridity in Theory, Culture and Race* offers useful insight on the social construction of whiteness and these efforts to collapse ethnic complexities into "imagined communit[ies] of homogeneous national identit[ies]."[15] Jim Crow Louisiana made it imperative that whiteness become solidified and unified against those on the other side of the color line.

Thus, *The Awakening* functions as a kind of racial project, defined by Michael Omi and Howard Winant as "an interpretation, representation, or explanation of racial dynamics, and an effort to reorganize and redistribute resources along particular racial lines."[16] Chopin's project in *The Awakening* involves an erasure of regional racial histories to reinforce the whiteness and privilege of the Pontellier family (themselves marked as ethnic "others" in a multiethnic South). The view of the South roiling under the Plessy decision and other white supremacist endeavors is suppressed within the novel to preserve the façade of white affluence and leisure. Slavery and Jim Crow exist in the novel solely in symbol and metonymy: Black servants are present to provide the necessary upkeep of Creole households, but the text does not portray their point of view, nor does it overly concern itself with the inconvenient details of their lives on the other side of the color line.

Instead, Edna Pontellier's story occupies a primary position; the text replaces the story of transatlantic slavery with the story of Edna's "soul's slavery," Chopin's wording for the drudgery of marriage and motherhood.[17] This replacement reveals itself upon consideration of the fragile but explicit link between Edna's struggle for freedom and the dangerous "voice of the sea," the force that calls to Edna in a voice that "is seductive; never ceasing, whispering, clamoring, murmuring, inviting the soul to wander in for a spell in abysses of solitude; to lose itself in mazes of inward contemplation."[18] In this voice, Edna finds her own freedom; however, she stops short of seeing the hypocrisy of the limits placed upon autonomy and equality in the Jim Crow

South. With an intersectional "contemplation" of subjugation, a very different portrait of New Orleans emerges—one that gives voice to the novel's buried racial history and brings into full relief the complexity of regional identities.

Black characters are present throughout the novel, largely in positions of silent servitude that demonstrate parallels between antebellum and postbellum forms of Black labor. For each character, the narrator carefully describes skin tone and comments upon racial heritage, illustrating the importance of racial transparency within the Creole community. Young notes that fears about racial impurity resulted in obsessive categorization of "miscegenated, mongrel" people, in order to "track any furtive vestiges of secreted blackness."[19] As proof, Young cites a table describing racial mixing in South America in which "twenty-three crosses can be determined, and have received names."[20] These varied forms of Blackness are evident in Chopin's cast of quadroon nursemaids, "light-colored mulatto" stewards;[21] Black kitchen women, "little negro" sewing assistants,[22] and romanticized "friendly dark[ies]."[23] In spite of these differences in color, the Black characters are united in their mute servility. These characters "[follow] at the respectful distance they [are required] to observe,"[24] sit "patient as [savages],"[25] submit to the "supervision" of white masters,[26] artfully manage household maintenance and childcare, and vanish seemingly into thin air when their presence is no longer convenient.

There are, however, a few rare moments in which servile silence is disturbed. For example, in one scene Madame Lebrun sits "busily engaged at the sewing-machine" while "a little black girl works the treadle of the machine."[27] Chopin writes that "the sewing machine made a resounding clatter in the room; it was of a ponderous, by-gone make. [. . .] Clatter, clatter, clatter, bang! For the next five or eight minutes."[28] Throughout the scene, the ancient sewing machine's "clatter, clatter, bang" noisily punctuates and interrupts the dialogue, providing an audible reminder of the labor underway (and the "by-gone" history of such work), with the Black child bearing the most difficult task to avoid "imperiling" the Creole woman.[29] Later in the novel, a second scene provides another encounter with Black labor made audible. Chopin describes the noisy inconvenience of a maid "talking back" to her Creole master: "Before she saw them Edna could hear them in altercation, the woman—plainly an anomaly—claiming the right to be allowed to perform her duties, one of which was to answer the bell."[30] Edna's disdain for the Black maid's backtalk ironically contradicts her own desire to cast off white male privilege. The wording here of the maid as "plainly an anomaly" speaks to

The Specter of Transatlantic Slavery in *The Awakening* 63

the importance of black folks knowing their place both during slavery and Jim Crow. In fact, the novel largely demonstrates an investment in avoiding such anomalies and inconveniences, dismissing altogether the burgeoning development of the civil rights movement; it posits the norm as a tightly enforced color line with silence filling the space of righteous expression of racial grievance.

On her side of the color line, however, Edna experiences growing dissatisfaction with her roles as a wife and mother, and the novel presents her emergent feminist yearning through the language of a narrative of racial justice. The novel begins in a Grand Isle vacation cottage with Léonce Pontellier's pronouncement: "'You are burnt beyond recognition,' he added looking at his wife as one looks at a valuable piece of personal property which has suffered some damage."[31] Edna's suntan (or sunburn) symbolically darkens her and relegates her to the status of a slave. Later in the novel, this sense of ownership is further conveyed in a description of the pleasure Léonce takes in his material possessions, which by extension include his wife: "He greatly valued his possessions, chiefly because they were his, and derived genuine pleasure from contemplating a painting, a statuette, a rare lace curtain—no matter what—after he had brought it and placed it among his household goods."[32] Once Edna begins to see herself as one of his collected objects, she succumbs to "an indescribable oppression, which seemed to generate in some unfamiliar part of her consciousness, filled her whole being with a vague anguish. It was like a shadow, like a mist passing across her soul's summer day. It was strange and unfamiliar; it was a mood."[33] It is significant that oppression is characterized here as a darkened "shadow," something "strange and unfamiliar," which again offers opportunity to access the experience of subjugation through the lens of slavery and racial othering. Edna embraces this thought in a scene in which she sails "across the bay to the Chênière Caminada, [and feels] as if she were being borne away from some anchorage which had held her fast, whose chains had been loosening—had snapped the night before when the mystic spirit was abroad, leaving her free to drift whithersoever she chose to set her sails."[34] Slavery as a metaphor runs throughout the novel, positing that it is the sea that must save Edna from her "soul's slavery," the oppression of marriage and motherhood.[35]

It is worth noting here the symbolism of water within African and African American folk practices. The spiritual "Wade in the Water," for example, famously highlights water as a source of healing and escape from bondage.

Throughout the Black diaspora, water carries folk symbolism as a passageway to the spiritual world, and under the influence of Christianity, water assumes new specific meanings associated with baptism and rebirth. The Middle Passage adds yet another dimension of meaning, as the sea becomes representative of both trauma and freedom from oppression. There are a number of Igbo legends about "flying Africans," those who could allegedly fly or swim across the Atlantic Ocean in a reverse Middle Passage; however, a more practical explanation for these beliefs in transmigration might come from the number of water suicides undertaken to provide release from enslavement. The complex symbolism of water within the Black community parallels the ambiguity that Chopin ascribes to Edna's relationship with the sea. On one hand, the sea stirs her desires for freedom; on the other hand, the novel ends with Edna's suicide, meaning that it is only in death that Edna finds escape from the "old terror" of patriarchal oppression.

Although Edna describes the voice of the sea as something that *awakens* her, the transformation is limited by her investment in white privilege. Chopin writes, "She could only realize that she herself—her present self—was in some way different from the other self. That she was seeing with different eyes and making the acquaintance of new conditions in herself that colored and changed her environment, she did not yet suspect."[36] Edna's experience "colors" her and makes her anew, and she is called to cast off the "loosened" chains of patriarchy. The limits of this difference, however, are well conveyed in the scene in which Edna paints her quadroon servant, who is described as sitting for "for hours before Edna's palette, patient as a savage."[37] Edna's burgeoning freedom parallels her artistic development, and her devotion to painting offers an opportunity for self-exploration and expression. When Edna shifts the focus of her paintings from her children to her maids, she once again symbolically casts off her interest in motherhood. Edna's maids are objectified under her gaze, reduced to the usefulness of their body in her study of their "classic lines." Additionally, the maids could function as a projection of Edna herself, a blank canvas for her to explore her own subjection. In the visage of her maid, Edna "could hear again the ripple of the water, the flapping sail. She could see the glint of the moon upon the bay, and could feel the soft, gusty beating of the hot south wind."[38] In her servant's objectified and subjugated body, Edna again hears the call of the sea and contemplates rising against her own oppression, even as she exercises her own privilege and authority. Although Edna fails to see to the hypocrisy of her situation,

The Specter of Transatlantic Slavery in *The Awakening*   65

the novel presents overt parallels between patriarchy and slavery. Uncovering these submerged traces meaningfully reinscribes the text within the history of the transatlantic slave trade and exposes a critical moment of racial and cultural negotiation at the end of the nineteenth century.

The Awakening also offers an important opportunity to study relationships (and the lack thereof) between women across the Jim Crow color line. By predicating Edna's liberation upon the symbolic metonymy of Black women's subjugation, Chopin creates a direct link—however flawed—between the experiences of Black and white women. In consideration of the mistress-maid dynamic in antebellum texts, Minrose Gwin asks these important questions:

> Placed as they were in an opposing but a similarly confining mythology, how did black and white women relate to one another? How much did their assigned roles in a culture based upon racial and sexual inequality affect their relationships with one another? How humanely or inhumanely did the white woman use her power? How did the slave woman vent her anger at her own powerlessness?[39]

Gwin's questions create space for consideration of a continuum of both antagonistic and cooperative relationships between Black and white women during slavery and beyond. She urges us to think about the gender-based similarities and differences between the mistress and Black maid, and the dynamic of racial inequality within this discussion. Although there are antebellum and postwar texts that portray mistress-maid devotion and a more one-sided view of Black compliance, narratives written by Black folks often tell a different story about the nature of the division between Black and white women.

Solomon Northup's 1853 narrative *12 Years a Slave* recounts in brutal detail the racial and sexual complexities of life during slavery, and its setting offers relevant opportunity to explore the dynamics of the Louisiana plantation household that underlie the fraught interactions in *The Awakening*. Northup, a free black man kidnapped and sold into southern slavery, suffers particular mistreatment in the household of Edwin Epps, a cruel Louisianan planter. Northup's narrative describes the painful misfortune of a fellow slave named Patsey, an object of physical and sexual abuse within the Epps household. Master Epps's desire for Patsey and his wife's hatred of the rival for her husband's attention binds the three in an unsettling triangle. In one especially heartbreaking scene, Epps orders that Patsey be whipped while his wife "gaz[es] on the scene with an air of heartless satisfaction."[40] Northup provides the following description of Patsey's situation:

> It had fallen to her lot to be the slave of a licentious master and a jealous mistress. She shrank before the lustful eye of the one, and was in danger even of her life at the hands of the other, and between the two, she was indeed accursed. In the great house, for days together, there were high and angry words, poutings and estrangement, whereof she was the innocent cause. Nothing delighted the mistress so much as to see her suffer.[41]

Patsey's position, caught between the licentiousness and jealousy of her masters, forecloses the possibility of an alliance between black and white women in the Epps household. It would hold that Mistress Epps would likely have experienced similar forms of domestic tyranny at the hands of her husband, yet rather than view Patsey as an ally, she holds neither empathy nor sympathy for the abused enslaved woman.

Northup suggests that when the women were younger (and Patsey was not yet a sexual rival), the women had a different relationship:

> Patsey had been a favorite when a child, even in the great house. She had been petted and admired for her uncommon sprightliness and pleasant disposition. She had been fed many a time, so Uncle Abram said, even on biscuit and milk, when the madam, in her younger days, was wont to call her to the piazza, and fondle her as she would a playful kitten. But a sad change had come over the spirit of the woman. Now, only black and angry fiends ministered in the temple of her heart, until she could look on Patsey but with concentrated venom. [...] The pride of the haughty woman was aroused; the blood of the fiery southern boiled at the sight of Patsey, and nothing less than trampling out the life of the helpless bondwoman would satisfy her.[42]

Mistress Epps's "kind" treatment objectifies Patsey as "playful kitten," and it reveals the difficulty in their having a relationship founded on anything other than problematic forms of patronizing attachment. Their fragile false affection is shattered by perceived competition for the master's attention. Elizabeth Fox-Genovese argues, "Women were bound to each other in the

The Specter of Transatlantic Slavery in *The Awakening*   67

household, not in sisterhood, but by their specific and different relations to its master."[43] In Fox-Genovese's view, the white male master of the plantation household is the authoritarian center who holds together his "family, white and black" even in his absence. Women in the plantation household relate to one another only through their place within *his* world.

In contrast with the view of Black and white women as romantic and sexual rivals in competition for the attention of the white male slave owner, there is also the view of Black women as asexual Mammy figures bound to white women as household managers. In this relationship, the women are still in tension with one another; although they are not sexual rivals, they compete for domestic and maternal authority. Kimberly Wallace-Sanders has traced the caricature of the Mammy to "depictions of African American mothers [. . .] popularized through literature, travel narratives, and religious propaganda between 1820 and the 1850s," noting that even in these early characterizations of the Mammy, "her maternity, her body size and shape, and her skin color contribute to our understanding of the mammy as an ultimate representation of maternal devotion."[44] The "stereotype's haunting power" is strongly at work in romanticized accounts of slavery written after the Civil War,[45] especially in Margaret Mitchell's 1936 homage to the Old South, *Gone with the Wind*. In both novel and film versions of *Gone with the Wind*, we see Mammy's domineering efforts to "run [the O'Haras'] lives and to hold Scarlett to ridiculous codes of Southern conduct,"[46] assisting in Scarlett's success as a "bearer of privileged [white] womanhood."[47] We see Mammy helping Scarlett sew a dress out of curtains to work her magic on Rhett Butler, lacing Scarlett's corset snugly to produce her much-lauded tiny waist, and protecting her on the crowded streets of Atlanta from "black trash" and other "wuthless niggahs." As Tara McPherson notes in her own study of *Gone with the Wind*:

> Throughout the narrative, Mammy's physical labor and "supporting" role allow Scarlett to perform femininity. [. . .] Paradoxically, Mammy here is figured as chief coconspirator in the production of a system of femininity that simultaneously works to deny her own status as a bearer of privileged womanhood. Mitchell consistently represents Mammy as the enforcer of southern etiquette, thus supporting her narrative claim that Mammy has authority over Scarlett and the whole plantation. But Mammy's "power" is only the power to labor in the maintenance of white femininity.[48]

The benign tension between Scarlett and Mammy is explained in this last sentence. Although Mammy polices Scarlett's behavior, telling her what is and what isn't "fittin'" her power is an illusion. She is held in her place by her "implicit acceptance of her own inferiority."[49]

These models for mistress-maid relationships situate Black and white women as sexual and domestic rivals for one another, bound in their competition for the white master's favor. *The Awakening* illustrates that once the desired alliance with patriarchy is diminished—symbolized by Edna's dissolution of her marriage—white and Black women are held together only tenuously. When she separates from her husband, Edna does not automatically find feminist solidarity with her Black sisters also laboring to survive in the patriarchal South; instead, the novel reveals an even more insistent grasping at white supremacist power as an attempt to garner what little privilege might be available to a woman on her own in the world. In her discussion of antebellum Black-white relations, Fox-Genovese describes this phenomenon as the failure of "poor women, poor slaves" ideology—the false conflation of women's rights with abolitionist sympathies:

> It has been, if anything, more seductive to reason that ladies, who themselves suffered male domination, were the primary, if secret, critics of their society—nothing less than closet feminists and abolitionists who saw slavery as a "monstrous system." "Poor women, poor slaves," in the widely quoted words of Mary Boykin Chesnut. But most ladies, like Mary Chesnut herself, were hardly prepared to do without slaves and enthusiastically supported secession.[50]

The application of Fox-Genovese's ideas to *The Awakening* thus explains how Edna could cast off patriarchal oppression while simultaneously reinforcing Jim Crow white supremacy. Edna is dependent upon the subjugation of Black women in order to assert her own independence.

Wishing that *The Awakening* could "do better" than this is a fruitless, revisionist desire; however, it is worthwhile to unpack the complexities of racial encounters and buried histories in the novel in order to understand slavery's racial and gendered implications in turn of the century New Orleans. In her analysis of later novels also authored by southern women, Sharon Monteith argues, "The extent to which black and white women can each be described as protagonists or antagonists, and as collaborators or conspirators, is indicative of wider social relations in the United States, not just in the

South."[51] Although Monteith is particularly interested in examples of what she terms the "friendship plot" in contemporary southern novels depicting cross-racial relationships, her argument is relevant to a text like *The Awakening*, which portrays the notable absence of such forms of interracial alliance. As much as *The Awakening* invites consideration of the shared status that could potentially bring Black and white women together, it also offers a powerful demonstration of the racist forces at work in the Jim Crow South that keep women from forming such alliances. In *Telling Memories: Domestic Workers and Their Employers in the Segregated South*, Susan Tucker renders a powerful analysis of the importance of "place and race" in considering these relationships: "For both black and white southern women, place and race are among the most obvious defining circumstances. And for both, place and race having meanings for their roles in the domestic sphere, meanings that both separate them from, and connect them to, each other."[52] The slipperiness of "place" in Tucker's writing could be taken to mean both class and regional identity, and I would argue that both have relevance for *The Awakening*'s representations of Black and white women. The novel keeps southern Black women in their "place" in order to allow privileged white women to escape theirs. By drawing upon explicit forms of slavery metaphors, the novel ironically calls for reexamination of exactly what it seeks to keep at arm's length: the buried stories of Gulf Coast black women endeavoring against their own bonds of oppression. Over one hundred years later, Beyoncé's "Formation" serves as its own kind of "awakening" for millennial Black feminist consciousness. The final image of Edna Pontellier walking into the waves of the Gulf finds its visual twin in the view of Beyoncé sinking into the post-Katrina floodwaters of New Orleans. Whether the act is one of rebirthing or drowning self-sacrifice is left open to interpretation, as it is in *The Awakening*: "How strange and awful it seemed to stand naked under the sky! how delicious! She felt like some new-born creature, opening its eyes in a familiar world that it had never known."[53]

Notes

1. Jon Caramanica, et. al. "Beyoncée in 'Formation': Entertainer, Activist, Both?" *New York Times*, February 6, 2016.

2. Kate Chopin, "The Awakening," *The Awakening and Other Stories*, ed. Sandra Gilbert (New York: Penguin Books, 2003), 81.

3. Chopin, *Awakening*, 49.

4. Chopin, *Awakening*, 44.

5. Chopin, *Awakening*, 175.

6. Elizabeth Ammons, *Conflicting Stories: American Women Writers at the Turn into the Twentieth Century* (New York: Oxford University Press, 1992).

7. Michelle Birnbaum, "'Alien Hands': Kate Chopin and the Colonization of Race," *American Literature* 66, no. 2 (1994): 303.

8. Sandra Gunning. "Kate Chopin's Local Color Fiction and the Politics of White Supremacy," *Arizona Quarterly: A Journal of American Literature, Culture, and Theory* 51, no. 3 (1995): 63.

9. Joyce Dyer, "Reading 'The Awakening' with Toni Morrison," *Southern Literary Journal* 35, no. 1 (2002): 140.

10. Toni Morrison, "Unspeakable Things Unspoken: The Afro-American Presence in American Literature," in *The Norton Anthology of African American Literature*, eds. Henry Louis Gates, Jr. and Nellie Y. McKay, 2nd ed. (New York: W. W. Norton & Company, 2004), 2306–7.

11. Morrison, "Unspeakable Things Unspoken," 2306.

12. Dale A. Somers, "Black and White in New Orleans: A Study in Urban Race Relations, 1865–1900," *Journal of Southern History* 40, no. 1 (1974): 38.

13. "Anti-Italian Mood Led to 1891 Lynchings," *Times Picayune* (New Orleans, LA), March 14, 1991. P. Cahill, M. (1991, March 14). Anti-Italian Mood Led to 1891 Lynchings. *Times-Picayune* (New Orleans, LA), p. B1. Available from NewsBank: Access World News: https://infoweb-newsbank-com.arclosrios.idm.oclc.org/apps/news/document-view?p=AWNB&docref=news/0FAC441F918A0D0B.

14. Andrew Jolivétte, *Louisiana Creoles: Cultural Recovery and Mixed-Race Native American Identity* (Lanham, MD: Lexington Books, 2007), 4.

15. Robert Young, *Colonial Desire: Hybridity in Theory, Culture, and Race* (London: Routledge, 1995), 17.

16. Michael Omi and Howard Winant, *Racial Formation in the United States: From the 1960s to the 1990s* (New York: Routledge, 1994), 56.

17. Chopin, *Awakening*, 175.

18. Chopin, *Awakening*, 175.

19. Young, *Colonial Desire*, 177.

20. Young, *Colonial Desire*, 176.

21. Chopin, *Awakening*, 100.

22. Chopin, *Awakening*, 79.

23. Chopin, *Awakening*, 123.

24. Chopin, *Awakening*, 55.

25. Chopin, *Awakening*, 108.

26. Chopin, *Awakening*, 70.

27. Chopin, *Awakening*, 66.

28. Chopin, *Awakening*, 66.

29. Chopin, *Awakening*, 66.

30. Chopin, *Awakening*, 110.

31. Chopin, *Awakening*, 44.

32. Chopin, *Awakening*, 99.

33. Chopin, *Awakening*, 49.

34. Chopin, *Awakening*, 81.

35. Chopin, *Awakening*, 175.

36. Chopin, *Awakening*, 88.

37. Chopin, *Awakening*, 108.

38. Chopin, *Awakening*, 109.

39. Minrose C. Gwin, *Black and White Women of the Old South: The Peculiar Sisterhood in American Literature* (Knoxville: University of Tennessee Press, 1985), 46.

40. Solomon Northup, *12 Years a Slave*. 1853 (Los Angeles: Graymalkin Media, 2014), 277.

41. Northup, *12 Years a Slave*, 247.

42. Northup, *12 Years a Slave*, 251.

43. Elizabeth Fox-Genovese, *Within the Plantation Household: Black and White Women of the Old South* (Chapel Hill: University of North Carolina Press, 1988), 101–2.

44. Kimberly Wallace-Sanders, *Mammy: A Century of Race, Gender, and Southern Memory* (Ann Arbor: University of Michigan Press, 2008), 13–14.

45. Wallace-Sanders, *Mammy*, 15.

46. Wallace-Sanders, *Mammy*, 126.

47. Tara McPherson, *Reconstructing Dixie: Race, Gender, and Nostalgia in the Imagined South* (Durham: Duke University Press, 2003), 55.

48. McPherson, *Reconstructing Dixie*, 55.

49. Wallace-Sanders, *Mammy*, 126.

50. Fox-Genovese, *Within the Plantation Household*, 47.

51. Sharon Montieth, *Advancing Sisterhood? Interracial Friendships in Contemporary Southern Fiction* (Athens: University of Georgia Press, 2000), 6.

52. Susan Tucker, *Telling Memories Among Southern Women: Domestic Workers and Their Employers in the Segregated South* (Baton Rouge: LSU Press, 1988), 16.

53. Chopin, *Awakening*, 189.

4

"MOVING FROM THE INSIDE OUT"
Malwida von Meysenbug and the Portrayal of a New Feminine Experience in *The Awakening*[1]

Heidi Podlasli-Labrenz

As early as the 1970s, scholars emphasized the European influences on Kate Chopin's work. In his article, "Kate Chopin's European Consciousness," Thomas Bonner asserts, "American writers sought the perspective of history and the inspiration of an established culture" and that Kate Chopin's "education, her reading, and her Grand Tour drew her to Europe."[2] Some thirty years later, Janet Beer still maintains that "Chopin's literary influences were emphatically European rather than American."[3] I would like to argue that one major source of European inspiration for Chopin was Malwida von Meysenbug, one of the nineteenth-century German women writers influenced by the German Revolution of 1848.[4] Born in Kassel in 1816 into a prestigious French Huguenot family with close affiliations to the reigning Hessian Court, Meysenbug strove early in her youth to separate herself from the social and moral views of her class. She was an ardent supporter of the German Revolution and a staunch Democrat. Because of her pronounced political views, she was forced to leave the country and sought exile, first in Paris and London and then in Italy, where she died in 1903. All through her life, she was close friends with Friedrich Nietzsche, whose lectures, Über die Zukunft unserer Bildungs-Anstalten (*About the Future of Our Educational Institutions*), she translated into Italian.[5]

Among her writings, it is in particular von Meysenbug's travel diary, *Mémoires d'une Idéaliste (entre deux revolutions 1830–1848)* [*Memoirs of an Idealist (Between Two Revolutions 1830–1848)*], published anonymously in

French in 1869, which might have been part of Chopin's reading canon. Meysenbug's acclaimed publication, which turned her into a nominee for the Nobel Prize in literature in 1903, was highly recommended by Nietzsche as indispensable literature for anyone seeking to understand the significance of the political and social uprisings in Germany all through the 1830s and 1840s, which were hailed by Nietzsche as "the signs of the new age."[6] While it is not unlikely that the *Mémoires* had already caught Katherine O'Flaherty's immediate attention in the French translation, it is just as probable that it was brought to Kate Chopin's attention by her mentor, Dr. Frederick Kolbenheyer, credited by Per Seyersted as a major influence on her writing career.[7] The native Austrian, who left his home country for political reasons around 1870, had become deeply immersed in the group of German émigrés who had settled in St. Louis; Carl Schurz was one of these émigrés. He kept a steady correspondence with Meysenbug, called her "his friend" and praised the *Memoirs* in his *Reminiscences* as an "exceedingly interesting book, which has so well held its place in literature that but recently, more than a quarter of a century after its first appearance, a new edition has been printed and widely read."[8] Kolbenheyer and Schurz, editors at the Pulitzer-owned *St. Louis Post Dispatch*, tried to disperse a publication within their community which derived its immense significance from closely documenting times of political and social upheaval. Quite incidentally, this was exactly the time when Kate Chopin had started to work on her writing career.

Indeed, the "signs of the new age," to which Nietzsche referred, emphasized the importance of the reform movements in Germany, notably the efforts to strive for more democracy by giving extended rights to its citizens. Especially German women of the higher and the middle classes benefitted from these societal changes, as they were now able to move around alone within and from city to city. Invested with these new opportunities, these women could cherish newly gained freedoms and strive toward more social and emotional independence. Likewise, Kate Chopin notes in her diary that while in Europe she developed the habit of walking alone, exploring peculiarities of European city life and making character studies of its inhabitants. Not only was she inspired and influenced by these experiences, but they also seem to have infiltrated the descriptions of city life in New Orleans in her later works of fiction. Her new insights were also visible in Chopin's development of themes, which often focused on the unorthodox behavior of her protagonists. I would like to point out some of the striking similarities between

Meysenbug's autobiographical writings and Kate Chopin's descriptions of Edna Pontellier, whose walking around alone in New Orleans is intrinsic to her search for personal independence. Both are very similar in tone and content, and I will show that Meysenbug's *Mémoirs* and Chopin's *The Awakening* focus on women who were challenging their existence by making enriching and rewarding experiences on their way to newfound freedom.

When discussing the similarities between Kate Chopin's and Malwida von Meysenbug's writings, it is significant to note that both writers were eyewitnesses to historic events that ignited critical changes in the social structures and political landscapes of Europe. Meysenbug talks about the hopes, but also the shattered illusions, of the German Revolution of 1848; Kate Chopin experiences the commotion surrounding the beginnings of the Franco-Prussian War of 1870–71. Describing the changing times, Meysenbug writes:

> Black-red golden flags fluttered from our train, a long row of carriages full of volunteers: young, enthusiastic men, who were going to Schleswig-Holstein, and Polish men on their way home. At every station they were cheered by the assembled crowd. . . . And now? The people had vanished, there were only poor workers, travelling artisans on business, frequenting the third and fourth class compartments; in the other classes there were elegant people of the "privileged classes," who, with their usual indifference, looked down on the others and seemed to say: "We want quiet at any cost."[9]

Quite similar in tone, Chopin notes in her diary on July 17, 1870:

> What an uproar! What an excitement! I do not see how we got out of Wiesbaden alive. News reached us last night of the declaration of war between France & Prussia; so this morning all the hotels emptied their human contents into the various depots. French women with their maids, their few children, their laces and velvets hastening to get started on their homeward journey.[10]

In the same manner, both Meysenbug and Chopin refer to the political consequences of the German Revolution. It was early in her travels when Chopin noted the still prevailing tensions between students and the bourgeoisie. On July 13, she writes about her stay in Bonn: "During the tableaux which followed the concert there was a little encounter between a citizen and

A New Feminine Experience in *The Awakening*   75

a student, brought about by some fancied slight on the part of the citizen. Bunnie feels it will end in a duel, which, he tells me are of frequent occurrence."[11] A few days later, on July 17, 1870, Chopin comments in a rather surprised tone on the unusual relationship between maids and mistresses: "I was struck on the way by the familiarity of an otherwise very refined German lady, with her maid. They seemed more like sisters, than mistress and maid."[12] Similarly, Meysenbug emphasizes her efforts to change the relationship with the female servants who were working in her house:

> I felt that I wanted to transmit the knowledge I had acquired to others. I began with our servant girls and went to see them every once in a while in order to convey clearer ideas to them while they were doing needlework. I told them, for instance, about the orbit of the earth around the sun, the alternation of the seasons and so on. They were delighted and said: "Oh. Miss, if only everyone were of your opinion that we poor people also enjoy learning something!"[13]

Among the most immediate and significant effects of the new rights given to German citizens were the different realms of independence which women were from now on able to explore. Their newly gained freedom of moving around alone within and from city to city particularly enhanced their mobility and their autonomous exploration of public spaces. Praising this significant gain as an outcome of the German Revolution, Meysenbug asserts: "The most beautiful, historically significant fruit of the movements of the past two years is perhaps: to have directed to the young continent the fertile stream of German life as far as intelligence, energetic action, and desire for freedom are concerned."[14] Travelling a considerable distance all by oneself, or any distance, for that matter, was a right, which had not been granted to women in Germany before 1848. Taking advantage of the new possibilities, embarking on voyages into the unknown, and benefitting from these experiences, however, was only possible in Meysenbug's opinion if women were self-assured and self-reliant:

> I feel sorry for the person who has never experienced the beautiful feeling of independence and or reposing in herself, in the face of distance, of the new and the unknown and the longing caused by them; that feeling or rather that knowledge of the eternally unalterable amid the pleasure of change, of expectation; of hurrying on to new new things worth exploration.[15]

A woman who was ready to risk this adventure could also benefit from the new means of travelling, the railway, which seemed to open the doors to a completely new reality at an even more accelerated pace. Meysenbug asserts:

> I don't know if my sisters share my taste, but with regard to the present safety of travel, even for single women, there is a rare delight in this independence, for one has a strong, compelling inner dignity. And no way of travelling increases this delight as much as the railway, that doesn't even slow down one's winged longing.[16]

When traveling through Europe, Kate Chopin also used the railway to traverse Germany at an increased pace, sometimes only spending a day or two in each city. She comments on the size of the country but remarks also, "[h]ow short the distance seems to us here, from one city to another; in comparison with those interminable miles and miles of night and day travelling in America."[17] In obvious recognition of the consequences of the German Revolution which had ushered in the mingling of the aristocracy with the "common" social classes, she goes on to write: "We took the 3 o'clock train and went about half an hour's ride up the Rhine. . . . I must not forget to note that we travelled on the same train this afternoon with the Queen of Prussia, who was going to attend a concert in Rollensberg."[18]

Meysenbug's new, cherished feeling of independence is also described by Chopin through Edna's habits of behavior that defy the social code of manners and risk her not being regarded as "respectable" anymore. It is also reflected in a variety of emotions, feelings, and perceptions. Kate Chopin, for instance, is doing wild, unheard of kind of things while travelling. She is "broiling under the sun"[19] and dares to get sunburnt (a sunburn was socially not acceptable for women of the higher classes as it indicated the unprotected toils of physical labor against the sun and therefore a lower class). Chopin also gets completely drenched from the rain but feels "with hands and feet almost frozen—beautifully festooned with icicles."[20] She gets tipsy from drinking quite a bit of the delicious Rhine wine and often feels like smoking a cigarette.[21] Her walking gait also reflects her various moods and states of health. In one entry, she notes, "[We] strolled leisurely through the quaint streets" of the city of Berne, the largest one in Switzerland,[22] while she complains in the city of Wiesbaden about "walk[ing] about town rather listlessly" because she "had been feeling badly all day."[23] On yet another occasion, "a long walk to Schaffhausen" leaves her in high spirits and deliciously fatigued.[24]

Most importantly, she develops and refines her physical skills. At "so idyllic a spot as the 'Rhein Fall,'"[25] she does not shy away from daring a precipitous ascent in the most inclement weather conditions: "Never had I felt such rain with a sprinkling of hail. We scrambled as best we could up the slippery path which a moment before had seemed so idyllic—drenched to the skin."[26] Similarly, when rowing on the "blue [Lake] Zurich's waters," she acknowledges: "I find myself handling the oars quite like an expert."[27] By developing this strength, she nurtures what Meysenbug identified as the "strong, compelling, inner dignity" that is a driving force in women.[28] Her writer friend and contemporary Fanny Lewald[29] shared this perception. In her autobiography, *Meine Lebensgeschichte* (*The Story of My Life*), she relates how, at age seventeen, she was for the first time allowed to take long walks by herself in the countryside. Reflecting on this experience, she emphasizes, both thoughtfully and enthusiastically:

> And just as the child, once it has discovered the designation of the ego with discovery of the word I, will never again let go of it, so the longing for a separate Independence never again left me, once I had learned to experience, on my quiet afternoon walks, how restricted a girl's existence is made within the family—down to the slightest movement—and how restricted I myself had been up until then.[30]

It is precisely this feeling that encourages Kate Chopin to walk alone and to defy conventions in the most daring way by displaying a type of behavior not commonly accepted for young women of the time. The recommendations in *Martine's Hand-Book of Etiquette, and Guide to True Politeness* from 1866 reads rather sternly: "Young married ladies may visit their acquaintances alone; but they may not appear in any public places unattended by their husbands or elder ladies. This rule may never be infringed, whether as regards exhibitions, or public libraries, museums or promenades. . . ."[31] Kate Chopin, however, leaves these societal norms behind: "I took a walk alone. How very far I did go. I wonder what people thought of me—a young woman strolling about alone"[32] Much later, in 1894, she would note in her essay "Impressions": "There are a few good things in life—not many, but a few. A soft, firm, magnetic sympathetic hand clasp is one. A walk through the quiet streets at midnight is another."[33]

Travelling and walking through the cities changed Chopin. Janet Beer contends that Chopin "laid claim to new freedoms, particularly the freedom to walk the city streets,"[34] a right which had also been demanded by Meysenbug just a few decades earlier. Formerly confined by the social restrictions and codes of their class, both women walked and traveled their way toward new challenges: social, emotional, and physical ones. At the same time, they felt sorry for other women still enclosed in their own little worlds. The German writer also scolds the men who still strive to "banish us [women] to a closed circle, like hothouse plants that have to be protected against rough wind and strong sun, so that one can enjoy their exquisite beauty."[35] In accordance with these changes in attitude, both women defy social norms: Kate Chopin walks alone, smokes, and combats the elements of nature; Meysenbug, on the other hand, travels by herself, discusses the rights of women and related moral and social issues, while insisting on associating with the so-called common people rather than members of her own class. On her journey, the German writer favorably records the comments of her female traveling companion: "I also go to third class by principle, for, on the one hand, when close to the common people to whom alone I want to belong, because my heart belongs to them, I feel better and safer than in the often very dubious vicinity of the people travelling first class."[36]

In summarizing Kate Chopin's experiences in Europe, Beer and Nolan conclude that "Chopin's account of their travels in Germany, Switzerland, and France reveals that it was at this time that she encountered many unfamiliar codes of behavior which both shocked, yet at the same time attracted her."[37] Are these seemingly captivating experiences reflected again in Kate Chopin's life in Louisiana and later in her fiction? It is known that after her return to New Orleans, Chopin would continue the habits which she had developed in Europe. Barbara Ewell points out: "According to a diary of the period which is now lost, she was especially fond of roaming about the city alone, an unconventional activity for women. She often walked or rode the mule-drawn streetcars, observing the cosmopolitan bustle of the French Market or Canal Street or the waterfront, where her husband's—and earlier her father's—business originated."[38]

In Chopin's literary works several heroines have a passion for walking through the streets of New Orleans. In "A Sentimental Soul," Chopin describes Mamzelle Fleurette's walking habits as a reflection of her moods, similar to the sensations Chopin described in her diary on the Grand Tour.

More specifically, the female protagonist faces subdued feelings when trying to cope with her passion for her customer, Monsieur Lacodie: "Mamzelle Fleurette did not walk down Chartres Street with her usual composed tread; she seemed preoccupied and agitated."[39] Walking, however, is also the activity that serves as a release for these feelings, eventually liberating her soul to admit her passion: "Mamzelle Fleurette did not ride back to her home; she walked. The sensation of walking on air was altogether delicious; she had never experienced it before."[40] It is after this walk that she decides to adorn Lacodie's tombstone with a personal token, turning from a spinster who had only conveyed "a pathetic desire and appeal to be permitted to exist"[41] into a woman who is courageous enough to defy the moral expectations of her society. Athénaise, the young, immature, and impulsive heroine in the short story of the same name, travels to New Orleans to escape the bondage of marriage. Her walking sprees through the city accompany and strengthen her on her way to selfhood: "She liked to be out of doors, and they [Athénaise and Gouvernail] strolled together in the summer twilight through the mazes of the old French quarter."[42] Not only does the bachelor Gouvernail protect Athénaise's respectability by not letting her walk alone, he also initiates her into the secrets and revelations of city life: "On Sunday morning, he arose at an unconscionable hour to take her to the French market, knowing that the sights and sounds there would interest her."[43] During her stay in the city, Athénaise discovers the limitations of urban life for women, but she also realizes that she will find fulfillment in her role as mother and wife: "She walked along the street as if she had fallen heir to some magnificent inheritance. On her face was a look of pride and satisfaction that passers-by noticed and admired."[44] Chopin creates two female characters in different times in their lives, yet each is fulfilled and satisfied, and for each, walking is the path to self-discovery.

Chopin's most famous walker, however, the one whose unfamiliar codes of behavior were extremely shocking to a contemporary audience, is Edna Pontellier of *The Awakening*. While some of the experiences of both the fictional heroine and her creator bear striking similarities, they often differ remarkably in their results. Knowing that she does not comply with the beauty standards of the time, Kate Chopin half mocks, half deplores the fact that she again has gotten sunburnt while on her Grand Tour[45] in contrast to *The Awakening*, where Léonce Pontellier disparagingly remarks right at the beginning of the novel that Edna "has been burnt beyond recognition."[46] Kate

Chopin notes in her diary that this "disfiguration" did meet with a particular disapproval on the part of Oscar Chopin. We also know from her diary that Kate Chopin started walking alone after she had successfully mastered the art of rowing on Lake Zurich in Switzerland."[47] Similarly, Edna also starts her habit of walking alone after coping with the challenges of water: mastering the art of swimming. After a few unsuccessful tries, Edna is invigorated by her discovery of personal strength. It is her first act as a self-determined human being, leaving her family and friends behind for the first time: "She started to walk away alone. They all called to her and shouted to her. She waved a dissenting hand, and went on, paying no further heed to their renewed cries which sought to detain her."[48] Edna continues this "habit of walking alone," which Madame Lebrun calls "capricious,"[49] after her return to the city, just like Kate Chopin did after her return from Europe. Unlike her heroine, however, Chopin was not reprimanded for it.

Venturing out on "her perambulations" by herself in New Orleans, Edna denounces all aspects of respectability. By doing so, she is emphasizing her personal independence just as Meysenbug did when riding alone on the train. By entering unknown grounds, both women discover their own strength and demonstrate their courage. Significantly, on one of her first walks to personal freedom, Edna leaves her home on one of her customary and expected social "Tuesdays."[50] She had rigorously and dutifully kept this routine of staying at home on that day to receive callers since she had been married, not only because it was considered part of her social obligations but also because it was a commonly accepted way of securing one's husband's business ties. By intuitively following what Meysenbug recognizes as a "winged longing"[51] within women, Edna instead starts exploring the world around her on her own terms. "I simply felt like going out, and I went out" is her explanation to an infuriated Léonce Pontellier when she returns home.[52] Fortified and invigorated by her walking spree, she does not deem it necessary to find acceptable excuses for her behavior in order to appease her exasperated husband. What then does this "habit of walking" mean to her? It seems worthwhile to look more closely at Helen Taylor's comment, in which she suggests that "Edna's progress within the city is signaled through a series of walks [where] she explores the meaning of femininity within an urban context."[53] If this is true, then Edna's experiences are arguably very similar to Meysenbug's.

Walking is an emotional outlet for Edna Pontellier, setting her mind free to admit openly to her feelings, or "infatuation" as she calls it, for Robert Lebrun,

A New Feminine Experience in *The Awakening*   81

her companion from Grand Isle. No longer the obedient, submissive wife, it is during her strolls through the city that she can admit openly to her passions: "As Edna walked along the street, she was thinking of Robert. She was still under the spell of her infatuation. She had tried to forget him, realizing the inutility of remembering. But the thought of him was like an obsession, ever pressing itself upon her."[54] Quite enthusiastic and invigorated by the news of his imminent return from Mexico just a few months later, "she splashed through the streets on her way home"[55] and took the liberty of asking him to stay for dinner after their first walk together through the streets of the French Quarter: "They went together, picking their way across muddy streets and sidewalks encumbered with the cheap display of small tradesmen."[56]

Furthermore, walking allows Edna to cast off her "old self," by transcending formerly restricted domains. When she walks to the home of Adele Ratignolle to discuss her sketches, Edna's gait and outward appearance express the beauty and self-assuredness of a woman who has taken control of her life and who no longer aims to be dependent on her husband: "She looked handsome and distinguished in her street gown. The tan of the seashore had left her face, and her face was smooth, white, and polished beneath her heavy, yellow-brown hair."[57] But walking places is not just a means for her to advance her artistic career.[58] She also rewards herself with a walk when taking a break from painting. This activity, which has replaced her customary and expected household routines, fills her with deep satisfaction. It is not only an expression of her innermost self, but it also makes her feel at one with the world: "She liked then to wander alone into strange and unfamiliar places. She discovered many a sunny, sleepy corner, fashioned to dream in. And she found it good to dream and to be alone and unmolested."[59]

It is on one of these early walks through the city of New Orleans that she discovers a place "so far out of the way" that it is "a good walk from the car."[60] Here, she enjoys spending her afternoons: "The place [of the old mulatresse] was too modest to attract the attention of people of fashion, and so quiet as to have escaped the notice of those in search of pleasure and dissipation."[61] Edna Pontellier, however, admits freely to her affinity for unfashionable places, and she tells Robert Lebrun about her refuge at Catiche's: "I am so glad it has never actually been discovered. It is so quiet, so sweet, here. Do you notice there is hardly a sound to be heard?"[62] It is again worth noting that Edna's personal preferences echo Meysenbug's diary entries. The German writer shows how strongly she feels about her beliefs when she applauds the outcry of another female traveler who exclaims: "What did the thing they call etiquette mean to me at that moment? They, who force even the most sublime feeling into the confinement of their rules?"[63] After her walks, Edna indulges freely in her appetite for the sensuous pleasures of food, savoring milk and cream cheese and enjoying tasty fried chicken prepared by Catiche. She blossoms in the peaceful serenity of the beautiful garden atmosphere, spends her time reading, thinking, and pondering "her place in the universe." At the end, she cannot but admit: "I almost live here."[64]

While walking Edna is able to absorb the intensity of the life surrounding her and explore the different facets of human existence. When she laments to Robert Lebrun that "we women learn so little about life on the whole,"[65] she is again echoing Meysenbug, who had provocatively asked another travelling companion, a Jesuit priest: "Where is it written that only one part of humanity may eat from the Tree of Knowledge and the other mustn't?"[66] While both women share their concerns about the limitations of women's existence with a male confidante, Edna with Robert and Meysenbug with the priest, they also use the same means to open up unfamiliar spheres of experience: they are moving around alone. Edna reasserts: "I don't mind walking. I always feel so sorry for women who don't like to walk; they miss so much—so many rare glimpses of life on the whole."[67] She is fully aware that her walking the streets alone prompts the disapproval of the passers-by when the inquisitiveness of "the glance of strange eyes had lingered in her memory, and sometimes had disturbed her."[68] But despite her deviating from the accepted social norms, she insists on her right to explore the world on her own terms. Like with Meysenbug, walking is a socio-political endeavor.

During her "perambulations" through the city of New Orleans, Edna also trespasses the confines of her social circles and transcended gender limitations. Just like the women walkers of the German Revolution, she is no longer interested in class differences. In her efforts to find Mlle. Reisz, "she did not linger to discuss class distinctions with Madame Pouponne. . . ."[69] Furthermore, while walking alone and learning about street life without "a protector" or "guide" to provide her with well-meant directives, she gains insight into the secrets of the human heart. Consequently, when Edna visits the Lebruns and Victor shares the intimacies of his city adventures, she knows all too well what he is talking about. His confession that "a man needed occasional relaxation" prompts Taylor to write that, "it is significant that Victor whispers his tale to a fully comprehending Edna while saying he cannot think of telling her since, as a woman, she could not comprehend such things."[70] Edna has begun to eat from "The Tree of Knowledge." She is no longer "banish[ed] to a closed circle, like hothouse plants that have to be protected against rough wind and strong sun." Instead, her behavior reflects the social and moral change that Malwida von Meysenbug had demanded for women. Even though Edna is fatigued from her "long tramps" through the city, the feeling of liberty and satisfaction that they have instilled start to show in her personality.[71] Realizing that she has lost much of her reserve and stiff formality, Victor cannot but acknowledge that "The city atmosphere has improved her. Some way she doesn't seem like the same woman."[72]

Edna herself uses this particular phrase when she walks to what will be her last meeting with Robert Lebrun. Although she had never seen him there before, she is not too surprised when he joins her at Catiche's garden restaurant. The self-assured, confident Edna turns what might have been a clandestine meeting with her lover, filled with ambiguous remarks, into a conversation in which she does not shy away from straightforward expression. Insisting on her right to say what she thinks and feels, she tells the completely confounded Robert, "You never consider for a moment what I think, or how I feel your neglect and indifference. I suppose this is what you would call unwomanly; but I have got into a habit of expressing myself. It doesn't matter to me, and you may think me unwomanly if you like."[73] Consequently, the habit of walking, choosing where and how far she wants to go, is reflected in her new habit of expressing her thoughts. Both are expressions of a self-determined woman who has transcended the societal expectations of femininity by defining her own concept of female identity.

Beer's observation that "the freedom of the woman to move in the wider world is [Chopin's] concern . . . challenging the male possession of the streets and the restricted and restrictive range of signification attached to the woman who goes out alone,"[74] expands on the argument made by Taylor.[75] I would add that Edna Pontellier is on her way to assert her personal individuality, by retrieving the "inner dignity" that Meysenbug talks about, the dignity which was concealed under the restraints of societal norms and expectations. It is to the utter dismay of Edna's husband that "she has abandoned her Tuesdays at home, has thrown over all her acquaintances, and goes tramping about by herself, moping in the street cars, getting in after dark."[76] When Léonce Pontellier seeks counsel with the family doctor to quiet his anxieties about the "peculiar" behavior of his wife, old Dr. Mandelet can only retort: "Madame Pontellier not well? Why, I saw her—I think it was a week ago—walking along Canal Street, the picture of health, it seemed to me."[77] For Edna, walking is both a manifestation of her unique personality and her human freedom. This becomes most obvious when she "perambulates" for the first time through the house on Esplanade Street, inspecting with great inner joy the all too familiar surroundings. She is finally able to set up her own relations to the world around her, taking charge of her life, defining and cherishing her responsibilities:

> A feeling that was unfamiliar but very delicious came over her. She walked all through the house, from one room to another, as if inspecting it for the first time. She tried the various chairs and lounges, as if she had never sat and reclined upon them before. And she perambulated around the outside of the house, investigating, looking to see if windows and shutters were secure and in order.[78]

Focusing on the importance of the city for women in their pursuit of personal freedom, Beer argues that "New Orleans in Chopin's fiction is the place where the women grow up."[79] In *The Awakening*, Edna's solitary walks through the city nurture and accompany her growing maturity and are largely responsible for her difference in personality. This obvious change does not go unnoticed by Dr. Mandelet when he joins the Pontelliers for dinner: "He observed his hostess attentively from under his shaggy brows, and noted a subtle change which had transformed her from the listless woman he had known into a being who, for the moment, seemed palpitant with the forces of life. Her speech was warm and energetic. There was no repression in her glance or gesture."[80] Edna herself concludes in a poignant moment of self-revelation: "Every step which she took toward relieving herself from obligations added to her strength and expansion as an individual. She began to look with her own eyes; to see and to apprehend the deeper undercurrents of life. No longer was she content to 'feed upon opinion' when her own soul had invited her."[81] Edna's insights about her personal development reflect in a striking and stirring way Meysenbug's assertions about personal, human rights:

> Freedom of individual convictions and a life in conformity with them is the first of the rights and the first of the duties of a person. Until then people had debarred women from their holy right and a duty just as holy . . . I realized

that it was time to lift this ban, and I told myself that I wouldn't be able to esteem myself any longer if I didn't have the courage to leave everything in order to justify my convictions by my action.[82]

In concluding her argument on the importance of city life for women's personal growth, Beer observes that "they are eventually also forced to grow down—to a sense of paucity of their opportunities."[83] In her opinion, this seems to be especially true for Edna Pontellier. Malwida von Meysenbug, however, did not see any justification for such imposed limitations. Instead, the German writer insists on a woman's right to her unique personality. She affirms: "For the first time I told myself quite clearly that you *have* to free yourself from the authority of the family, as painful as it may be, as soon as it leads to the death of individuality and tries to submit the freedom of thought and conscience to a certain form of conviction."[84] Edna, who vigorously states in a conversation with Mlle. Reisz that she never wants to miss this "feeling of freedom and independence,"[85] keeps insisting that, "whatever came, she had resolved never again to belong to another than herself."[86]

I would argue that Edna never forfeits her right to express her individual convictions, independent of her family bonds and societal expectations. It is as if she had listened to Meysenbug's appeal when the German woman advises: "You women of the upper classes, the so-called educated ranks: if you go to Ostend, visit the cottage near the lighthouse and observe how the nature and grace, the strength and independence that woman and a truly feminine sense can go together so well."[87] Edna Pontellier, a woman of the upper classes, had been to the sea where she, in Taylor's words had "explore[d] the meaning of femininity"[88] by discovering her physical strength and her social and emotional independence. While walking through the city of New Orleans, she intensified this quest for her true sense of self. Her return to the sea and her final decision to drown herself have, consequently, nothing to do with "growing down" but rather with upholding the "inner dignity," which Meysenbug calls for. Edna is insisting on her personal beliefs rather than giving up her individuality by agreeing to conform to society's demands and expectations. In this respect, her final action with all its consequences dramatizes the German writer's way of thinking.

Striving for independence and freedom of thought, the German female walkers, whom Meysenbug described in her travel literature, traversed long distances and transcended social and emotional limitations by not only associating with members of different classes but also by showing empathy for their needs and desires. Invigorated and strengthened by the ideals of the German Revolution, walking allowed these women to see the world with their own eyes, setting up the relations they wanted, exploring, growing and maturing at their own pace. Familiar surroundings gained new meaning because they were now able to experience them on their own terms, viewing and evaluating them by their own standards. Meysenbug's thoughts and demands, which are reflected in the behavior and attitudes of her German women walkers, anticipate in sometimes striking similarities all of Chopin's "walking heroines." In particular, Edna Pontellier reflects that "there was with her a feeling of having descended in the social scale, with a corresponding sense of having risen to the spiritual."[89] All of these parallels strongly suggest that Kate Chopin must have been familiar with and influenced by Meysenbug's work and her description of the important role of the perceptive, courageous German female walker, especially since Chopin herself began her own wandering while in Germany. In considering her contributions to urban literature, Taylor asserts that "Chopin transformed that European figure of the solitary, disillusioned, aimless male flâneur into a complex, 'daring and defying' female walker who symbolically challenged the gendered meanings of fin-de-siècle urban space."[90] Some thirty years earlier, Malwida von Meysenbug had preceded her in that endeavor.

Acknowledgment

I would like to dedicate this essay to my late friend and neighbor Gisela Tecklenborg, who was another one of those courageous German woman walkers who dared and defied.

Notes

1. A shorter version of this essay was first presented at the New Orleans conference of the American Literature Association in 2015, in a session organized by the Kate Chopin International Society. I would like to thank the conference participants and the members of the Society for their comments and suggestions. I am especially indebted to Nancy Dixon and Leslie Petty for their careful readings of the manuscript.

2. Thomas Bonner, "Kate Chopin's European Consciousness," *American Literary Realism* 9 (1975): 281.

3. Janet Beer, "Walking the Streets: Women Out Alone in Kate Chopin's New Orleans." In Janet Beer and Elizabeth Nolan, *Kate Chopin's The Awakening: A Sourcebook* (London, New York: Routledge, 2004), 93.

4. The Revolutions of 1848 were series of violent uprisings in Germany and other European countries where legal attempts at economic and political change had not been successful. Initiated by peasants who had revolted against developing practices that were causing even greater poverty, the uprisings quickly swept over to students and members of the middle class and nobility, who began demanding constitutional and representative governments.

5. Wulf Wuelfing, "On Travel Literature by Women in the Nineteenth Century: Malwida von Meysenbug" in *German Women in the Eighteenth and Nineteenth Centuries: A Social and Literary History*, eds. Ruth Ellen B. Joeres and Mary Jo Maynes (Bloomington: Indiana University Press, 1986), 289–304.

6. Malwida von Meysenbug, *Eine Reise nach Ostende* (1849) (Berlin und Leipzig: Schuster & Loeffler, 1905), 290.

7. Per Seyersted, *Kate Chopin: A Critical Biography* (Baton Rouge: LSU Press, 1969), 49.

8. Carl Schurz, *The Reminiscences of Carl Schurz. Vol. Two*, 1852–1863 (New York: Doubleday, Page, & Co., 1907), 15. https://en.wikisource.org.wiki.

9. Meysenbug, *Eine Reise*, 292.

10. Per Seyersted and Emily Toth, *A Kate Chopin Miscellany* (Natchitoches, LA: Northwestern State University Press, 1979), 76.

11. Seyersted and Toth, *Miscellany*, 75.

12. Seyersted and Toth, *Miscellany*, 76.

13. Meysenbug, *Eine Reise*, 298.

14. Meysenbug, *Eine Reise*, 298.

15. Meysenbug, *Eine Reise*, 291.

16. Meysenbug, *Eine Reise*, 291.

17. Seyersted and Toth, *Miscellany*, 76.

18. Seyersted and Toth, *Miscellany*, 73–75.

19. Seyersted and Toth, *Miscellany*, 72.

20. Seyersted and Toth, *Miscellany*, 85.

21. Seyersted and Toth, *Miscellany*, 74–75.

22. Seyersted and Toth, *Miscellany*, 83.

23. Seyersted and Toth, *Miscellany*, 75.

24. Seyersted and Toth, *Miscellany*, 79.

25. Seyersted and Toth, *Miscellany*, 80.

26. Seyersted and Toth, *Miscellany*, 79.

27. Seyersted and Toth, *Miscellany*, 81.

28. Meysenbug, *Eine Reise*, 291.

29. Fanny Lewald was among the most renowned and successful German women writers of the nineteenth century. Renate Möhrmann emphasizes that next to Ida Hahn-Hahn, Lewald was one of the first women in the country who could manage to live on her writing (*Die andere Frau*, 2).

30. Quoted in Margaret Ward, *Fanny Lewald—Between Rebellion and Renunciation*, 59.

31. Beer and Nolan, *Kate Chopin's The Awakening: A Sourcebook*, 26.

32. Seyersted and Toth, *Miscellany*, 81.

33. Seyersted and Toth, *Miscellany*, 96.

34. Janet Beer, "Walking the Streets: Women Out Alone in Kate Chopin's New Orleans." In *The Awakening: A Sourcebook*, 93.

35. Meysenbug, *Eine Reise*, 293.

36. Meysenbug, *Eine Reise*, 294.

37. Beer, Nolan, *Sourcebook*, 46.

38. Barbara C. Ewell, *Kate Chopin* (New York: Ungar, 1986), 14.

39. Kate Chopin, "A Sentimental Soul," in Per Seyersted, *The Complete Works of Kate Chopin* (Baton Rouge: LSU Press, 1969), 389.

40. Chopin, "A Sentimental Soul," 396.

41. Chopin, "A Sentimental Soul," 389.

42. Kate Chopin, "Athénaise," in Per Seyersted, *The Complete Works of Kate Chopin* (Baton Rouge: LSU Press, 1969) 449.

43. Chopin, "Athénaise," 449.

44. Chopin, "Athénaise," 452.

45. Seyersted and Toth, *Miscellany*, 78.

46. Kate Chopin, *The Awakening and Selected Stories* (New York: The Modern Library, 1981), 211.

47. Seyersted and Toth, *Miscellany*, 81.

48. Chopin, *Awakening*, 213.

49. Chopin, *Awakening*, 214.

50. Chopin, *Awakening*, 249.

51. Meysenbug, *Eine Reise*, 291.

52. Chopin, *Awakening*, 249.

53. Helen Taylor, "Walking through New Orleans: Kate Chopin and the Female Flaneur," *Symbiosis* 1, no. 1 (April 1997): 82.

54. Chopin, *Awakening*, 254.

55. Chopin, *Awakening*, 298.

56. Chopin, *Awakening*, 325.

57. Chopin, *Awakening*, 254.

58. Chopin, *Awakening*, 295.

59. Chopin, *Awakening*, 261.

60. Chopin, *Awakening*, 336.

61. Chopin, *Awakening*, 334.

62. Chopin, *Awakening*, 336.

63. Meysenbug, *Eine Reise*, 296–97.

64. Chopin, *Awakening*, 335.

65. Chopin, *Awakening*, 337.

66. Meysenbug, *Eine Reise*, 296–97.

67. Chopin, *Awakening*, 336–37.

68. Chopin, *Awakening*, 277.

69. Chopin, *Awakening*, 262.

70. Taylor, "Female Flaneur," 83.

71. Chopin, *Awakening*, 263.

72. Chopin, *Awakening*, 266.

73. Chopin, *Awakening*, 336.

74. Beer, "Walking the Streets," 93.

75. Taylor, "Female Flaneur," 82.

76. Chopin, *Awakening*, 273.
77. Chopin, *Awakening*, 272.
78. Chopin, *Awakening*, 283.
79. Beer, "Walking the Streets," 95.
80. Chopin, *Awakening*, 279.
81. Chopin, *Awakening*, 317.
82. Meysenbug, *Eine Reise*, 299.
83. Beer, "Walking the Streets," 95.
84. Meysenbug, *Eine Reise*, 298.
85. Chopin, *Awakening*, 295.
86. Chopin, *Awakening*, 296.
87. Meysenbug, *Eine Reise*, 296.
88. Taylor, "Female Flaneur," 82.
89. Chopin, *Awakening*, 317.
90. Taylor, "Female Flaneur," 84.

5

"THE UNJUST SPIRIT OF CASTE" IN CHARLES W. CHESNUTT'S AND GEORGE WASHINGTON CABLE'S NEW ORLEANS NOVELS

Matthew Teutsch

Charles Chesnutt wrote *Paul Marchand, F. M. C.* in 1921, two years after the Red Summer of 1919 and on the threshold of the Harlem Renaissance. However, the novel remained unpublished until 1998 because companies, such as Houghton Mifflin, Harcourt Brace, and Alfred Knopf, showed no interest in publishing it.[1] Set in Antebellum New Orleans, *Paul Marchand* can be viewed partly as an anomaly through its continuation of the "local color" movement during a period that saw the rise of modernism. However, I would argue that the novel should be seen in relation to George Washington Cable's and Chesnutt's deconstruction of ongoing beliefs that biology rather than environment created "racial" differences between people. By choosing New Orleans as the setting, Chesnutt placed his novel in a city and time that would best highlight the flaws of the Black and white binary that existed in the Jim Crow South while at the same time commenting on contemporaneous de facto segregation and racism in the North.

Antebellum New Orleans's unique social structure provided Cable and Chesnutt with a locale that, as Thadious Davis has noted, served "as an alternative space for modeling a more expansive and less binary construction of race within the United States from the nineteenth century onward" because of the legal recognition of free people of color as a distinct class in the social structure.[2] Matthew Wilson also argues "that Chesnutt used New Orleans strategically as the only place in the antebellum period known for its class

"The Unjust Spirit of Caste" in Chesnutt's and Cable's Novels

of persons, the quadroons, between whites and blacks, a class that Chesnutt himself lived in and wrote about for much of his career."[3] I would like to expand on these statements by exploring how Cable and Chesnutt set their novels in New Orleans to comment on a society that sought to maintain a specific separation between people based solely on the belief that race exists as a biological truth and that one drop of African blood eliminates an individual from participating equally in that social order.

Focusing on heredity and economic status, Chesnutt's and Cable's use of the term *caste* works to critique the thoughts surrounding the term *race* during the latter part of the nineteenth and early part of the twentieth centuries. As Mia Bay notes, the turn of the century saw a shift in thinking that counteracted the beliefs regarding race as being biologically determined. Instead, Franz Boas and others came "to the conclusion that culture and environment—rather than racial characteristics—were the main arbiters of human difference"; however, whites would not embrace these ideas until after World War II.[4] Written at the end of the nineteenth century and during the early part of the twentieth century, respectively, Cable's *The Grandissimes* (1880) and Chesnutt's *Paul Marchand, F. M. C.* (1921) can be seen as contributing to this shift by dismantling the racist theory based on supposed biological differences and pointing out that societal segregation exists because of factions that seek to subjugate groups through legal means so wealthy whites may maintain sole power. Rather than situating characters' identities as inborn, both authors present identity as a choice. As Stephanie Foote notes when discussing *The Grandissimes*, "By framing identity as a choice of affiliation, the [novel] appears to offer the figure of the individual Creole as a working model of cultural heterogeneity in a homogenous nation."[5] Cable does this with the Creole inhabitants of New Orleans during the Americanization of the city after the Louisiana Purchase, and Chesnutt, rather than using the Creole as the "working model of cultural heterogeneity," expands the multiculturalism of the "homogeneous nations" by having Paul choose to identify as a F. M. C. after the revelation of his true ancestry comes to light.

Antebellum New Orleans as a true heterogeneous community made it the ideal locale for Cable and Chesnutt to challenge contemporaneous views of race at the turn of the twentieth century. Consisting of three distinct social classes—white Creoles, *gens de couleur libres* (free people of color), and slaves—antebellum New Orleans provided both authors with a setting in which they could construct narratives that consist of ambiguities based on the idea of race, especially with Honoré Grandissime, F. M. C. and Paul Marchand, F. M. C. For this essay, Creole refers to individuals of French or Spanish descent born in the colonies. Existing in a space between white Creoles and Black slaves, the *gens de couleur libres*, typically mixed-race individuals, could own property and slaves; however, they could not fully take part in the society due to their mixed-blood ancestry. For both Cable and Chesnutt, the *gens de couleur libres* allowed them to attack the prevailing thoughts that biology constitutes racial identity. As a group who existed between Black and white, the *gens de couleur libres* maneuvered in a precarious space, free to experience some freedoms but still constricted because of their lineage.

Early in his career, Cable tackled the issue of race in "'Tite Poulette" (1874), a story that provides an example of his movement towards deconstructing the Black-white binary through focus on caste and identity choice. Writing to his mother about Poulette, Kristian Kopping conflates caste and race when describing Poulette's position: "I see none so fair as the poor girl who lives opposite me, and who, alas! though so fair, is one of those whom the taint of caste has cursed."[6] Even while the law classifies Poulette racially because of the "supposed" drop of African blood in her veins, Kristian turns the focus on *caste*. As Kristian does this, the law remains, creating a specific binary that separates Poulette from Kristian. Poulette's "mother," Zalli, asks her to promise that when a man loves her she "will not tell him [she is] not white."[7] Poulette cannot make this promise to her mother because of the law which says that she cannot marry a white man due to the drop of African blood and because she fears becoming separated from Zalli, a free woman of color, because of the law. Eventually Zalli informs Poulette that she can marry Kristian because she is in fact white, and Zalli produces the papers to prove this fact.

While the story has a "happy ending," it leaves a lot of issues which fail to get settled. James Nagel states that Kristian's Dutch, Protestant immigrant status, his clumsiness with the French language, and his outstanding conflict with Monsieur de la Rue remain unresolved. The main aspect that remains unsettled, according to Nagel, "is the background social issue of the vulnerability of the quadroon mistress [Zalli]" which remains "a problem compounded by the *Code Noir* proscription against interracial marriage" that caused Monsieur John and Zalli to remain unmarried.[8] Zalli still exists within a structure that places her on the outskirts, free to have a relationship with M. John but not free to experience the full benefits of that relationship.

In addition, Zalli's announcement of Poullete's whiteness could be false. Rather than acknowledging Poulette as mixed-blood, which would not allow her to marry Kristian, perhaps Zalli constructs Poulette's identity through the pronouncement and revealing of signed papers that claim Poulette's parents were Spanish. At the end of "'Tite Poulette," Cable has the reader believe that Poulette's parents were white; he has Zalli conclude the story by telling Kristian, "I never had a child—she is the Spaniard's daughter."[9] Zalli, throughout, counters the idea of Poulette being white when she tells M. de la Rue and Kristian, "Of courses she is my child!"[10] It could be argued that Zalli serves as a surrogate mother for Poulette; however, the revelation of Poulette's Spanish parentage appears while Kristian comes in and out of consciousness. During his delirium, Kristian tells Zalli that he cannot marry Poulette because of her "race," but then he even refuses her because of her whiteness. These ambiguities create a fluid idea of race and the social construction of race in the story. In this way, Poulette's position, becomes malleable in much the same way that Paul Marchand's does in Chesnutt's novel.

In 1882, two years after the publication of *The Grandissimes*, Cable gave the commencement address at the University of Mississippi where he discussed the state of literature in the southern states. Speaking on the South's "belief that slavery was vitally necessary to the existence of society," Cable mentioned that the institution of slavery "established caste" by creating a "fixed aristocracy and a fixed peasantry."[11] Here, Cable centers in on the word *caste*, a word that eliminates the widely held biological ideas regarding race during the period and turns the focus to class and economics. Cable goes on to show how the continued binary of Black and white would not allow individuals "from the ranks of that peasantry" to elevate themselves "so long as a drop of its blood was discernible in the veins."[12] Rather than relying on other factors, the legal designations based on blood continuing after Reconstruction served to maintain social distinctions based on "biological factors." Karla F. C. Holloway calls the construction of race to create and maintain legal superiority over others "[America's] most visible, predictable, persistent, and paradoxical social convention," and Cable and Chesnutt throughout their writings confront the "legal fictions" that serve the ruling class by classifying African Americans, mixed-race individuals, and others as inferior to white citizens because of the blood that flows through their veins.[13]

Cable addresses the economic system of caste that perpetuates racism in *The Grandissimes* when Frowenfeld speaks with Aurora and Clotilde. After

Aurora comments on the American government possibly freeing the slaves, Frowenfeld tells her that while that may happen "there is a slavery that no legislation can abolish,—the slavery of caste."[14] This slavery exists because the ruling class does not want to even consider anything different, seeking "to preserve its established tyrannies" by becoming an "armed aristocracy" that keeps free people of color and slaves in place.[15] When Clotilde comments that they should consider freeing the quadroons because they appear phenotypically white, Frowenfeld simply tells her that the quadroons "want a great deal more than mere free papers can secure them."[16] While they may be technically free, Frowenfeld points out that they will not achieve true freedom "until they achieve emancipation in the minds and good will of the people."[17] Until that time, they will be subjugated to a position by the white aristocracy that allows them some semblance of freedom but ultimately keeps them in a liminal space between Black and white even though their fathers, in the majority of cases, were wealthy white Creoles.

Just as the caste system relegates the mixed-blood population to a level below the white Creoles, it also leads them to create their own identity and class which reinforces a society based on race while trying to eliminate racial distinctions at the same time. After seeing Honoré Grandissime, F. M. C. try to take his own life, Honoré Grandissime tells Frowenfeld that immigrants may complain about gaining acceptance in society, but people with mixed blood have an even larger complaint. Even though he may have drowned himself for love, Honoré Grandissime points out that Honoré Grandissime, F. M. C.'s life stands as "an accusation . . . against that 'caste' which shuts him up within that narrow and almost solitary limits!"[18] His very existence appears as an affront to the white, hegemonic class that seeks to keep him and other people of mixed blood in a subordinate position. However, even though Honoré Grandissime, F. M. C.'s presence confronts the system that oppresses him, the mixed-race community seeks to keep others out by isolating itself from Blacks and whites alike. Continuing, the Creole Honoré Grandissime says, "this people esteem the very same crime of caste, the holiest and most precious of their virtues."[19] Being ostracized from fully participating in society, the mixed-blood community, according to Honoré Grandissime, seeks to keep those who could not pass as white or who had mixed blood outside. In this way, they choose, like the white Creoles, to define their own identity based on legal fictions centered around blood and shared cultural experiences.

"The Unjust Spirit of Caste" in Chesnutt's and Cable's Novels   95

The community must maintain its own existence because the white Creoles work consciously to subvert the mixed-race lineage of their ancestors and themselves. As Frowenfield and Honoré Grandissime continue, their conversation moves to the "shadow of the Ethiopian" that intermingles with the Creoles. Honoré Grandissime tells his companion:

> [The shadow] is the *Némésis* w'ich, instead of coming afteh, glides along by the side of this morhal, political, commercial, social mistake! It blanches . . . ow whole civilization! It drhags us a centurhy behind the rhes' of the world! It rhetahds and poisons everhy industrhy we got!—mos' of all our-h immense agrhicul-tu'e! It brheeds a thousan' cusses that nevva leave home but jus flutter-h up an' rhoost . . . on ow heads; an' we nevva know it!—yes, sometimes some of us know it.[20]

Honoré Grandissime, a white man who struggles with his own views of identity in a society whose structure he does not totally agree with but nevertheless benefits from, sees the "shadow" lengthening over interracial relationships, that while known, must exist as private liaisons. Honoré Grandissime's half-brother exists as such, emaciated at times and continually referred to as a "shadow," an entity that has no true identity in and of itself, only an antecedent to a subjugated group of people. In this way, Honoré Grandissime's comments foreshadow his uncle Agricola's desire to maintain a "pure" lineage while ignoring, and burying, the mixed-race ancestors.

Before Honoré Grandissime, F. M. C. murders Agricola in Frowenfield's shop near the end of the novel, the white Creole Agricola speaks with the men gathered in the apothecary about the punishment for his slave Clemence whom Palmyre enlisted to kill Agricola by conjuring. Cassandra Jackson argues that this scene "conveys the desire of Creoles to suppress the history of cross-racial contact despite the presence of the sign of interracial history—the mixed-race individual."[21] To further emphasize this desire to suppress interracial history, Cable has Honoré Grandissime, F. M. C. enter Frownfeld's shop: "As [Agricola] spoke, a shadow approaching from the door caused him to turn."[22] Again, Honoré Grandissime, F. M. C. becomes a shadow, devoid of identity. He exists as the spectre of the secret rendezvous between slaves and masters or, in this case, *gens de couleur libre* and white Creoles. Agricola tries to expel his biological nephew from the shop, and a scuffle ensues in which Honoré Grandissime, F. M. C. stabs his uncle. Agricola's attempt to expel his nephew "demonstrates the desire to exclude the complicated history of race relations that produced Honoré F. M. C."[23] Agricola does this because, as he states earlier in the novel, "h-tradition is much more authentic than history."[24] For Agricola, identity exists because of "tradition" and social constructions, not because of biological factors; he uses race to maintain his position of power.

Almost fifty years after the publication of *The Grandissimes*, Chesnutt wrote about the publication of *The Conjure Woman* in his essay "Post-Bellum—Pre-Harlem" that appeared in *Colophon* in June 1931. In the essay, Chesnutt zeroes in on the aspects of caste and "people of mixed blood," like himself, that occupy his works. He claims that his writings "have dealt with the problems of people of mixed blood, which, while in the main the same as those of the true Negro, are in some instances and in some respects much more complex and difficult of treatment, in fiction as in life."[25] Chesnutt deals with this, of course, in *Marrow of Tradition* (1901), *House Behind the Cedars* (1900), and of course *Paul Marchand, F. M. C.* Interestingly, Chesnutt notes that the "people of mixed blood" show some similarities with the "true Negro."[26] Writing about Chesnutt's nonfiction, SallyAnn Ferguson notes, "Although he does not begrudge darker-skinned blacks whatever residual gains may accrue to them from his advocacy of racial equality, his nonfiction makes quite clear that Chesnutt writes, above all, to prompt white acceptance of color-line blacks."[27] Through this position, Chesnutt extends caste to intraracial relationships as well as interracial ones. Examples of this intraracial stratification in *Paul Marchand, F. M. C.* occurs when he relegates "true Negro" characters like Terence, the carriage driver, and slaves to the outskirts, and they never become fully developed; Zabet, alone, serves as the only exception in the novel because she has a prominent role; however, she still comes across as less than Paul because he treats her as he would a slave.

In the conclusion of "Post-Bellum—Pre-Harlem," Chesnutt marks a specific aspect of fiction, caste. He writes, "Caste, a principal motive of fiction from Richardson down through the Victorian epoch, has pretty well vanished among white Americans. Between the whites and the Negroes it is acute, and is bound to develop an increasingly difficult complexity, while among the colored people themselves it is just beginning to appear."[28] Chesnutt's multifaceted remark echoes Cable's novel when Honoré Grandissime explains to Frowenfeld the differences between white Creoles and immigrants to Louisiana, telling the German immigrant that he is right, "We are not a separate people . . . it is time to stop calling those who come and add themselves

"The Unjust Spirit of Caste" in Chesnutt's and Cable's Novels

to the community, aliens, interlopers, invaders."[29] If an immigrant appears phenotypically white, as Frowenfeld does, he can assimilate, thus flattening the community by eliminating those signs of Creole and immigrant. While whiteness may level the field for some, like it does Frowenfeld under American rule, it only exacerbates the differences when it comes to the gaps between whites, mixed-race individuals, and Blacks. Honoré Grandissime, F. M. C. experiences this when Agricola Fusilier tells him that he cannot buy Palmyre because she is wed to the slave Bras-Coupé. Agricola makes it known that even though Honoré Grandissime, F. M. C. is heir to the Grandissime fortune, he is nonetheless not the white heir: "You did this [tried to purchase Palmyre] for impudence, to make a show of your wealth. You intended it as an insinuation of equality. I overlook the impertinence for the sake of the man whose white blood you carry."[30] While immigrants, based on their supposed pure whiteness may become equals with the likes of Honoré Grandissime and Agricola Fusilier, their respective brother and nephew Honoré Grandissime, F. M. C. suffers because of his mixed race.

The word *caste* appears eighteen times throughout *Paul Marchand, F. M. C.*, a 148-page novel. Wilson points out that Chesnutt's use of *caste* provided him with "a way to conceptualize race as a social construct, but he saw, more clearly than Cable himself, how Cable was still implicated in the very racism he was attempting to critique."[31] While Cable espouses the idea that *caste*, not blood, causes separation and segregation, in his book *The Negro Question* he writes of "the black [as] 'an inferior race,' though how, or how permanently inferior, remains unproved."[32] Immediately after this statement, Cable moves into the "core of the colored man's grievance," the fact that instead of being treated with "regard to person, dress, behavior, character, or aspirations," he becomes judged through the lens of his "African tincture."[33] "'Tite Poulette" and *The Grandissimes* focus on individuals who could supersede distinctions based on race due to their phenotypes, and *Paul Marchand, F. M. C.* presents a case study, if you will, of Cable's comments above.

From the very beginning of the novel, Paul Marchand lacks the ability to define his own identity. Instead, society constructs one for him based on the "legal fictions" of the period. Even when he finds out his true parentage, the legal system, through the power of the pen, defines who he should be within New Orleans society, a white Creole property owner who must relinquish every aspect of his life as a free man of color because the law nullifies his marriage to Julie just as it refuses a union between Zalli and

M. John in "'Tite Poulette." Dean McWilliams compares Paul's lack of agency to a castration; Paul becomes impotent "within the linguistic order" unable to signify.[34] McWilliams points to the scene at the Cotton Exchange where Paul's cousin Hector makes the auctioneer ignore Paul's bid and calls him, "*Cochon!* . . . pig of a Negro!"[35] At this point, Paul cannot respond because the *Code Noir* forbids him from confronting a white man, and he becomes symbolically impotent.

When the revelation of Paul's "true" identity becomes known later in the novel, he still does not have any voice in deciding his true existence. Instead, he fluctuates between the quadroon caste and the white Creole caste. Throughout the novel, the narrator refers to Paul in varying ways, typically calling him "Paul Beaurepas, hitherto Marchand" or "Paul Beaurepas, late Marchand."[36] For the most part, though, he appears as "Paul Beaurepas." Paul's biological father Pierre Beaurepas, in his will, tells Paul that he will no longer be called Paul Marchand, F. M. C.; instead, he will become Paul Beaurapas. Here, the pen determines Paul's impotence, not allowing him to signify himself: "In one moment, by the stroke of a decrepit old man's pen, [Paul] was raised from a man of color to a white man."[37] Pierre's pen stroke, deliberately or not, upends the caste system based on blood within New Orleans by showing that race does not exist as an inborn biological fact but as a social construct. Numa Grandissime appears to upend the caste system in Cable's novel when he leaves Honoré Grandissime, F. M. C. "the bulk of his fortune"; however, the "black Honoré" still does not find acceptance, he merely appears as a shadow and secret.[38] Even with this stroke, the pen also serves as a tool that can damn. Commenting on Paul's new status as a "white" man, the narrator speaks of the "legal fiction" that classifies a man as "black for all social purposes, so long as he acknowledged or was known to carry in his veins a drop of black blood."[39]

Ultimately, Paul Marchand has the opportunity to choose his racial identity according to early nineteenth-century Louisiana social and racial constructs. After "trying" on whiteness, as Keith Byerman says, Paul chooses to remain a free man of color. Paul tells his cousins that he once heard his cousin Henri Beaurepas say "that blood without breeding cannot make a gentleman."[40] Here, Henri essentially supports the idea that race is a construct as Agricola does in *The Grandissimes*. Paul continues by pointing out that environment plays a large role in creating this social construct of race: "It may be said with equal truth that the race consciousness which is the strongest of Creole

"The Unjust Spirit of Caste" in Chesnutt's and Cable's Novels

characteristics, is not a matter of blood alone, but in large part the product of education and environment; it is social rather than personal."[41] As Paul tells the cousins, he cannot forget the social conditions that worked to shape him into the person standing before them, and because of this, he decides to no longer live as a man who "must be of one caste or another" and as a man "without a race."[42] His lack of identification in the New Orleans society in which he lives, leads him to make good on the long thought out decision to return to France with his family where they can live on "equal" terms with others.

Before Paul leaves, though, he transfers Pierre Beaurepas's property to his youngest cousin Philippe. Based on information from the slave Zabet, Philippe appears to be an imposter in the Beaurepas family because of his mixed blood. Only Paul knows this, and after transferring the property, he tells the cousins that one of them is a quadroon. Byerman points to this scene as the culmination of Paul "trying out" whiteness. The closing scene serves as a *denouement*, wherein race identification becomes a choice in much the same way that white Creole identification occurs in *The Grandissimes*. Paul learns the power that comes with identifying as white, and he realizes "[h]e can destroy or enhance lives not based on character or achievement, but simply on the basis of skin color."[43] By choosing to gainsay whiteness, Paul shows that blood does not hold any sway over one's position in society. Likewise, his decision to remain married to Julie works to create a "model of cultural heterogeneity" that could ultimately exist and serve as a model for the nation.[44]

While Paul's choice to maintain his relationship with Julie could possibly serve as an example, it fails to do so because the couple emigrate to France, thus escaping the torment of continual racism at home. In this way, Paul acts like Honoré Grandissime, F. M. C. because rather than staying to fight back against the oppression head on, he flees. However, Paul does fulfill Chesnutt's proposal in "The Future American" (1900) to ameliorate the problems of racism by remaining with Julie. In that essay, Chesnutt systematically presents his thoughts on the race question, arguing that the way to solve the problem lies in interracial relationships. Speaking about the intermarriage between whites, African Americans, and Native Americans, Chesnutt argues that if intermarriage is legal "in three generations the pure whites would be entirely eliminated, and there would be no perceptible trace of the blacks left."[45] Chesnutt provides for this resolution in the novel by having Julie and Paul remain married, and in a way, it could be argued that Cable does as well in "'Tite Poulette" when Zalli tells Poulette she is white.

Along with Chesnutt, others saw selective racial mixing as a way to rectify the continued atrocities caused by the legal construction of race. As such, eugenics played a role in not only modernist but also African American thought during the early part of the twentieth century. Daylanne K. English notes that the "association of a more vigorous Americaness with racial mixture would be more fully and explicitly articulated during the 1920s and 1930s, particularly by several writers of the Harlem Renaissance," and I would add Chesnutt.[46] Through this intermixture, equality would be achieved. However, to even consider such a proposal, the whites needed to eliminate the idea of race based on biology, and this, as stated earlier, did not come about until after World War II. The ideas in Chesnutt's "The Future American" do not only appear in his penultimate novel; they also occur in his final novel, *The Quarry* (1928).

In this novel, which remained unpublished until 1999, Donald Glover, an orphan, believes he is of mixed-race ancestry. His white adoptive family, the Seatons, decide to give Donald to an African American family when they discover his mixed-race lineage. However, as the novel unfolds, we discover, like Paul, he does not have any African American blood. When approached with this revelation by Mr. Seaton, Donald chooses to remain, as Paul before him, within the African American community and to fight for racial equality and racial uplift. To this end, he marries a quadroon woman, Berta, and unlike Paul, Donald remains in the United States, settling in New York. Likewise, when Mr. Seaton tells Senator Brown, the man who finds an African American family to raise Donald, about Donald's ancestry, he responds with a statement that directly echoes Chesnutt's "The Future American":

> I see no ultimate future for the Negro in the Western world except in his gradual absorption by the white race.... It is already far advanced.... There is obviously much white blood among the so-called Negroes, and among the white people much black blood that is not obvious. We'll not live to see the day, but as sure as the sun rises and sets the time will come when the American people will be a homogenous race.[47]

Here, Senator Brown illuminates the "private" relationships between whites and Blacks that produce mixed-race children rather than subtly hinting at them like Honoré Grandissime does when speaking with Frowenfield. Chesnutt made a similar move in 1900 when in "The Future American" he

"The Unjust Spirit of Caste" in Chesnutt's and Cable's Novels

pointed out that "one need only read the literature and laws of the past two generations to see how steadily, albeit slowly and insidiously, the stream of dark blood has insinuated itself into the veins of the dominant, or, as a Southern critic recently described it in a paragraph that came under my eye, the 'domineering' race."[48] Chesnutt continues by noting the presence of the Quadroon Caste in Cable's work and that people would have to have their heads buried in the sand to ignore the intermingling. Agricola, while he does not bury his head, blatantly ignores the mixed-race progeny of these relationships, and Chesnutt, in his own way, counters Agricola's dismissal in *Paul Marchand, F. M. C.* when he places the presumably mixed-race Phillipe at the head of the Beaurepas household.

When the Beaurapas's servant Zabet arrived in New Orleans, fleeing the Haitian Revolution with Pierre Beaurepas's nephews, she came with four boys. However, Paul finds out, once he takes "possession" of the household, that Réné, Pierre's brother, had three sons and one daughter. Realizing this difference, Paul confronts Zabet and asks about the fourth boy. Zabet informs Paul that the fourth child was "[y]our uncle Réné's child, master, and my daughter's!"[49] We do not know who the anonymous, mixed-race Beaurepas is, but we assume that is Phillipe because when he hears the name from Zabet, Paul's demeanor changes from one of revenge towards those who have wronged him "to an expression of disappointment" because Phillipe has been the only Beaurepas to treat Paul honorably.[50]

The mixed-race Beaurepas never sees the light of day as a quadroon, thus remaining in the shadows as Honoré Grandissime, F. M. C. does, but unlike the quadroon Honoré Grandissime F. M. C., Phillipe remains within the Creole society that seeks to keep those like Paul and Honoré Grandissime, F. M. C. in subjugation. Ultimately, Phillipe marries Josephine Morales, the daughter of another white Creole landowner, and while their fortunes never really take off, their marriage "proved a happy one."[51] With this relationship, Chesnutt mirrors the one between Paul and Julie, an interracial relationship that does not cause the end of civilization but one that results in happiness. As discussed above, Chesnutt reinforces his argument that environment, not biology, creates caste when he has Paul respond to his cousin Henri's comments near the end of the novel about honor and "blood without breeding" failing to make a man.[52] Throughout his writings, Chesnutt argues that identity hinges on environmental factors, not biological. Without the environment, the identity does not become fully formed. Donald experiences this in *The Quarry* just like

Paul, and both decide to remain within the community where they grew up, thus rejecting the "white" blood and choosing their own identities respectively.

Cable's and Chesnutt's novels focus on the white-Black binary not as something innate within individuals, but rather, as a constructed binary. To accomplish this, the two deploy the term *caste* to show the ways that these distinctions existed as a result of social hierarchies, not biology, and they explore the ways that identity, rather than being something one is able to construct on one's own, becomes a concept as well, either through cultural experiences or the pen. Through their affronts to the popular race science of the time, both writers worked to alleviate the suffering caused by the "race problem" in their writing. In this way, their discussions of race cause us to reexamine the ways that the some constructed or challenged the terminology to either exacerbate the continued infection of racism or to eradicate it from the cultural consciousness. Further examination needs to be done on this topic, specifically in regards to Chesnutt's later novels and their relationship to *passé blanc* of the Harlem Renaissance, specifically those of Nella Larsen, James Weldon Johnson, and others.

Notes

1. William L. Andrews, *The Literary Career of Charles W. Chesnutt* (Baton Rouge: LSU Press, 1980), 265.

2. Thadious M. Davis, *Southscapes: Geographies of Race, Religion, & Literature* (Chapel Hill: University of North Carolina Press, 2011), 186.

3. Matthew Wilson, introduction to *Paul Marchand F. M. C.*, by Charles Chesnutt (Jackson: University Press of Mississippi, 1998), xxiv–xxv.

4. Mia Bay, *The White Image in the Black Mind: African-American Ideas About White People, 1830–1925* (New York: Oxford University Press, 2000), 187.

5. Stephanie Foote, *Regional Fictions: Culture and Identity in Nineteenth-Century American Literature* (Madison: University of Wisconsin Press, 2001), 100.

6. George Washington Cable, "'Tite Poulette," in *Old Creole Days* (Gretna: Pelican Publishing Company, 1997), 222.

7. Cable, "'Tite Poulette," 223.

8. James Nagel, *Race and Culture in New Orleans Stories: Kate Chopin, Grace King, Alice Dunbar-Nelson & George Washington Cable* (Tuscaloosa: University of Alabama Press, 2014), 27.

9. Nagel, *Race and Culture*, 243.

10. Nagel, *Race and Culture*, 241.

11. George Washington Cable, "Literature in the Southern States," in *The Negro Question: A Selection of Writings on Civil Rights in the South*, ed. Arlin Turner (New York: Doubleday, 1958), 38.

12. Cable, "Literature," 39.

13. Karla F.C. Holloway, *Legal Fictions: Constituting Race, Composing Literature* (Durham: Duke University Press, 2014), 2.

14. George Washington Cable, *The Grandissimes* (Athens: University of Georgia Press, 1998), 143.

15. Cable, *The Grandissimes*, 143.

16. Cable, *The Grandissimes*, 144.

17. Cable, *The Grandissimes*, 144.

18. Cable, *The Grandissimes*, 155.

19. Cable, *The Grandissimes*, 155.

20. Cable, *The Grandissimes*, 156.

21. Cassandra Jackson, *Barriers Between Us: Interracial Sex in Nineteenth-Century American Literature* (Bloomington: Indiana University Press, 2004), 81.

22. Cable, *The Grandissimes*, 318.

23. Jackson, *Barriers Between Us*, 81.

24. Jackson, *Barriers Between Us*, 19.

25. Charles Chesnutt, "Post-Bellum—Pre-Harlem," in *The Conjure Stories*, ed. Robert Stepto and Jennifer Rae Greeson (New York: W. W. Norton & Company, 2012), 226.

26. Chesnutt, "Post Bellum," 226.

27. SallyAnn Ferguson, "Chesnutt's Genuine Blacks and Future Americans," *MELUS* 15, no. 3 (1988): 111.

28. Chesnutt, "Post-Bellum—Pre-Harlem," 227.

29. Ferguson, "Chesnutt's Genuine," 151.

30. Ferguson, "Chesnutt's Genuine," 186.

31. Matthew Wilson, "Introduction," in *Paul Marchand, F. M. C.* by Chalres Chesnutt (Jackson: University Press of Mississippi, 1998), xxiv.

32. George Washington Cable, *The Negro Question*, in *The Negro Question: A Selection of Writings on Civil Rights in the South*, ed. Arlin Turner (New York: Doubleday, 1958), 126.

33. Cable, *The Negro Question*, 126.

34. Dean McWilliams, *Charles W. Chesnutt and the Fictions of Race* (Athens: University of Georgia Press, 2002), 199.

35. Charles Chesnutt, *Paul Marchand, F. M. C.* (Jackson: University Press of Mississippi, 1998), 21.

36. Chesnutt, *Paul Marchand, F. M. C.*, 83, 104.

37. Chesnutt, *Paul Marchand, F. M. C.*, 126–27.

38. Cable, *The Grandissimes*, 109.

39. Cable, *The Grandissimes*, 131.

40. Cable, *The Grandissimes*, 138.

41. Cable, *The Grandissimes*, 138.

42. Cable, *The Grandissimes*, 139.

43. Keith Byerman, "Performing Race: Mixed-Race Characters in the Novels of Charles Chesnutt," in *Passing in the Works of Charles W. Chesnutt*, eds. Susan Prothro Wright and Ernestine Pickens Glass (Jackson: University Press of Mississippi, 2010), 90.

44. Foote, *Regional Fictions: Culture and Identity in Nineteenth-Century American Literature*, 100.

45. Charles Chesnutt, "The Future American," *MELUS* 15, no. 3 (1988): 99.

46. Daylanne K. English, *Unnatural Selections: Eugenics in American Modernism and the Harlem Renaissance* (Chapel Hill: University of North Carolina Press, 2004), 17.

47. Charles Chesnutt, *The Quarry* (Princeton: Princeton University Press, 1999), 266.
48. Chesnutt, "The Future American," 99–100.
49. Chesnutt, *Paul Marchand, F. M. C.*, 96.
50. Chesnutt, *Paul Marchand, F. M. C.*, 96.
51. Chesnutt, *Paul Marchand, F. M. C.*, 144.
52. Chesnutt, *Paul Marchand, F. M. C.*, 138.

6

MORE THAN ONE CITY OF NEW ORLEANS
Eudora Welty and Zora Neale Hurston's Crescent City

Ruth R. Caillouet

For decades, the city of New Orleans, with its rich gumbo of cultural influences and history, has been home to a host of creative geniuses—from writers to musicians to street performers and talents of both palette and palate. Many of these artists, born and raised in the city, may ridicule the state's crooked politicians and gloomy economic outlook but fiercely proclaim with pride that New Orleans, with its unique blend of cultures, is like no other city. But what about all of those folks, especially the writers, for whom New Orleans and Louisiana are not home? What is the lure, the purpose, and the response of those who are not "from" New Orleans? What has this city meant to them? We have countless tales of Faulkner, Twain, Williams and many other male authors who found a spiritual connection to the Crescent City—men not from there who spent months in the city drinking in the history along with its gin fizzes, rum, and mint juleps and absorbing the culture and language of the place. And there are many stories of Kate Chopin, a native of St. Louis, who came to New Orleans early in her marriage to Oscar Chopin and lived at three different residences from 1870–1879.

But the city of New Orleans also had a profound effect and lasting literary impression on two women writers of the WPA era who never got to call the city home but were lured by its gumbo pot of cultures, history, and traditions. Eudora Welty and Zora Neale Hurston, very different southern writers separated by race, economics, and upbringing, spent much of their writing careers capturing the pastoral settings of their home states, but in the city of New Orleans each found a rich roux to flavor her unique stories. By examining

Hurston and Welty's nonfictions—biographies, letters, essays, and photographs centered around the city—we can begin to see the power of this city's influence on more than one generation, more than one race, more than one story.

Eudora Welty and Zora Neale Hurston never met, and although their paths were very different, one born and raised by her moderately wealthy parents in Jackson, Mississippi, and the other isolated at an early age by her mother's death and her father's remarriage in rural Florida, their lives were also surprisingly similar. Both Welty and Hurston lived much of their lives and died in their own southern home states of Mississippi and Florida, respectively, and both through their WPA work ventured out to rural communities to collect representations of the South, one through photography and the other through folklore. And although they were seasoned travelers, each having escaped the South to live in New York and experience the excitement of the city, both seemed drawn to the places of their roots—to their own people—to home. For each writer, New Orleans provided stark contrast to her hometown roots and served as inspiration for creative energy long after she left the city. And although neither ever called New Orleans home, each was uniquely influenced by the city's rich cultural heritage, including its diverse people, music, and food.

Almost fifty years after Kate Chopin and family left the city of New Orleans for the pastoral setting of Cloutierville, Louisiana, Zora Neale Hurston at age thirty-seven arrived in the Crescent City on a folklore-gathering trip sponsored by her white benefactor, Charlotte Osgood Mason. According to biographer Valerie Boyd's *Wrapped in Rainbows: The Life of Zora Neale Hurston*, in August of 1928, Hurston wrote Langston Hughes, "I have landed here in the kingdom of Marie Laveau and expect to wear her crown someday."[1] Hurston's primary reason for traveling to New Orleans was to learn more about hoodoo by meeting with the city's leading practitioners. While the term *voodoo* comes from a West African word for spirit or deity, Hurston used the term *hoodoo*, the Americanization of *voodoo*. In *Mules and Men*, Hurston explains this term for conjuring:

> Hoodoo, or Voodoo, as pronounced by the whites, is burning with a flame in America, with all the intensity of a suppressed religion. . . . It adapts itself like Christianity to its locale, reclaiming some of its borrowed characteristics to itself, such as fire-worship as signified in the Christian church by the altar and the candles and the belief in the power of water to sanctify as in baptism.[2]

In New Orleans, Hurston felt she could study with the best hoodoo practitioners in America. According to Hurston, "Belief in magic is older than writing. So nobody knows how it started."[3] She firmly believed that Hoodoo was a legitimate religion and even describes the Christian creation myth as "six days of magic spells and mighty words."[4]

Hurston's trip to New Orleans was part of her second folklore-gathering venture. Her first attempt in Florida two years prior was inspired by her Barnard instructor Franz Boas and had resulted in limited findings and even an accusation of plagiarism. In her autobiography *Mules and Men*, Hurston blames her failure on her Barnard accent and mannerisms:

> The glamor of Barnard College was still upon me . . . I went about asking, in carefully-accented Barnardese, "Pardon me, but do you know any folk-tales or folk-songs?" The men and women who had whole treasuries of material just seeping through their pores looked at me and shook their heads. No, they had never heard of anything like that around there. Maybe it was over in the next county. Why didn't I try over there?[5]

On her second attempt in Florida and then on to New Orleans, Hurston was inspired and funded by Charlotte Osgood Mason, the same wealthy white benefactor who funded Langston Hughes and many other Black scholars. Although Mason contributed "between $50,000 and $75,000 to black writers and artists"[6] during the Harlem Renaissance, she was also rather prescriptive with her "godchildren," controlling not only the kind of art they would produce but also how African Americans were portrayed in the work. Hurston, contracted to travel back to the South to collect stories, games, hoodoo, poetry, and songs, was paid $200 per month and given a motion picture camera and car for use on the trip.[7] Unlike other contracts negotiated by Mason, this one gave Hurston the focus of collecting the material, "obtaining and compiling certain data"[8] as a researcher, rather than concentrating on any of her own literary creations, but giving Mason "full control of any material Hurston collected."[9] The contract also gave Hurston a sense of freedom as she left her husband and friends behind in New York, receiving more money per month from Mason than even Langston Hughes had received.[10]

Hurston travelled by train to Mobile in December of 1927, where she worked to correct her failure from her first interview with a slave ship survivor, Cudjo Lewis, and after purchasing a "shiny gray Chevrolet,"[11] she journeyed back to Florida for a stop in Eatonville and then on to the lumber mill town of Loughman, just south of her home county. These few months back in Florida were crucial to Hurston's success in New Orleans, as it was in the lumber mill community that, with the freedom of an employer many miles away, she truly shirked most of her academic anthropological training to get her material. After several nights of drinking with the locals and working to keep her Barnard training at bay, she still felt like an outsider even though she was just a few miles from her hometown. Through the confidence of one young man, she learned that her shiny Chevy had folks fearing that she was either a detective or revenue officer, so she began spreading the word that she was a bootlegger escaping from the law. Soon, people relaxed and after Zora led the group in a few rounds of John Henry, "Zora's car was everybody's car."[12] She learned to inspire storytelling by organizing competitions and blending in with the locals, becoming the life of the party—until a bar brawl and death threats scared her into getting out of town fast.

After leaving Florida and a few months of gathering folklore in Alabama, in August of 1928, Hurston moved on to New Orleans to begin her quest for lore about hoodoo. "So I slept at night, and the next morning I headed my toenails toward Louisiana and New Orleans in particular," claims Hurston in *Mules and Men*.[13] "New Orleans is now and has ever been the hoodoo capital of America. Great names in rites that vie with those of Hayti in deeds that keep alive the powers of Africa."[14] Hurston claims that the "way we tell it, hoodoo started way back there before everything" and describes the creation myth, the work of Moses, and many other scenes from the Bible as episodes of conjuring.[15] She lived first in Algiers, a short ferry ride from the French Quarter, paying ten dollars per month for rent and furnishing her place for another sixteen:[16]

> Now I was in New Orleans and I asked. They told me Algiers, the part of New Orleans that is across the river to the west. I went there and lived for four months and asked. I found women reading cards and doing mail order business in names and insinuations of well known factors in conjure. Nothing worth putting on paper. But they all claimed some knowledge and link with Marie Leveau [*sic*].[17]

So Hurston began the search for stories and practices of Marie Laveau, spending much of her time in New Orleans with Luke Turner, the voodoo doctor who claimed to be Laveau's nephew.

Hurston devotes only about two pages of her 1942 autobiography, *Dust Tracks on a Road*, to this trip to New Orleans, but she published "Hoodoo in America" in the *Journal of American Folklore* in 1931, centered half of *Mules and Men* on the subject, and continued to explore the topic for the rest of her life. In her autobiography, she tells of her experiences studying with the Frizzly Rooster and his wife Mary and learning about how to break up marriages, get rid of enemies, and change the minds of judges and juries. She also tells of the initiation she had to go through with each Hoodoo doctor. Other stories detail the trips into the swamp to perform ceremonies with black cats and of long nights waiting to meet the devil. She describes one frightening night in the swamp outside New Orleans:

> The most terrifying was going to a lonely glade in the swamp to get the black cat bone. The magic circle was made and all the participants were inside. . . . The fire was built inside, the pot prepared and the black cat was thrown in with the proper ceremony and boiled until his bones fell apart. Strange and terrible monsters seemed to thunder up to the ring while this was going on. It took months for me to doubt it afterwards.[18]

In another tale, Hurston describes how her finger was cut so that she became "blood brother to the rattlesnake" and how they "were to aid each other forever. I was to walk with the storm and hold my power, and get my answers to life and things in storms. The symbol of lightning was painted on my back. This was to be mine forever."[19] Hurston's repetition of the word *forever* in the passage speaks to her belief in the importance of these days in New Orleans toward understanding her own strength and giving her the confidence she needed for both life and fiction. A few years later, Hurston uses the storm image in *Their Eyes Were Watching God*. Janie reassures Teacake as the hurricane rages by saying, "Ah'm wid mah husband in uh storm, dat's all. . . . If you kin see de light at daybreak, you don't keer if you die at dusk. It's so many people never seen de light at all. Ah wuz fumblin' round and God opened de door."[20] Hurston and Janie both recognize the transformative powers of nature and do indeed learn to "walk with the storm" and "get the answers to life and things in storms."[21]

Prior to writing *Dust Tracks in a Road* or *Their Eyes Were Watching God*, however, Hurston published her collection of folklore gathered from across the South from Alabama to Florida to Louisiana from 1928–1930. Hurston focuses on hoodoo in part two of this 1935 collection, *Mules and Men*, and devotes each section of her text to a different "two headed doctor," including stories from six different New Orleans hoodoo practitioners. Hurston poured herself into truly understanding the ceremonies and beliefs, devoting her mind and body to the rituals, from snake skins to days of fasting to studying the spirits of dead chickens and black cats as well as countless swamp and cemetery ceremonies. The text is filled with stories that Hurston gathered from each experience, including details about the habits of ghosts, the special properties of herbs and roots, methods for getting revenge, stories of eggs and entrails, black chickens and black cats, lavender oil, incense, and a host of other crucial ingredients for hoodoo. She writes with conviction about each experience but is careful not to reveal too many secrets of hoodoo practices, claiming, "I studied under Turner five months and learned all of the Leveau [*sic*] routines, but in this book all of the works of any doctor cannot be given."[22] The New Orleans stories range from Urquhart Street to St. Claude and St. Ann and from Lake Pontchartrain to Bayou St. John, from the Cabildo to Belleville Court, and from the Vieux Carré to Tremé.

With techniques that she learned from the Florida lumber mill community, Hurston slowly gained the trust of these hoodoo doctors by telling each that she wanted to learn the trade—and perhaps, in the end, that is exactly what she desired. From Luke Turner she heard the story of Marie Laveau, who was born in 1827. According to Turner, "She was very pretty, one of the Creole Quadroons and many people said she would never be a hoodoo doctor like her mama and her grandma before her."[23] Turner explained that, in time, people came from all over the world to Laveau's house on St. Ann Street asking for her help. Even Queen Victoria is said to have sought Marie Laveau's services. As part of the training that Turner gave to Hurston, she had to complete an elaborate initiation ceremony that lasted for several days:

> I was made ready and at three o'clock in the afternoon, naked as I came into the world, I was stretched, face downwards, my navel to the snake skin cover, and began my three day search for the spirit that he might accept me or reject me according to his will. Three days my body must lie silent and fasting while my spirit went wherever spirits must go that seek answers never given to men as men.[24]

According to Hurston, she lay for sixty-nine hours with no food or drink and had "five psychic experiences" and was then painted with a lightning bolt across her back because "the Great One was to speak to me in storms."[25] Hurston's training with Turner went on for five months before she was eventually offered a partnership that she had to turn down. Each of the other doctors offered unique initiations and training sessions, and from each Hurston gained more stories and more confidence.

Hurston biographer Valerie Boyd claims that the experience in New Orleans transformed Hurston as a scholar and writer but also influenced her spiritual growth: "Hurston's immersion in New Orleans conjure completed her transition from an enthusiastic rookie folklorist to an adept and mature scholar."[26] Hurston stayed in New Orleans through the winter of 1928–29 and was so carefully trained by the leading voodoo doctors that at least one hoped that she would take his place. According to Boyd, "Zora's deep dip into the well of New Orleans spirituality had matured her on another level that was beyond scholarship, beyond words. She had experienced a gradual ripening from within."[27] Hurston not only gained confidence in her abilities to gather folklore but also in her own conjuring talents as she gained the respect of several voodoo experts. On Hurston's last night in the city, she gave a poetry lecture at New Orleans University (now Dillard University), and then returned home to Florida. Hurston's experience in New Orleans formed the beginnings of her scholarship as a folklorist but also helped her see herself as a serious anthropologist, and she soon began plans for how she would publish and develop the material.

New Orleans not only helped shape Hurston's future research projects including her stint with the Works Progress Administration (WPA) and later trips to Haiti and Jamaica, but the experiences also filtered through to her future fiction and life itself. While New Orleans did not become the setting for any of Hurston's fiction, the conjuring arts that Hurston learned from the city's fascinating residents in back streets, alleys, and nearby swamps became plot elements for many of her works. Janie, for instance, is accused of placing a voodoo spell on her first husband to speed up his death in *Their Eyes Were Watching God*, a book written in Haiti while Hurston continued her research of voodoo. The snakes and storms of *Their Eyes Were Watching God* and so many other stories may indeed have been inspired by Hurston's rattlesnake blood brother and lightning on her back. A year later, *Tell My Horse*, the personal account of her research in Haiti and Jamaica, was published, continuing the descriptions of ceremonies and customs that Hurston began researching in New Orleans. Conjuring is also an important plot element in Hurston's first novel, the 1934 *Jonah's Gourd Vine*, a book that she patterned after her own parents' lives. Published just six years after her trip to New Orleans, the novel tells the story of John Buddy Pearson and his wife Lucy as well as the jealous Big 'Oman, a conjurer who works to steal John from his loving wife. "You b'lieve in all dat ole stuff 'bout hoodoo and sich lak?" is the question asked by Hattie, the very one who uses conjuring powers to win her love.[28] Over and over, after her experiences in New Orleans, Hurston returned to the conjuring arts in her fiction and folklore. Even later divorce documents filed by Hurston's second husband listed his fears of "black magic" and "voodoo-ism" as the reason for the divorce.[29] And almost thirty years after Hurston studied with the Frizzly Rooster and slept with snakeskins in New Orleans, her final publication ran in the *Fort Pierce Chronicle* from 1957–1959, a column called "Hoodoo and Black Magic." Without a doubt, the city of New Orleans, its stories and characters, its mysticism and magic, its history and hoodoo did indeed season the art and life of Zora Neale Hurston, giving her that first taste of freedom, confidence, a little black magic—and, of course, the lightning on her back.

Just over six years after Zora Neale Hurston left New Orleans, Eudora Welty arrived at age twenty-seven for a photography expedition, and it is a testament to the city's diverse offerings that Welty, a white, middle-class Mississippian, would find the ingredients for cooking up an entirely different pot of gumbo than Zora Neale Hurston. Since Jackson is just over 180 miles north of New Orleans, a quick trip by train at the time, Welty, with family or friends, easily visited the city for day trips throughout her life. But, like Hurston, Welty was not from New Orleans, and always remained an outsider, an observer of the city's customs and celebrations. Like the characters described in *The Optimist's Daughter*, "New Orleans was out-of-town for all of them."[30] According to biographer Suzanne Marrs, in the early 1930s Welty and a group of friends who called themselves the Night-Blooming Cereus Club—self-named for the flower that many Jacksonian social groups celebrated through all night vigils—took many road trips during Welty's youth. These young men and women, home from college, entertained themselves with trips around the state of Mississippi, visits to the county fair, nights of charades, music, talking and drinking, and, of course, trips to New Orleans.[31] According to another biographer, Ann Waldron, the group often made day trips to the Crescent City, sometimes taking the early morning train, getting a meal at Galatoire's, a drink at Pat O'Brien's, and then back on the train for home at night. Most of the group members were too poor to stay overnight but occasionally they stayed at the Monteleone Hotel and would go to Preservation Hall to hear jazz. According to Waldron, "Jackson people tended to choose either New Orleans or Memphis for their big-city activities; Eudora always went to New Orleans."[32] Since funds were low, New Orleans served as the group's replacement for New York during those Depression years with quick trips to soak in music, food, and fun.

But in 1936, Welty journeyed to the city to photograph Mardi Gras celebrations. It was, in fact, Welty's photography in New Orleans that seemed to most influence her later fiction. While working with the WPA as a publicist, Welty traveled the state of Mississippi from 1935–1936. Although she was not hired as a WPA photographer, she often sent pictures with her writings and tried to capture images of people in everyday life. In New Orleans, she photographed Mardi Gras costumes and street scenes. According to Waldron, she later used the photographs to help her with details while writing *The Optimist's Daughter*. In the novel, the main character, Laurel, who is in the city to help her father through an operation, takes a late-night cab ride during the Mardi Gras season:

> The interior of the cab reeked of bourbon, and as they passed under a street-light she saw a string of cheap green beads on the floor—a favor tossed from a parade float. . . . Then she heard more than one band, heard rival bands playing up distant streets. Perhaps what she had felt was no more than the atmospheric oppression of a Carnival night, of crowds running wild in the streets of a strange city.[33]

The carnival festivities and raucous celebrations provide a stark contrast to the silence of the clean, sterile hospital room and hallways in Welty's story, and the images of her fiction seem to be a retelling of the images of her camera. Welty, in fact, saw her photography and writing as running on "parallel lines," one capturing "interior feelings and apprehensions," while the other captured the exterior, the "look of things."[34] Later, in examining the photographs, Welty says, "All these lives began to take on meaning for me, and soon the settings of my stories changed. . . . They stopped being in an imaginary world and began to appear in a real place."[35]

Welty spoke of the importance of her photographer's eye in the introductory interview of *Eudora Welty Photographs*. When asked whether the

Mardi Gras scene from *The Optimist's Daughter* was a reflection of one of her photographs, she said this was not exactly true:

> Not as a reflection; I've seen it directly in life. But I went back and looked up my photographs after I had written this to get some exact costume that I could give a person. You can't make up something fantastic. So I used in the way I might refer to notes, certain snapshots of costumes, but it was the Mardi Gras itself, the living experience, working in my imagination, that made me put it in the story in the first place. My fiction's source is living life.[36]

In the essay "Literature and the Lens," published in the collection edited by Pearl Amelia McHaney, *Eudora Welty Occasions: Selected Writings*, Welty describes the scene of a picture that she snapped on Royal Street while on one of her trips to New Orleans. Three old women wanted to know why she was taking the picture: "It is hard to guess why the act of taking a picture with a camera is always suspect. You can do all kinds of other things in public without a question of being asked—but if you click your camera at something people from nowhere run up and ask 'Why did you take that?'"[37] She goes on to explain how some cultures believe that snapping a picture is an attempt to steal a soul:

> It is clear that the fascination of a photograph of anything is that it imprisons a moment in time—and is that really different from stealing its spirit, its soul? Perhaps one does right to protest. Yet this must be in a sense, the purpose of nearly everything we do—certainly in the arts; painting, and writing, we steal spirits and souls if we can, and in love and devotion, what do we do but pray: Keep this as it is, hold this moment safe?[38]

"Keeping that moment safe" is exactly what Welty went on to perfect in her fiction as she became the master of capturing a moment, a place, and the characters who inhabit it. Her short story, "No Place for You, My Love," begins and ends in New Orleans, and through the text, Welty reveals a very different side to the city than that portrayed in Zora Neale Hurston's fiction and folklore. The story, published in the *New Yorker* in 1952, is the tale of a couple who meets for the first time at Galatoire's with friends and takes a day trip south of the city to Venice, Louisiana. Welty's description of the restaurant, the journey, the oppressive heat, the Cajun and African American people, and the sounds of insects on their journey out of town, captures the details of South Louisiana. Welty uniquely alternates the point of view in the story, creating a two-sided narrative of a couple's first meeting.

The city of New Orleans serves as the frame of the story but also functions as a marker of civilization, and in some ways, as an additional character, like a matronly chaperone who keeps the young couple in check and mindful of the rules of society. While many may assume the Galatoire's address on Bourbon Street would represent wild abandon and an escape from order, nothing could be farther from the truth. The cultured, jackets-only clientele, black-tie waiters and formal setting of Galatoire's represent "old" New Orleans and the wealthy social set who demand polite conversation and a proper place setting along with their white tablecloths and several courses of fine dining. The restaurant serves as the backdrop for the story that begins with the line, "They were strangers to each other, both fairly well strangers to the place."[39] Welty is careful to use New Orleans as a setting for characters not from there, providing a sense of the displaced person in her fiction and perhaps reflecting on her own experience as a "stranger" just outside New Orleans society and customs, always separated by her own lens.

In the story Welty explains the relationship of this couple: "What they amounted to was two Northerners keeping each other company."[40] There is a constant reminder that the couple in the story is not from New Orleans and not from the South. When the stranger asks her if she would like to ride with him, the young woman asks, "South of New Orleans? I didn't know there was any south to *here*. Does it just go on and on?"[41] "No Place for You, My Love" is very much a story about place—from knowing one's place to feeling vulnerable because of a place to being put in one's place. And as the couple drives out of the city, the characters are moved by the wild abandon of the country roads, dark swamp, and deafening cacophony of insects:

> Below New Orleans there was a raging of insects from both sides of the concrete highway, not quite together, like the playing of separated marching bands. The river and the levee were still on her side, waste and jungle and some occasional settlements on his—poor houses. Families bigger than housefuls thronged the yards. . . . As time passed and the distance from New Orleans grew, girls ever darker and younger were disposing themselves over porches and the porch steps, with jet-black hair pulled high, and ragged palm leaf fans rising and falling like rafts of butterflies.[42]

The description of a lonely drive through the marshland and countryside seems a direct reflection of Welty's camera lens, images of the South's rural landscape and its people. The fictional trip was also based on a real drive with Carvel Collins, a young professor and acquaintance.[43] In "Place and Time: The Southern Writer's Inheritance," an essay published in McHaney's collection, *Eudora Welty Occasions: Selected Writings*, Welty writes about the unique position of southern literature and its connection to place. Her words help characterize the setting of this New Orleans short story as well as her thoughts on what makes southern literature unique:

> One thing Yoknapatawpha County has demonstrated is that deeper down than people, farther back than history, there is the Place. All Southerners must have felt that they were born somewhere in its story, and can see themselves in line. The South was beautiful as a place, things have happened to it, and it is beautiful still—sometimes to the eye, often to the memory. . . .[44]

For the young northern couple in "No Place for You, My Love," struggling against the oppressive heat and insects of south Louisiana, this exotic place is less than inviting. "It was a strange land, amphibious—and whether water-covered or grown with jungle or robbed entirely of water and trees, as now, it had the same loneliness. He regarded the great sweep—like steppes, like moors, like deserts (all of which were imaginary to him); but more than it was like any likeness, it was South."[45]

As the couple returns to New Orleans from their journey from "far down here in the South—south of South, below it,"[46] they also return to their former lives. "For their different reasons, he thought, neither of them would tell this . . . that, strangers, they had ridden down into a strange land together and were safely back."[47] And as they drive over the levee, "like an aurora borealis, the sky of New Orleans, across the river, was flickering gently."[48] She is dropped off at her hotel where someone crosses the lobby to greet her and he heads for his own room and parks the car with intentions of heading back to Syracuse and his wife the next morning. The final scene is very much like the late-night drive in *The Optimist's Daughter*. The city of New Orleans is alive with festivities and music, but the characters in the story remain apart from the celebrations:

> As he started up the car, he recognized in the smell of exhausted, body-warm air in the streets, in which the flow of drink was an inextricable part, the

signal that the New Orleans evening was just beginning. In Dickie Grogan's, as he passed, the well-known Josefina at her organ was charging up and down with "*Clair de Lune*."[49]

New Orleans serves as the setting for the start and end to the story, but it also functions as a marker of society—reminding the characters that they are not of this city, that they are strangers who must eventually return to their former lives. In many ways, Welty uses New Orleans in her fiction as she did in her own life—as a plot element and setting but also as a bit of escape from "normal" routines, like so many Mississippians.

New Orleans had a profound impact on these two writers, but that impact was also profoundly different for each. While each set very few of her fictional works in the city of New Orleans—both preferring more pastoral settings and characters—the city influenced each author and her stories. Zora Neale Hurston took away the secret society of voodoo practices as well as the respect of its leaders, giving her a new confidence and direction that she had not experienced before. And Eudora Welty found escape in the city but also rediscovered the South through her camera lens and developed an eye for detail in capturing the moment. More than anything we can see that New Orleans has been and continues to be more than one city, impacting its visitors and writers in a variety of ways but always having an undeniable impact. From swamp meetings with voodoo doctors to black-tie waiters at Galatoire's, the varied experiences of Hurston and Welty in New Orleans could not have been more different. And perhaps that is what makes New Orleans so unique—that it can serve as the muse for so many artists and their diverse stories. Without question New Orleans helped to shape the art of Zora Neale Hurston and Eudora Welty and the writers they would become.

Notes

1. Valerie Boyd, *Wrapped in Rainbows: The Life of Zora Neale Hurston* (New York: Scribner, 2003), 175.

2. Zora Neale Hurston, *Mules and Men* (New York: Harper Perennial, 1935), 183.

3. Hurston, *Mules and Men*, 183.

4. Hurston, *Mules and Men*, 183.

5. Zora Neale Hurston, *Dust Tracks on a Road* (New York: Harper Perennial, 1942), 127–28.

6. Boyd, *Wrapped in Rainbows*, 158.

7. Boyd, *Wrapped in Rainbows*, 160.

8. Boyd, *Wrapped in Rainbows*, 159.

9. Boyd, *Wrapped in Rainbows*, 160.

10. Boyd, *Wrapped in Rainbows*, 160.

11. Boyd, *Wrapped in Rainbows*, 162.

12. Boyd, *Wrapped in Rainbows*, 164.

13. Hurston, *Mules and Men*, 183.

14. Hurston, *Mules and Men*, 183.

15. Hurston, *Mules and Men*, 183.

16. Boyd, *Wrapped in Rainbows*, 174.

17. Hurston, *Mules and Men*, 191.

18. Hurston, *Dust Tracks*, 140.

19. Hurston, *Dust Tracks*, 140.

20. Zora Neale Hurston, *Their Eyes Were Watching God* (New York: Harper and Row, 1937), 151.

21. Zora Neale Hurston, *Dust Tracks*, 140.

22. Hurston, *Mules and Men*, 202.

23. Hurston, *Mules and Men*, 192.

24. Hurston, *Mules and Men*, 199.

25. Hurston, *Mules and Men*, 200.

26. Boyd, *Wrapped in Rainbows*, 182.

27. Boyd, *Wrapped in Rainbows*, 183.

28. Zora Neale Hurston, *Jonah's Gourd Vine* (New York: Harper and Row, 1934), 147.

29. Carla Kaplan, ed. *Zora Neale Hurston: A Life in Letters* (New York: Knopf, 2003), 431.

30. Eudora Welty, *The Optimist's Daughter* (New York: Vintage Books, 1969), 10.

31. Suzanne Marrs, *Eudora Welty: A Biography* (Orlando: Harper, 2005), 49.

32. Ann Waldron, *Eudora: A Writer's Life* (New York: Doubleday, 1998), 61–62.

33. Welty, *Optimist's Daughter*, 41–42.

34. Waldron, *Eudora*, 76.

35. Waldron, *Eudora*, 77.

36. Eudora Welty, *Photographs* (Jackson: University Press of Mississippi, 1989), xvi.

37. Pearl Amelia McHaney, ed. *Eudora Welty Occasions: Selected Writings.* (Jackson: University Press of Mississippi, 2009), 71.

38. McHaney, *Eudora Welty Occasions*, 71.

39. Eudora Welty, *The Collected Stories of Eudora Welty* (New York: Barnes and Noble Books, 1980), 465.

40. Welty, *Collected Stories*, 466.

41. Welty, *Collected Stories*, 466.

42. Welty, *Collected Stories*, 467.

43. Waldron, *Eudora*, 223.

44. McHaney, *Eudora Welty Occasions: Selected Writings*, 164.

45. Welty, *Collected Stories*, 479.

46. Welty, *Collected Stories*, 479.

47. Welty, *Collected Stories*, 480.

48. Welty, *Collected Stories*, 480.

49. Welty, *Collected Stories*, 480–81.

7

NEW ORLEANS IN WALKER PERCY'S WORKS
Place, Placement, Nonplacement, and Misplacement[1]

Edward J. Dupuy

"I alight at Esplanade in a smell of roasting coffee and creosote and walk up Royal Street. The lower Quarter is the best part. The ironwork on the balconies sags like rotten lace. Little French cottages hide behind high walls. Through deep sweating carriageways one catches glimpses of courtyards gone to jungle"[2] So muses Binx Bolling in Walker Percy's first and most well-known novel, *The Moviegoer*. While he describes a lush scene in this passage, Binx also says that he "can't stand the old world atmosphere of the French Quarter or the genteel charm of the Garden District."[3] Having lived in the Quarter, he grew tired, he says "of Birmingham businessmen smirking around Bourbon Street . . . and [the] patio connoisseurs on Royal Street."[4] When he tries to live in the Garden District, on the other hand, he is either in a "rage, during which [he] develop[s] strong opinions on a variety of subjects and write[s] letters to editors," or in a "depression during which [he] lie[s] rigid as a stick for hours staring straight up at the plaster medallion in the ceiling of [his] bedroom."[5] So he lives an "uneventful" and "peaceful" life in Gentilly, a suburb near Lake Pontchartrain, away from both the Quarter and the Garden District. Throughout the novel, Binx engages with both, though in his own peculiar, detached, and "in between" way. In this manner he's like Walker Percy himself, who though he lived in New Orleans for a while in the mid-1940s, moved to the Northshore of Lake Pontchartrain in 1948, first on Military Road North of Covington, and in 1961, just before *The Moviegoer*'s publication, to Jahnke Avenue, then on the outer edges of Covington. From this "in between" place, he observed New Orleans and the South for the rest of his life. Walker Percy is not Binx Bolling, of course, yet Binx's "in betweeness" reflects a philosophical stance Percy developed throughout his linguistic essays and novels. Following a line of continental philosophers, Percy sought to place characters such as Binx Bolling, Will Barrett, and Tom More, in a place, as Simon Critchley might say, that has a "goal of individual or collective emancipation"—a place between the bifurcated poles of nihilism let loose since the Enlightenment."[6] In doing so, Percy looks at the self and place from an "interesting" perspective, and I use "interesting" in its root sense here as "being concerned about" and also as "*inter-esse*" or "being between."[7] Percy's characterization of Binx Bolling, his characterization of New Orleans and his search, coupled with Percy's nonfiction essays on Covington, Louisiana, and New Orleans, including his engagement of the "race question" that beset the South of the 1960s, all suggest Percy's attempt to find a middle way, an interstitial and "interesting" place for himself, his characters, and ultimately his readers.[8]

By most conventional standards, Binx Bolling is an upstanding citizen—a stock and bond broker from a good family who wants for very little. And yet the novel uncovers an underlying "dis-ease" or "malaise" in Binx's character. As he notes at one point,

> For some time now the impression has been growing upon me that everyone is dead.
>
> It happens when I speak to people. In the middle of a sentence it will come over me: yes, beyond a doubt this is death. There is little to do but groan and make an excuse and slip away as quickly as one can.[9]

And thus Binx sets out on a search for something beyond this "death." In *The Moviegoer*, the bifurcated poles of nihilism might best be expressed by "consumerism" and "scientism." In the former, the self is sunk in the consumption of the abundant goods and services made possible in the West. The stance of scientism is the stance of theory, of standing outside the world looking in—orbiting the world, as Percy will come to say in his later works. Binx searches for a place between the death (nihilism) of consumerism and scientism he sees all around him. His highly self-conscious narration seeks a way between these two poles, and his attempt at finding such an in betweeness carries over not only into where he lives in New Orleans, thus reflecting Walker Percy's own attempts at finding a habitable place for himself, but also his attempt at reconciling what Percy sees as a bifurcation in the self which contributes to the myriad social ills besetting New Orleans and the South, and he would say the "modern city." Self, place, placement, and displacement recur throughout Percy's fiction and nonfiction, thus emphasizing its centrality to what dogged him for the more than forty years of writing.

In Percy's famous "self-interview," published originally in the December 1977 issue of *Esquire* and reprinted in both *Conversations with Walker Percy* (1985) and *Signposts in a Strange Land* (1991), Percy asks himself at the outset about place, "Do you regard yourself as a southern writer?" His ironic and pugilistic alter ego responds: "That is a strange question, even a little mad. Sometimes I think that the South brings out the latent madness in people.... Would you ask John Cheever if he regarded himself as a northern writer?" The hapless interviewer persists: "How do you perceive your place in society?" Answer: "I'm not sure what that means." The interview continues:

> But what about those unique characteristics of the South? Don't they tend to make the South a more hospitable place for writers?
>
> Answer: "Well, I've heard about that, the storytelling tradition, sense of identity, tragic dimension, community history and so forth. But I was never quite sure what it meant.... People don't read much in the South and don't take writers very seriously.... I've managed to live here [in Covington, Louisiana] for thirty years and am less well-known than the Budweiser distributor.... If one lived in a place like France where writers are honored, one might well end up like Sartre, a kind of literary-political pope, a savant, an academician, the very sort of person Sartre made fun of in *Nausea*. On the other hand, if one is thought an idler and a bum, one is free to do what one pleases. One day a fellow townsman asked me: 'What do you do, Doc?' 'Well, I write books.' 'I know that doc, but what do your really do?' 'Nothing.' He nodded. He was pleased and I was pleased."[10]

This hilarious "self-interview" not only touches on the notion of physical placement of writers (Percy in the South, John Cheever in the North, Jean-Paul Sartre in Paris) but their place (or lack of it) in the culture at large. The Budweiser distributor has a greater "place" in Covington, Louisiana, than does Walker Percy. Its format, furthermore, with Percy as interviewer and interviewee, displays a split, with the author himself between the two "characters" in the interview, thus displaying even here Percy's nagging quest for "in betweeness."

Despite his protestations about not wanting to be called a "southern writer," Percy said in another interview (one with someone other than himself) that "without the southern backdrop, Mississippi, Louisiana (New Orleans)—the [*Moviegoer*] does not work—it doesn't work at *all*. Try to imagine Binx Bolling in Butte, Montana. There has to be a contrast between this very saturated culture in the South . . . whether it's French, Creole, uptown New Orleans, or Protestant. It's a very dense society or culture which you need for Binx to collide with."[11] While *The Moviegoer* is a very understated book and while it doesn't follow a traditional novelistic structure, part of its dramatic tension rests in the place—New Orleans and the Gulf South—Percy uses as its backdrop. *The Moviegoer* explores New Orleans and its environs richly and, of all Percy's works, most thoroughly.

Of Percy's other novels, *Lancelot* deals with New Orleans also, but to a lesser extent than *The Moviegoer*. Ostensibly set in the old city as well—because Lancelot Lamar tells his story to Fr. John in a detention facility in New Orleans—most of *Lancelot* takes place at Belle Isle, away from New Orleans. In characteristic fashion, Lance provides a trenchant assessment of the city:

> New Orleans! Not a bad place to spend a year in prison—except in summer. Imagine being locked up in Birmingham or Memphis. What is it I can smell, even from here, as if the city had a soul and the soul exhaled an effluvium all its own? I can't quite name it. A certain vital decay? A lively fetor? Whenever I think of New Orleans away from New Orleans, I think of rotting fish on the sidewalk and good times inside. . . . The city's soul I think of as neither damned nor saved but eased rather, existing in a kind of comfortable Catholic limbo somewhere between the outer circle of hell, where sexual sinners don't have it all that bad, and the inner circle of purgatory, where things are even better.[12]

Like Binx's observations in *The Moviegoer*, Lance tries to name the "effluvium" and "soul" of the city, but he does so only by placing it among opposites—in an "in between" space, "vital decay" or "lively fetor," "neither damned nor saved."

Both Lance and Binx are obsessed with the idea of place and placement and their counterparts, nonplacement and misplacement. A scion of the aristocratic South, like Binx and Lancelot Lamar, Percy knew well the American and Southern lineage of Faulkner, Robert Penn Warren, Welty, and O'Connor, among many others. These writers are likewise concerned with "place" in their fiction—recall Welty's "Place in Fiction"—but Percy approaches place in a different way. Faulkner, Warren, Welty, and O'Connor help define the southern "backdrop" Percy uses in *The Moviegoer* and thus set the stage for what I think are Percy's unique explorations of it and what Percy calls Binx's "collisions" with it. The character of Aunt Emily, for example, is based on Percy's second cousin, William Alexander Percy, a lawyer, planter and poet who is also the author of *Lanterns on the Levee*, which, among other things serves as an extended paean to a South the elder Percy sees vanishing. After his father's suicide when Percy was thirteen and his mother's death two years later, Walker and his two brothers were adopted by "Uncle Will," as they called him. Walker Percy dedicated *The Moviegoer* to him. Percy uses Uncle Will and his novelistic incarnation, Aunt Emily, as part of the backdrop against which Binx collides. And they do collide, especially after Kate, his suicidal second cousin and would be fiancée, concocts the plan to leave New Orleans for Chicago without telling Aunt Emily of her intentions.

Binx is detached, adrift, on a search for a place, a way of being in the world, that the South can no longer provide as it once did for Uncle Will *cum* Aunt Emily. Neither is Percy's approach to place the same as that developed in Faulkner, Warren, or Welty. By having Binx live in Gentilly, Percy places him outside the two "centers of the city," in the "nonplace" of suburban America. He writes: "Except for the banana plants in the patios and the curlicues of iron on the Walgreens drugstore one would never guess [Gentilly] was part of New Orleans. Most of the houses are either old-style California bungalows or new-style Daytona cottages. But this is what I like about it."[13] In the nonplace of Gentilly, Binx presents himself as "a model tenant and model citizen and take[s] pleasure in doing all that is expected of me."[14] As he says: "What satisfaction I take in appearing the first day to get my auto tag and brake sticker. I subscribe to *Consumer Reports* and as a consequence I own a first-class television set, an all but silent air conditioner and a very long lasting deodorant. My armpits never stink."[15] He is, as Percy develops later in the novel, at times the perfect consumer and at times a scientist, developing theories of rotation and repetition. But he seeks something more.

The search for a place between scientist and consumer has entered his consciousness and "complicated" his model suburban existence.[16] Binx defines the search as "what anyone would undertake if he weren't sunk in the everydayness of his own life."[17] Percy's use of Heidegger's category of "everydayness" in this definition indicates the irony with which Binx plays at being the "model citizen." He recognizes his self-conscious placement as precarious at best.

Binx describes two types of searches: the vertical and the horizontal. During his vertical, scientific, search Binx reads only "'fundamental' books, that is key books on key subjects:"[18] books such as *War and Peace, A Study of History, What is Life?*, and *The Universe as I See It*. As he says, "during those years I stood outside the universe and sought to understand it. I lived in my room as an Anyone living Anywhere. . . . Certainly it didn't matter to me where I was when I read such a book as *The Expanding Universe*."[19] He goes on to say,

> The greatest success of this enterprise, which I call my vertical search, came one night when I sat in a hotel room in Birmingham and read a book called *The Chemistry of Life*. When I finished it, it seemed to me that the main goals of my search were reached or were in principle reachable. . . . The only difficulty was that though the universe had been disposed of, I myself was left over . . . obliged to draw one breath and then the next.[20]

The vertical search "displaces" Binx clear out of the world, above it (in orbit, if you will). For Binx, as for Percy, this is the displacement of scientism. One can understand the universe, but the "self" is left over, adrift and without a place to anchor it. Before he became a stock and bond broker Binx had spent a summer doing research with Harry Stern, who he says, "was absolutely unaffected by the singularities of time and place."[21] He goes on to say that Harry "is no more aware of the mystery which surrounds him than a fish is aware of the water it swims in."[22] Harry is a scientist, outside of time and place, while Binx is troubled and in search of its "mystery" and "singularities." And thus Binx sets out on a "horizontal" search, seeking these "singularities of time and place."

Percy develops this idea of the scientistic displacement of "orbiting the world" further and much later in *Lost in the Cosmos* (1983), his satirical, wildly funny, and at the same time, very serious attempt to view the self from a semiotic point of view.[23] Like Kierkegaard before him, Percy sees the self always as a particularity, and any attempt to encompass the self through science, which *de facto* depends on looking at particulars in terms of generalities, falls short. Furthermore, the self is not a thing as a chair might be. In naming a chair with the word "chair," Percy says, we give it a place in the world. While the thing and the word are distinct, we "know" the chair in naming it. It has a place through a mutual naming between "you and me." There is no name for the self, however; the self cannot be encompassed by signs, and thus it is quite literally unspeakable. Lost, then, the self seeks any manner of ways to avoid its unspeakableness, to place itself as a thing among the other things of the world. Such an enterprise leads to despair. *The Moviegoer* is dedicated to William Alexander Percy, but its epigraph comes from Kierkegaard: ". . . the specific character of despair is precisely this; it is unaware of being despair."

Here again Percy can be seen as developing a strand of continental philosophy. In Simon Critchley's terms, the "true crisis of the European sciences or what Heidegger calls 'the distress of the West' is felt in the absence of distress: 'crisis, what crisis?' The real crisis is the absence of crisis, the real distress is the absence of distress."[24] The real despair, to continue the analogy, is the unawareness of despair. The problem of placement is the unawareness of the problem of placement. And so Binx participates in, while he is also dimly aware of, his own despair. *The Moviegoer*, following in the continental tradition, seeks "a critique of the present conditions, as conditions not amenable to freedom, and toward the emancipatory demand that things be otherwise, the demand for a transformative practice of philosophy, art, thinking, or politics."[25] Binx's becoming aware of his despair is part of the "emancipatory demand" Percy's seeks for the reader as well. As Walker Percy's widow, Mary Bernice Townsend ("Bunt") Percy once told me in a casual conversation: "Walker wanted people to wake up!" Today's proponents of so-called "antiwoke" philosophy are perhaps most deeply lost in the despair that does not know itself as despair.

Again, since the vertical search leaves the "universe disposed of" (lost), Binx has "undertaken a different kind of search, a horizontal search. . . . What is important is what I shall find when I leave my room and wander the neighborhood."[26] The horizontal search might be described as the search for the "singularities of time and place."[27] The vertical search leaves one displaced, what Binx calls being an "anyone, anywhere"—and this is the "crisis" of placement, or better nonplacement, that of which he becomes aware. "The malaise," he says, "is the pain of loss. The world is lost to you, the world and the people in it, and there remains only you and the world and you no more able to be in the world than Banquo's ghost."[28] Note that the "malaise" is similar to the vertical search in that one stands outside the world to understand it. The world is disposed of (lost) through "fundamental" books but "there remains you and the world" and you, adrift from the singularities of time and place, are nevertheless obliged to find a place in the world—obliged to take one breath and then the next. Placement is the problem and the backdrop of New Orleans, with its richness of placement, allows Binx's search to come into relief.

At one point in the novel, Binx's Uncle Jules, the owner of the stock and bond company he works for, asks Binx to travel to Chicago on business. Binx expresses an extreme anxiety at having to do so:

> It is nothing to [Uncle Jules] to close his eyes in New Orleans and wake up in San Francisco and think the same thoughts on Telegraph Hill that he thought on Carondelet Street. Me, it is my fortune and misfortune to know how the spirit-presence of a strange place can enrich a man or rob a man but never leave him alone, how, if a man travels lightly to a hundred strange cities and cares nothing for the risk he takes, he may find himself No one and Nowhere.[29]

And when Binx arrives in Chicago, he reflects on the "genie-soul" of a place in language similar to Lance's about New Orleans. He thinks of an earlier trip to Chicago he made with his father, of which he remembers "not a thing" but this:

> . . . the sense of the place, the savor of the genie-soul of the place which every place has or else is not a place. . . . Nobody but a Southerner knows the wrenching rinsing sadness of the cities of the North. Knowing all about genie-souls and living in haunted places like Shiloh and the Wilderness and Vicksburg and Atlanta where the ghosts of heroes walk abroad by day and are more real than people. . . . The wind and the space, they are the genie-soul [of Chicago]. . . . This Midwestern sky is the nakedest loneliest sky in America. To escape it, people live inside and underground.[30]

Acutely aware of place and afraid of misplacement or displacement, Binx is haunted by place's genie-soul, and thus his attitude is at once there and not there, placed and not placed, in between.

Recall Lance's oxymoronic description of New Orleans noted earlier. Neither damned nor saved, neither vital nor fetid, Lance describes the soul of New Orleans as somewhere between both. Lance's absolutist character would do away with such in between qualities in favor of what he thinks is more solid footing. He cannot abide the mixed nature of New Orleans or of his fellow humans, and so he goes on a search as well. But his search, unlike Binx's, is for "pure evil."[31]

Percy is so preoccupied with the betweeness of place and placement, then, it is useful to examine the place that he chose for himself—Covington, Louisiana. Covington is near enough to New Orleans but not so near that he would be overcome by its strong sense of place. In his 1980 essay, "Why I live Where I Live," Percy explores the issue of his own placement in Covington:

> The reason I live in Covington, Louisiana, is not because it was listed recently in *Money* as one of the best places in the United States to retire to. The reason is not that it is a pleasant place but rather it is a pleasant nonplace. . . . Covington occupies a kind of interstice in the South. It falls between places.
>
> Technically speaking, Covington is a nonplace in a certain relation to place (New Orleans), a relation that allows one to avoid the horrors of total placement or total nonplacement or total misplacement.[32]

Note Percy's desire to avoid total placement, nonplacement, or misplacement. For Percy total placement would be to live in "Charleston or Mobile where one's family has lived for two hundred years. . . . Such places are haunted," he writes. "Ancestors perch on your shoulder while you write."[33] For Binx, total placement was living in the Garden District of New Orleans, where his family haunts him. Recall his continual musing over the photo on Aunt Emily's mantelpiece, searching it continually for clues to his own placement. He concludes that in the picture his father has a "smart-alecky" and "ironical" look about him. Like Binx, he's out of place with the other Bollings. Total nonplacement for a southern writer, Percy writes, "is to live in a nondescript Northern place, like Waterbury, Connecticut, or become writer in residence at Purdue." Again, Binx in Gentilly is an analogue of nonplacement. Total misplacement is

> to live in another place, usually an exotic place, which is so strongly informed by its exoticness that the writer, who has fled his haunted place or his vacant nonplace and who feels somewhat ghostly himself, somehow expects to become informed by the exotic identity of the new place. . . . Hemingway in Paris and Madrid. Sherwood Anderson in New Orleans, . . . Vidal in Italy.[34]

Such misplacement can be conducive to writing, though the "self" of the writer is still lost. Binx finds the exoticness of the French Quarter a misplacement for him.

When Percy first visited Covington, having driven over from New Orleans, he says: "I took one look around, sniffed the ozone, and exclaimed unlike Brigham Young: 'This is the nonplace for me!' It had no country clubs, no subdivisions, no Chamber of Commerce, no hospitals, no psychiatrists (now it has all these). I didn't know anybody, had no kin here. A stranger in my own country. A perfect place for a writer!"[35] But things changed. As Percy writes: "Covington is now threatened by progress. It has become a little jewel in the Sunbelt and is in serious danger of being written up in *Southern Living*."[36] All this in 1980. After Hurricane Katrina, Covington has become a refuge for many displaced New Orleanians, and it suffers from overdevelopment and traffic.

Earlier in his writing life, Percy described New Orleans in similar "in between" terms—not as the "exotic" place that made it possible for Sherwood Anderson to write, but more in line with how he describes Covington—as a place "between." In 1968, he published in the September issue of *Harper's*, "New Orleans Mon Amour." In this essay, he focuses on New Orleans as an interstice of the South: "It has something to do with the South and with a cutting off from the South, with the River and with history. . . . [New Orleans is] cut adrift not only from the South but from the rest of Louisiana, somewhat like Mont-St.-Michel awash at high tide."[37] "The city," he goes on to say,

> is a most peculiar concoction of exotic and American ingredients, a gumbo of stray chunks of the South, of Latin and [Black] oddments, German and Irish morsels all swimming in a fairly standard American soup. What is interesting is that none of the ingredients has overpowered the gumbo, yet each has flavored the others and been flavored.[38]

In 1968, racial tensions were high, of course. It was the year of the Chicago riots at the Democratic National Convention, the assassinations of Martin Luther King Jr. and Bobby Kennedy. The long shadow of the Watts riots in 1965 lingered. The TET Offensive in the Vietnam War, furthermore, caught United States troops and the Johnson administration off guard, and led to an escalation of US troops (composed largely of poor blacks and other minorities) being sent there to fight for an increasingly unpopular and ill-defined

New Orleans in Walker Percy's Works   129

cause. The mood in the country was, not unlike the mood today, rancorous and divisive. In "New Orleans Mon Amour," Percy seeks a middle way, a way between—an interstice, one might say—regarding the so-called "race question," something that anyone writing about New Orleans must address.

And so he makes the bold statement at the outset that New Orleans, because of its interstitial character, can serve as a model for the rest of the nation:

> If the American city does not go to hell in the next few years, it will not be the likes of Dallas or Gross Pointe, which will work its deliverance. . . . But New Orleans just might. Just as New Orleans hit upon jazz, the only unique American contribution to art, and hit upon it almost by accident and despite itself, it could also hit upon the way out of the hell which has overtaken the American City.[39]

Percy certainly recognized the deep problems of the city: "many of the streets look like the alleys of Warsaw. In one subdivision, feces empty into open ditches. Its garbage collection is whimsical and sporadic. . . . It has some of the cruelest slums in America."[40] And, furthermore, he acknowledges its complicated history: "New Orleans was the original slave market, a name to frighten Tidewater [Blacks], the place where people were sold like hogs, families dismembered, and males commercially exploited, the females sexually exploited. And yet it hit upon jazz."[41]

Percy counters nearly every serious problem in New Orleans with an "and yet." A "mediocre" newspaper is offset by an outstanding television station. A Jesuit-owned media outlet could do more for social justice, and yet, a Jesuit, Fr. Louis Twomey, has "translated Catholic social principles into meaningful action." And while other elements of the Catholic church have "been content to yield moral leadership to the federal bench," and Catholic schools integrate "only when public schools are forced to," New Orleans was also the place the Catholic Church installed the first [Black] bishop in the United States.[42]

Percy troubled over the place of African Americans in New Orleans and he sought, through "New Orleans Mon Amour," a middle way between the complete submission of Blacks to the white agenda and the riots in the streets that had beset much of the nation. Three prominent Black characters appear in *The Moviegoer*: Mercer, Aunt Emily's houseman, who, Binx says, "is thought to be devoted to us and we to him. But the truth is that Mercer and I are not at all devoted to each other. My main emotion around Mercer is unease that in threading his way between servility and presumption, his foot might slip. I wait on Mercer, not he on me"[43] Mercer is himself displaced, trying to walk the line between "old retainer," figuring out how to "harness his powers" and yet also presenting himself as the new man acquainted with politics and science. He tries to be "faithful retainer" for Aunt Emily, up to date on science and politics with Binx, but holds onto a "well-thumbed volume put out by the Rosicrucians called *How to Harness Your Secret Powers*."[44] The second is Cothard, "the last of the chimney sweeps." He appears in the background when Aunt Emily is telling Binx off (the "collision" that occurs after his ill-fated trip to Chicago) in her no-uncertain-terms-aristocratic-southern-way. His cry: "*R-r-r-ramonez la chiminée du haut en bas!*" is a foreshadowing of Binx's subtle change at the end of the novel when he at last finds a tentative solution to his "crisis," agrees to go to medical school, gets married to Kate, and finds a place for himself in the city. And finally there is the middle-class Black whom Binx sees at the church on the corner of Elysian Fields and Bons Enfants on Ash Wednesday, the day after Mardi Gras, which in the novel, happens also to be Binx's thirtieth birthday—the day he told Aunt Emily he would make a decision about his future. Because the African American is "sienna colored and pied," Binx cannot tell if he received ashes at the church, and thus he wonders if God is or is not present at the corner of Bons Enfant and Esplanade. "It is impossible to say," are the final words of the novel before the Epilogue.[45]

Except perhaps for Cothard, the chimney sweep, these characters of color in Percy's fiction are not the sort revealed to the world in the aftermath of Hurricane Katrina. Katrina unmasked the ugliness lurking beneath the seductive notion of "The Big Easy." In the flood waters, the storm paradoxically uncovered what the city had so arduously kept covered for the majority of its history since the civil rights movement—that Blacks and whites in New Orleans—despite Percy's "and yets"—have never really been on an equal footing. Percy does say in "New Orleans Mon Amour" that the real trouble in these race issues is that "as long as [Blacks] do not lose [their] temper nobody is apt to do anything about [them] and when they do it is too late." But this attitude—that someone should do something "about them"—does not sit well today, in these "dread latter days of the old violent beloved U.S.A.," as the start of Percy's third novel, *Love in the Ruins*, has it. And the degenerated attitude of *noblesse oblige* of Uncle Will and other "Southern Stoics" is part of what Percy writes against in his 1956 essay, "Stoicism in the South." The old Southern Code of honor, which made "place" inhabitable for many, no longer holds, if it ever did. The code which led "to generosity toward [one's] fellow men and above all to [one's] inferiors" was always at odds with seeing the individual as individual. The Southern Stoic attended to his "inferiors," as Percy says, "not because they were made in the image of God and were therefore loveable in themselves, but because to do them an injustice would be to defile the inner fortress which was oneself."[46] In *Love in the Ruins* Black "Bantu Guerillas" have overtaken "Paradise Estates"—a fairly clear metaphor that all is not well with in the so-called paradise of the Sunbelt South.

One can praise Percy's attempt to find a middle way for New Orleans in 1968—to take on the race issue at all—and to present the city, with all its foibles, as a possible way out of the "hell" of the American City. His attempt to place it as an interstice in the South, while recognizing also its squalor and *de facto* segregation, evinces a civil discourse flexible enough to accommodate the tumult of the present moment.

A recognition of lostness for both Black and white people, an acknowledgement of a precarious placement, which inevitably becomes misplacement, and an appreciation of the fundamental nonplacement that comes about from the attempt to name the self, all form the basis of Percy's explorations in his novels and essays of the self's desire to place itself. And his attempts to describe New Orleans and Covington, furthermore, take on the in betweeness he sees as sorely needed for his characters. In many respects, Percy overturns the Delphic question—not who am I, but where am I? And what he finds is an in betweenness—between consumer and scientist in *The Moviegoer*, between immanence and transcendence in *The Last Gentleman*, between angel and beast in *Love in the Ruins*. How does one place oneself when confronted with such nihilistic bifurcations? His characterization of the places he knew best, New Orleans and Covington, fall into the same in betweenness he develops about the self and language, thus making his explorations of self, place, and placement all of a piece. From this interesting place (again in the root sense of interest—as *inter-esse*—between being), Percy carves out an uneasy, interstitial space for himself and his readers.

Notes

1. This essay appeared first in the *Xavier* (New Orleans) *Review*. I am grateful to the *Review* for giving me permission to use it here in a slightly modified form.

2. Walker Percy, *The Moviegoer* (New York: Vintage International, 1998; originally published in 1961 by Alfred A. Knopf), 6.

3. Percy, *Moviegoer*, 14–15.

4. Percy, *Moviegoer*, 6.

5. Percy, *Moviegoer*, 6.

6. Simon Critchley, *Continental Philosophy: A Very Short Introduction* (Oxford: Oxford University Press, 2001), 8.

7. I develop this category of "inter-esse" more fully in my *Autobiography in Walker Percy: Repetition, Recovery, and Redemption*. I don't address it, however, with specific reference to New Orleans or Percy's characterizations of it or the South, or of Covington, Louisiana, as I try to do here.

8. The idea of search of a search amidst nihilistic options is not new to Percy criticism, having been suggested from Binx Bolling's search itself. Thus, Jay Tolson's biography is called *Pilgrim in the Ruins*, and William Rodney Allen's work is titled *Walker Percy: A Southern Wayfarer*. Going further back, the first full-length study of Percy's work, Martin Luschei's *The Sovereign Wayfarer: Walker Percy's Diagnosis of the Malaise* complements Robert Coles's *Walker Percy: An American Search*. And more recently, Win Riley's *Walker Percy: A Documentary Film* highlights Percy as an American seeker. John Desmond's *Walker Percy's Search for Community* likewise incorporates the theme of the search. My essay, however, looks at this theme of search with its correlated and putative goal—place—and thus I hope it will add to the rich and complex criticism of Walker Percy and his work.

9. Percy, *Moviegoer*, 99–100.

10. Lewis A. Lawson and Victor A. Kramer, eds., *Conversations with Walker Percy* (Jackson: University Press of Mississippi, 1985), 158, 161–62.

11. Lawson and Kramer, *Conversations*, 301.

12. Walker Percy, *Lancelot* (New York: Ivy Books, 1977), 18–19.

13. Percy, *Moviegoer*, 6.

14. Percy, *Moviegoer*, 6.

15. Percy, *Moviegoer*, 7.

16. Percy, *Moviegoer*, 10.

17. Percy, *Moviegoer*, 13.

18. Percy, *Moviegoer*, 69.

19. Percy, *Moviegoer*, 69–70.

20. Percy, *Moviegoer*, 70.

21. Percy, *Moviegoer*, 52.

22. Percy, *Moviegoer*, 70.

23. I won't develop Percy's linguistic philosophy deeply here. Readers who wish to explore this more fully should read the forty-page "Intermezzo" of *Lost in the Cosmos* called "A Semiotic Primer of the Self." They should also turn to *The Message in the Bottle* and *A Thief of Peirce*, the letters Percy exchanged with Kenneth Laine Ketner about the works of the mostly forgotten nineteenth- and early twentieth-century American Philosopher, Charles Sanders Peirce. Let me say only that in *Lost in the Cosmos*, the vertical search is the attitude of science, a removing of the self from its own particularity in favor of generality.

24. Critchley, *Continental Philosophy*, 72.

25. Critchley, *Continental Philosophy*, 72–73.

26. Percy, *Moviegoer*, 70.

27. Percy, *Moviegoer*, 52.

28. Percy, *Moviegoer*, 120.

29. Percy, *Moviegoer*, 99.

30. Percy, *Moviegoer*, 202–3.

31. If God exists, Lancelot says, the existence will not be proven by the old philosophical arguments; instead the discovery of evil will, paradoxically, show God's existence: "What would happen if you could prove the existence of sin, pure and simple? Wouldn't that be a windfall for you? A new proof of God's existence! If there is such a thing as sin, evil, a living malignant force, there must be a God!" Lance seeks this sin, thinks he has found it in his wife's (Margot's) sexual infidelity, and thus he destroys her and the "place" it occurs (Belle Isle, his ancestral home). He will begin a new life, a new age, in a new place, the mountains of Virginia.

32. Patrick H. Samway, S.J., ed., *Signposts in a Strange Land* (New York: Farrar, Straus and Giroux, 1991), 3.

33. Samway, *Signposts*, 3.

34. Samway, *Signposts*, 4.

35. Samway, *Signposts*, 7.

36. Samway, *Signposts*, 4–7.

37. Samway, *Signposts*, 11–12.

38. Samway, *Signposts*, 12.

39. Samway, *Signposts*, 11.

40. Samway, *Signposts*, 16.

41. Samway, *Signposts*, 17.

42. Samway, *Signposts*, 17–20.

43. Percy, *Moviegoer*, 20.

44. Percy, *Moviegoer*, 23–24.

45. The power of Percy's first novel derives in large part because he has kept its religious undertones extremely subtle and ambiguous. The question Percy asserts here, of course, is whether God has in fact appeared to Binx in his seeing this man receive ashes? If so, the issue of placement for Binx could be resolved.

46. Samway, *Signposts*, 85.

Part 2

POETRY

8

LES CENELLES AND CENSORSHIP[1]

Nancy Dixon

Armand Lanusse (1812–1867), a free Creole of color in New Orleans, was a writer and educator who published the first collection of poetry by African Americans in the United States in 1845, *Les Cenelles* (*The Mayhaws*).[2] *Les Cenelles* was a group of seventeen free Creoles of color, some of whom were the product of *plaçage*, the arrangement of a union between young Creole women of color and white men of means, a practice that resulted in a unique class of wealthy, educated, Creole men of color, like some of the members of *Les Cenelles*.[3] The seventeen contributors to the collection *Les Cenelles* were Valcour B., Bowers (Bo . . . rs), Jean Boise, Louis Boise, Pierre Dalcour, Desormes Dauphin, Nelson Desbrosses, Armand Lanusse, Numa Lanusse, Mirtil-Ferdinand Liotau, August Populus, Joanni Questi (Joanni), Nicol Riquet, Michel Saint-Pierre, Victor Séjour, Manuel Sylva, and Camille Thierry. Discussed in this essay are the works of Valcour B., Armand Lanusse, Mirtil-Ferdinand Liotau, Michel Saint-Pierre, Victor Séjour, and Camille Thierry.[4]

In 1843, a time when the most popular form of literature published by people of color in this country was the slave narrative, Armand Lanusse, an educator, poet, and publisher, began a monthly journal of literature in New Orleans penned by free Creoles of color, *L'Album Littéraire, Journal des Jeunes Gens, Amateurs de Littérature*.[5] Although the journal was short lived, it did inspire Lanusse to publish *Les Cenelles* two years later. Many of the poems in the latter collection are clearly inspired by the French Romantic style popular at the time, but they also address very serious issues facing the free Creoles of color in New Orleans. In the mid-nineteenth century, New Orleans had the largest number of free people of color of any city in the South, in large part due to the emigration of free Blacks from Saint-Domingue (now Haiti), and to a lesser degree to the practice of *plaçage*. Lanusse and his fellow poets were fiercely proud of their Creole heritage, which is apparent in much of their poetry, but they were also concerned with the dubious tradition of "placing" young, Creole women of color in these "arranged" marriages, thus diminishing their roles as wives and mothers in the Black Creole community.

Up to the 1830s, New Orleans was unique in its three-tiered racial hierarchy: white, free people of color, and enslaved Black citizens. According to the editors of *Louisiana: A History*, after "*Walker's Appeal*, the plea of a free black man in Boston that the slaves of the South rise in revolt, had made its appearance in New Orleans in 1829..., it became a capital crime in Louisiana not only to distribute printed matter which might incite insurrection, but also even to say anything from pulpit, bar, stage, bench or anywhere else that might breed discontent or encourage rebellion."[6] Therefore, nonwhites in New Orleans, including free Creoles of color, could say nothing to criticize whites or any of their dubious practices, such as *plaçage* and slavery. The laws passed in 1830 placed such restrictions on the writing of *Les Cenelles* that their works are sometimes difficult to follow, particularly for readers outside of New Orleans.

The first poet of *Les Cenelles* whose works are included in this anthology is Valcour B. One of the largest contributors, having penned eleven poems in the collection, he was educated in Paris and was an admirer of many of the popular French writers of the time, including poet and songwriter, Pierre-Jean de Beranger (1780–1857), whom he claims inspired one of his poems, "The Louisiana Laborer," which is to be sung to the tune of Béranger's "*Amis, voici la riante semaine*." In this poem Valcour B. touches on the subject of race in the line, "Misunderstood sons of New Orleans," a subject so often addressed by these proud Creole poets of color. For the most part, Valcour B. wrote love poems, but he writes a fine tribute, "Letter to Constant Lépouzé (on the receipt of a volume of his poems)" to his teacher and mentor, Constant Lépouzé, thanking him for his dedication and guidance and for all his "poetic tastes."

The next poet is Armand Lanusse, the editor and largest contributor to the collection, whose dedicatory poem, "Fair Sex of Louisiana," lauds the virtue of the women of the state, or more specifically the young, Creole women, a subject not only of his poetry, but of his short story also discussed here, "A Marriage of Conscience."[7] In his poems "To Elora," "The Priest and the Young Girl," and "Epigram," he laments the lost virtue of young Creole women of color and criticizes the Catholic Church for its role in "placing" these young women with the wealthy, white Creole men in a union recognized by neither the church nor the state. He addresses the topic humorously in his poem "Epigram," in which a mother assures a priest that she wishes to renounce Satan, but before doing so asks, "Why can't I, father—what?—*establish* my daughter?" In his poems and his short story, he also chastises mothers for the roles they play in the corruption of their daughters.[8]

Michel Saint-Pierre wrote six poems for *Les Cenelles*, and he too laments the pitfalls of *plaçage* for young creole women in "The Dying Young Girl." He writes of the dying girl's mother "finding a suitor who better fit her plans" than the sixteen-year-old dying girl's lover. Saint-Pierre congratulates the young girl for taking with her to her grave "innocence and honor!" Both Lanusse and Liotau address the state of the Catholic church—particularly the St. Louis Cathedral—in the 1830s, Lanusse in his short story "A Marriage of Conscience" and Liotau in his poem "An Impression." At that time, the newly appointed Bishop Antoine Blanc had refused to capitulate to the lay "wardens" of the cathedral who claimed that they had the right to name their own pastor, so these wardens withheld all church revenue from the diocese. In response, Bishop Blanc withdrew all priests, and therefore all sacraments, including baptism and marriage, from the cathedral. The wardens sued, lost, and a new Archdiocese of Louisiana was formed with Blanc as the first archbishop. New Orleans readers would have understood Lanusse's reference to the "schism" in the church and Liotau's to "Church of Saint-Louis . . . / empty and deserted!" but few others would have. Both authors raise the issue of the church's moral failings when it comes to the issue of race and slavery in New Orleans.[9]

Camille Thierry was a product of *plaçage*, with an octoroon mother and white French father, from whom he inherited a small fortune. He turned to writing poetry and at the age of thirty-seven left New Orleans for Paris to escape the stifling racism in the city, a topic he addresses in his poem "The Sailor," in which the narrator begs his lover to flee with him to escape her father, who "refused your hand to me / And vilified my race." In his poem "Farewell," he laments having to leave New Orleans, the city he has come to love, and in fact, he never did return, dying in Bordeaux in 1874.[10]

The last writer, and perhaps the most well-known, Victor Séjour, was born in New Orleans in 1817 to a Haitian father and New Orleans mother, both free people of color. He left New Orleans in 1834 to live in France, where he remained until his death. There he became friends with Alexandre Dumas, and Napoleon attended at least one of his plays. In his only poem included in *Les Cenelles*, "The Return of Napoleon," a lavish encomium to the former emperor, in which he calls him ". . . grand, superb, and handsome too," he chastises France for exiling Napoleon to Saint Helena. Indeed, Séjour is the only of *Les Cenelles* poets to identify so strongly with the French. He considers himself a Frenchman when he praises Napoleon upon his death: "Ah! Our honor, Frenchmen, is linked to his death throes!" Yet, his short story, "The Mulatto" published in the Parisian abolitionist journal *La Revue des Colonies* in 1837, is often considered to be the first written by an African American.

Lanusse's short story "A Marriage of Conscience" was also published before the *Les Cenelles* collection in New Orleans in the journal *L'Album Littéraire, Journal des Jeunes Gens, Amateurs de Littérature* in 1843 and is also the tale of a tragic mulatta exposing the dangers in the practice of *plaçage*. Although the female protagonist is a free woman of color, she is still not legally permitted to marry her white lover, and when he tires of her and their child, she has no rights at all and is driven to suicide.

Lanusse's story opens with an unnamed narrator, having recently returned to the city, strolling in the French Quarter, when he hears the bells of the St. Louis Cathedral and decides to attend Sunday mass. And although Lanusse does not tell us that the narrator is white, readers would know so because of the fact that he is freely walking about the Quarter, and he later brazenly addresses a white woman outside the church. Once at the church door, he overhears a group of young men talking, and "the words 'schism,' 'priests,' 'sacristans' caught [his] attention."[11] Here Lanusse addresses the state of the Catholic church—particularly the St. Louis Cathedral—in the 1830s after Bishop Blanc had withdrawn the priests in protest. Once again, New Orleans readers would have understood Lanusse's reference to the schism in the church, but few others would have. Even the narrator himself, who has been away from the city for some time, knows nothing of it and is surprised to find "only two or three people kneeling in the church . . . [and] an absolute silence reigned in the interior of the edifice," but his attention soon turns elsewhere, to a "remarkable unknown woman."[12] In fact, Lanusse writes this story to point to the dangers of leaving the church in the hands of a faction of white laymen.

He describes this remarkable unknown woman as "young and beautiful . . . her hair messed, her clothes in disarray," yet he gives her no name, nor does he tell us her race.[13] She is, however, praying on the steps of the altar: "O saint Mary, my patron!" so local Catholic readers could assume that her name is Mary, or probably the French, Marie, which, to lessen confusion, is how she will be known here. Perhaps Lanusse knew that readers could infer her name, but more likely he assigns her no name because she is "everywoman" or every free woman of color who finds herself poorly "placed." Marie continues, and the narrator disappears until resurfacing at the end of the story. Lanusse uses the rather awkward device of her own confession to divulge most of the story, in part because he cannot have a white narrator relating to the reader the story of a *roué* such as Gustave, Marie's love interest.

Marie tells us: "[u]ntil the age of sixteen, my life was as calm as the innocent thoughts which occupied me then . . . as a result of the lessons of a pious aunt . . . with whom I lived from a young age, I practiced with love the wonderful precepts of the Christian faith."[14] Her story begins like so many of the formulaic "tragic mulatta" tales popular in the nineteenth century. An innocent, young, Christian beauty, whose devout guardian suddenly dies, must move to the corrupt city (often New Orleans) where she is exposed to a way of life she does not understand, and where, due to her artlessness in such an environment, she is ruined and dies. That is indeed what happens to Marie, but her story is unique in that she is a free woman of color who is all but forced into the system of *plaçage* by her own mother.

At first she resists for a year and cannot make herself "come to terms with the frivolous language of [her] older sisters who did nothing but occupy themselves with balls, feasts, and finery."[15] These balls to which she refers are of course quadroon or octoroon balls popular in the city at the time. Arnold R. Hirsch and Joseph Logsdon, in their book, *Creole New Orleans, Race and Americanization*, describe these balls as "assemblages of [women of color] more often than not, simple prostitutes, who pandered to the concupiscence of the New Orleans male."[16] However, Lanusse, in his short story, proves them wrong. Marie is truly innocent and not a "simple prostitute" like so many of the victims of this practice. They go on to describe "the institution of *plaçage* [which] enshrined the tradition in which [white] creole men established particularly favored mulatto girls as mistresses of their own *ménages*, giving them place as 'second wives' in an arrangement unknown to the law but cherished in local custom."[17] Marie succumbs to this practice innocently, by attending several of these balls in order to please her mother.

She describes her time there "alone in the middle of a crowd of men who spoke a different language, with bold stares and daring gestures.[18] She is, of course, talking about American men attending such balls and speaking in

English, a language that she did not understand, but this might not be clear to readers. She also reveals the fact that none of the women attending such balls have the protection of a brother or husband, a real problem in the Black Creole community. Free men of color were not admitted to these balls; nor could they protect creole women from *plaçage*, and Lanusse conveys their feelings of inadequacy in the face of such a practice.

Marie does a good job of remaining "unnoticeable" until she meets "a young man whose manners were so full of distinction that they made him stand out from all the other men of the ball."[19] Her fall is almost immediate, which is also typical of the typical tragic mulatta, and she "rejoiced with all [her] soul at the love, which [she] believed [she] had truly inspired in him."[20] One remarkable aspect of this tale of the fallen mulatta is the role her mother plays in her demise. She badgers her daughter into attending these quadroon balls in the first place, then after Marie meets and falls for her lover, Gustave, her mother is the one who persuades her to enter into a "marriage of conscience." From the absent brothers and husbands to the scheming mother and sisters, Lanusse emphasizes the communal involvement in the corruption of young free women of color; yet the *coup de grace* for Marie is the role that the church plays in her sham marriage.

Again, as a tragic mulatta, Marie is a devout Christian, so when her mother explains that a marriage of conscience "'is a pact that is not recognized under the law, but to which a priest gives all the appearance of a legitimate engagement,'" Marie replies, "'Who would dare to violate its sanctity?'"[21] Indeed, her mother is the one pushing to have her daughter "placed." Such corruption in the church harks back to the opening paragraph and the discussion of the "schism" in the cathedral. This is a low point in the history of the St. Louis Cathedral. In fact, it is not even mentioned on the St. Louis Cathedral official website. However, Lanusse calls attention not only to the organizational problems that the Church is experiencing but also to the widespread corruption among its priests. Marie, like most young, free women of color, is helpless and alone in her efforts to remain chaste. Thomas F. Haddox, in his article, "The 'Nous' of Southern Catholic Quadroons: Racial, Ethnic, and Religious Identity in *Les Cenelles*" states that the writers of *Les Cenelles* "register ambivalence toward the Church's tolerance for [interacial marriage]." Although they praise the Church's kindness toward the children of such unions, the poets also criticize Catholic acquiescence in *plaçage*, the system of concubinage that simultaneously contributed to the material well-being of some *gens de couleur libres* and ensured continued sexual exploitation."[22] For Marie it is a double whammy, as the two voices of reason and comfort that she relies on, her mother and the Church, are both willing to sacrifice her to the sexual whims of a wealthy white man. However, Lanusse has yet to mention the fact that Marie is a free Creole of color and that Gustave is a white Creole. He was forbidden by law to do so.

When her mother tells her that Gustave had "first obtained her consent [and] had undertaken to propose that [Marie] unite . . . with him," she also had to explain that "this man, occupying a more elevated position than they, could not legitimately join himself with [her]."[23] Lanusse continues to avoid the subject of race, and at this point, most readers see this as a story about class and not race, but it is about both, which he tries to convey, but within very strict parameters. He is forbidden to criticize whites or the Church, so he has to do so cautiously. He cannot blatantly say that Gustave is a wealthy, white Creole searching for a mistress among young, free women of color; nor can he criticize the practice of *plaçage* or the Catholic priests who are so willing to dupe young women like Marie into such a union. So instead he goes on to describe a practice very well known to his New Orleans readers and makes Gustave a most despicable character, and rightly so.

Gustave proves to be even more of a cad when he dumps Marie in less than a year's time, even after they have had a child together, a child who dies after only eight days. He tells Marie that "motivations of interest required him to take a new wife,"[24] suggesting here that he is marrying a wealthy white woman for her money. Yes, Gustave is of a higher class than Marie, but perhaps due more to his race than to his material wealth, since he is "required" to marry. However, the only way that readers can surmise that his new wife is white is due to the fact that "his new wedding would be celebrated with pomp," hardly a resounding confirmation of her race.[25] Nonetheless, the wedding was a very public affair, unlike his earlier "marriage" to Marie, and the bridal carriage conveniently passes by the cathedral in which Marie was praying. The narrator then reappears to tell us that the carriage runs over Marie, killing her. In the end, Gustave ruins the young, beautiful Marie, both body and soul. Gustave's new bride asks if Marie was mad, and the narrator's final response summarizes Lanusse's views of *plaçage*: "She became mad because a coward, abusing her simplicity, had shamefully deceived her."[26]

In the end, Armand Lanusse writes a subversive story in order to shed light on the disgraceful consequences of the custom of "placing" young Creole women of color. It robs them of their innocence. It robs the Creole men of color of suitable partners. It even robs the often oblivious white wives of the white Creole men of suitable partners as well. However, his subversion was limited by racist laws imposed upon not only artists like Lanusse, but on all people of color in New Orleans in 1830. Haddox suggests that such works as this contain a "'hidden transcript' with a definite but disguised political message," but that Lanusse's "abhorrence of the practice is straightforward and unambiguous."[27] It does not seem as straightforward as it might if writers like Lanusse had been able to openly criticize white Creole[28] males who exploited these young Creole women of color along with the Catholic priests who publicly condemned such a practice while privately facilitating it. Armand Lanusse and the rest of the writers of *Les Cenelles*, proud mixed-race Catholics themselves, some even children of *placées*, were fiercely protective of their heritage and standing as *gens de couleur libres* or free Creoles of color; yet they criticized the church and its role the victimization of free women of color, a complicated stand and one not made any easier for readers to interpret due to the racist laws imposed upon them at the time.

Notes

1. A version of this essay first appeared in *Turning Points and Transformations: Essays on Language, Literature, and Culture*, eds. Christine DeVine and Marie Hendry. Cambridge Scholars Publishing, 2011), 111–24. I am grateful to them for allowing me to publish this version here.

2. Johnson, Jerah, "*Les Cenelles*: What's in a Name?" *Louisiana History* 31, no. 4 (Winter 1990): 407–10.

3. Hirsch, Arnold and Joseph Logsdon, *Creole New Orleans, Race and Americanization* (Baton Rouge: LSU Press, 1992).

4. For more biographical information see Regina Latortue and Gleason R. W. Adams, trans. *Les Cenelles: A Collection of Poems by Creole Writers of the Early Nineteenth Century.* (Boston: G.K. Hall & Co., 1979).

5. *The Literary Album, Journal of Young Men, Lovers of Literature.*

6. Wall, Bennett H. et al., *Louisiana, A History* (Boston: The Forum Press, Inc, 1984), 166–68.

7. "A Marriage of Conscience" was originally published in French in *Les Cenelles' L'Album Litteraire* in 1843. I am using an unpublished 1998 translation by Wendy Castenell and Linda Blanton for the University of New Orleans English Department.

Les Cenelles and Censorship

8. For more on *Les Cenelles* and the Catholic Church see Thomas Haddox, "The 'Nous' of Southern Catholic Quadroons: Racial, Ethnic, and Religious Identity in *Les Cenelles*," *American Literature* 73, no. 4 (2002): 757–78.

9. For more see Charles E. Nolan, "A History of the Archdiocese of New Orleans: The Antebellum Years: 1835–1860," *Archdiocese of New Orleans* (Eckbolsheim, France: Editions du Signe, 2000).

10. Tortue and Gleason, Preface, *Les Cenelles: A Collection of Poems by Creole Writers of the Early Nineteenth Century* (GK Hall & Co., 1979), xxiii.

11. Lanusse, Armand, *Les Cenelles*, trans. Wendy Castenell and Linda Blanton, unpublished manuscript, 1998, 1.

12. Lanusse, 1, 2.

13. Lanusse, 2.

14. Lanusse, 3.

15. Lanusse, 3.

16. Hirsch and Logsdon, *Creole New Orleans, Race and Americanization*, 149.

17. Hirsch and Logsdon, *Creole New Orleans, Race and Americanization*, 149–50.

18. Lanusse, 3.

19. Lanusse, 4.

20. Lanusse, 5.

21. Lanusse, 5.

22. Haddox, Thomas, "The 'Nous' of Southern Catholic Quadroons: Racial, Ethnic, and Religious Identity in *Les Cenelles*," *American Literature* 73, no. 4 (2001): 757–78, 760.

23. Lanusse, 5.

24. Lanusse, 7.

25. Lanusse, 8.

26. Lanusse, 9.

27. Haddox, "The 'Nous' of Southern Catholic Quadroons," 763.

28. The term "Creole" is often debated and has changed over the centuries. It once referred to those of European descent who lived in New Orleans. Now it more commonly refers to people of color in the city of European descent.

9

(RE)MAPPING THE COLONIAL CITY
Joy Harjo's Composite Poetic in "New Orleans"

Tierney S. Powell

For the Western *flâneur*, New Orleans is a dynamic city with vibrant nightlife and cultural flair, a city nestled within the "glistening, perfumed South,"[1] as Whitman and others have often portrayed it. To this wandering urban subject, the commercial corridors of New Orleans appear as a glamorous urban public space. The Western imaginary conjures tourist and commercial dimensions of the city, those that emphasize seductive social districts and filigreed buildings. However, this social stronghold is a contested terrain contoured and defined settler colonialism and its afterlives. Forged from the complex and layered histories of racialized, classed, and gendered violence, the space of New Orleans is its own particular site of developmentalist colonial logics, as it is also emblematic of long-standing and global spatial practices of expropriation and deracination.

In her 1983 poem "New Orleans," Muscogee (Mvskogee) Creek artist and United States Poet Laureate, Joy Harjo maps the city as undergirded by settler-colonial violence as well as Indigenous knowing. Though the contemporary site of the city appears absent of the subject's Creek history, Harjo's poem recuperates Indigenous epistemology in the landscape that is buried beneath and layered within the materially and psychologically dense space of the southern port city. What I describe as Harjo's composite poetic—a formal and thematic layering evocative of the doubly exposed photographic image—enables the material, psychological, colonial, and Indigenous histories of New Orleans to be held together, formalizing a politics of decolonial (re)mapping. "By recognizing the historic processes of enframing space and its corresponding cyclical turns and layering," Mishuana Goeman (Tonawanda Band of Seneca) writes in *Mark My Words: Native Women Mapping Our Nation*, "the tangled threads produced in the claiming of Native lands and erasure of bodies begin to unravel."[2] I describe Harjo's poetic as composite in order to theorize the aesthetic praxis of bringing these "tangled threads" into representation, while leaving room to place Harjo's poetic in conversation with decolonial, multi-ethnic, and transnational political and aesthetic movements aiming to abolish settler-colonial maps and (re)imagine alternative ones.[3]

In much of Harjo's poetry, urban space functions as a critical site of inquiry, addressing relatedly biopolitical and spatial practices of erasure, from colonization to gentrification. In "The Woman Hanging from the Thirteenth Floor Window," Harjo's subject exists in densely nested liminal space—hanging suspended from the "13th floor,"[4] in "east Chicago,"[5] "on the Indian side of town."[6] Residing in tenements with a collective memory of urbanization's violent processes, Harjo's spatial construction maps both the particular brutalities of urbanization for Indigenous land and peoples and also maps onto that same "gray plane" of the city "all the women of the apartment / building who stand watching her, watching themselves," their own experiences of liminality accumulating with the subject's.[7] Los Angeles, "this place of recent invention," Harjo writes in "The Path to the Milky Way Leads Through Los Angeles," "appears naked [. . .] in the illusion of the marketplace,"[8] while New York City, in "The Place the Musician Became a Bear," is recuperated by Harjo's subject; the city is "sung into place," incorporated into Indigenous geography, even as it is also a place of territorial violence.[9] Harjo's representations of urban centers simultaneously draw together global colonial logics at diverse national sites while (re)territorializing these sites of violence and exploitation as always already, unforgettably, and perpetually Indigenous. Even as these itineraries of violence are differentially applied to diverse populations throughout the long history of colonial, racial capitalism, Harjo uses built spaces—and most pertinent to this essay, the built space of New Orleans—to map and (re)map the modern city and the spatial practices reinforcing ongoing attempts at Indigenous erasure.

Harjo's poem "New Orleans"—published in the 1983 collection *She Had Some Horses*—positions the poem's subject in New Orleans, maneuvering through the streets of the city, "down Conti Street, Royal, or Decatur" through the French Quarter, surveying shops and bars and tourist traps amidst a proudly commercialized built space.[10] The subject searches for "remnants of voices," "evidence / of other Creeks," or "tobacco brown bones" (Harjo 1–3).[11] Passing pleasure boats and storefronts, the subject is lost among the "stale rooms" and street cars, searching for indexes of Creek heritage, "to know in another way / that memory is alive."[12] This search is what propels Harjo's subject through the built city space of New Orleans. The subject's wandering gaze charts urbanization and commercialization of the geographic and cultural space—socio- and geo-political imperatives reinforcing the erasure of the subject's Native identity. Embedded in the commercial landscape of the city, Harjo's subject takes stock of the imagery and infrastructure of settler-colonialism and succeeding regimes of racial capitalism. The legacy of settler-colonialism endures in the very fabric of the city, the poem argues; the text registers this historical space and experience through her subject's walking observations of the city.

Harjo's poem opens declaratively: "This is the south."[13] Harjo orients the reader to the geography that symbolizes some of the United States' most mythologized and historically commodified terrain. If the opening sentence's period indicates a statement, the succeeding "I look for evidence," dangling before the line break, unsettles such a sense of certainty, throwing the place, the ostensibly certain "south," into question. What does it mean to identify this place as "the south"? Under what spatial logics and regimes of territorial and ideological power has the American South been mapped? Or, as Goeman asks in *Mark My Words*, "what power structures have deterred certain maps and produced others?"[14] Where Whitman pines for his descriptively defined "home" in his own construction of the South in "Longings for Home,"—"O Magnet South! My South"—Harjo's subverted declarative investigates the landscape, searching for her subject's own "birth-things,"[15] "for evidence / of other Creeks, for remnants of voices." Harjo's subject experiences their own "irrepressible longing" in this politically charged geography, the site of Harjo's subject's contemporary urban *flânerie*.

Moving through modern New Orleans, Harjo's subject is a critical invocation of *le flâneur*, or the strolling spectator of the modern city. In Baudelaire's terms, *le flâneur* exhibits an unencumbered privilege of mobility; he may "be away from home, and yet feel oneself everywhere at home."[16] *Le flâneur* strolls through the city as "prince" and "passionate spectator," a privilege rooted in gendered, classed, and racialized hierarchies of Eurowestern modernity. As Rita Felski examines in the opening of *The Gender of Modernity*, modernity is constructed across differential treatments of gender, class, and race which impact not only the "factual content of historical knowledge—what is included and what gets left out,"—or in the case of the city, what is erected, what is buried, and the perennial question, 'whose city is it?'—but also, as Felski continues, "the philosophical assumptions underlying our interpretations of the nature and meaning of social processes."[17] Le flâneur is one such example of a key figure of modern cultural and geosocial production whose cosmopolitan freedom and unquestioned autonomy is predicated on distinctly Western notions of global expansion, bourgeois subjectivity, and the domination of space. Thus the figure of le flâneur "carries within it the seeds of domination," Felksi writes;[18] le flâneur asserts a socially-constructed gaze and engagement with the urban, itself a reflection of a certain rectilinear logic imposed on Indigenous land. Harjo's subject, whose very presence in the city is contested, inhabits this discourse of wandering urban ethnographic observation, even as they simultaneously deepen and subvert it.

Harjo's subject, an ungendered first person "I" whose "spirit comes [to the city] to drink," to recover those "voices buried in the Mississippi mud,"[19] is faced with the dissonance of being home, and yet simultaneously appearing absent from it. Where le flâneur is unbounded by filial or communal ties, to borrow Felski's formulation, and the Western flâneuse exhibits a restricted, often sexualized female urban subjecthood, Harjo's urban wanderer projects onto the space of the city the uncanny tension of liminality—being both at home and displaced. Harjo's subject faces the dissonance of experiencing the land, sites of mound-building and meaning-making, and the regimes of spatial violence that forcibly moved the Creek Nation across the Mississippi. The subject searches for a sense of place, for the filial—for the "ancestors and future children / buried beneath the currents stirred up by / pleasure boats going up and down."[20] The subject's sense of place is "made of memory"—a memory that is hidden beneath the historical and geo-political attempts at Indigenous erasure, existing despite the extraction and commercialization of the land, and "in another way / [. . .] alive" in the survival of the Muscogee Nation.[21] Harjo subverts the traditional and often still gendered orientations of flânerie discourse, joining works of writers, artists, and critics invoking the urban wanderer as an "imperfect vehicle" for the study of the city.[22] Harjo complicates both being in and perceiving the modern city, unsettling both the figure of observer—and the differentially constructed mobility politics accompanying his/her/their movement[23]—and the perceptual faculties used in observing the city.

Mapping the poem's course "down Conti Street [and] Royal, or Decatur," the subject leads the reader to the edges of Jackson Square, the historic park in the Vieux Carré, or French Quarter, named for former US President Andrew Jackson. The subject comes upon the square and "see[s] a blue horse / caught frozen in stone."[24] The equine trapped in stone refers to the statue of Andrew Jackson posed on his horse, erected in the center of the French Quarter in 1851 to commemorate Jackson's role in the Battle of New Orleans early in the nineteenth century. The statue, designed by American sculptor Charles Mills, figures the horse as perpetually balanced on its hind legs—as if forever being charged into battle, or perhaps, rearing in endless fear of its own imperial exploitation. "Brought in by the Spanish on / an endless ocean voyage," Harjo's subject recounts, the horse's objectification—as vehicle and commodity of war—trapped him; "he became mad / and crazy."[25] The figure of the horse bears a metonymic power in much of Harjo's poetry, from the seminal "She Had Some Horses" to Jackson's blue horse figured here. Horses connote European contact and the disparate ways in which Native peoples (from localized Muscogee peoples to the broader pan-Indian collective) have responded to, found resilience through, and survived despite ongoing regimes of oppression, violence, and deracination that extend from contact through colonization to the contemporary. The horse in "New Orleans" appears himself as a logistical object of Spanish colonization,[26] as he is simultaneously and transhistorically a logistical object in Andrew Jackson's motivations to control land and push forward the violent forced removal of Native American nations across the United States.[27] "Frozen in stone," the horse's confinement is materially forged in stone, a somewhat literal building block of urban infrastructure and construction, as the domination of space and peoples throughout a long history of colonization is also foundational to the construction and everyday practices of the modern city. These spatial practices of colonial mapping sought the erasure of Native peoples through expropriation of land and the institution of new social, political, and epistemological systems of governance, ones that continue to evolve throughout the development of the territories that eventually became the United States.

Harjo's systematic maneuvering through the city, on Royal Street, Decatur Street, and Conti Street, reveal the colonial history planned into the very spatial organization of the city. Royal Street connotes the royal houses which pushed armies into the "New World"; Decatur honors eighteenth-century American naval officer, Stephen Decatur, who is known for establishing key principles of naval warfare and America's attitude in military and/as commercial pursuits; and Conti refers to the French princely houses of Conti, a branch of the royal house of Bourbon. Conti, much like Royal, acknowledges the dynastic history of European (French) power (whereby French and Spanish rulership was linked under the House of Bourbon) and ambitions of European extraction of wealth in territories of the present-day US Mapping these avenues in the poem demonstrates the ways in which the landscape is literally shaped by a politically ordered socio-cultural imaginary, one predicated on territorial control and capital accumulation.

Overlaying her subject's walking experience of contemporary New Orleans with the place-based memory "swim[ming] deep in blood," Harjo's subject walks among the memory of "Creeks [who] lived in earth towns" as well as alongside the memory of Spanish conquistador, slave trader, and colonial officer of the state, Hernando De Soto.[28] Though the present space of the city is overwhelmed with tourism, the subject perceives the space as also inhabited by the memory of both Creek community and Spanish colonial forces. "There are ancestors and future children / buried beneath the currents [. . .] I remember DeSoto," Harjo's subject announces.[29] De Soto's colonial expedition through the interior of southeastern North America in the early sixteenth century is used as the historical and metonymic nexus of the subject's cultural trauma. The historical memory Harjo creates is one of the conquistador who arrives to survey and extract value from the land. De Soto "came looking for gold cities, for shining streets / of beaten gold to dance on with silk ladies."[30] De Soto expects gold, copper, and other commodifiable materials when arriving in La Florida in 1539.[31] After years of living as slave trader in Peru and colonially-appointed governor of Cuba, De Soto's quest into the southern territories of the now United States represents an explicitly extractive enterprise, one calibrated to maximize profit and exploit the territory and its peoples.

De Soto's violent enterprise in the interior continent was a continuation of the violence inflicted on Incan peoples during Francisco Pizarro's conquest of Peru in 1531. While much of the Eurowestern historical record has celebrated De Soto's bravery, Harjo's subject offers the important corrective: "blood is the undercurrent."[32] De Soto's expedition was marked by tactics including setting fire to Indigenous communities, taking Indigenous leaders captive as forced "guides," stealing crops, trafficking Indigenous women, and murdering any Indigenous opposition. However, as if inked with hubris, De Soto's imperial maps, which were incomplete and left much of the continental interior unidentified, failed him. De Soto died in 1542 when, after becoming disoriented, low on supplies, and fatally determined to find prized minerals, he succumbed to a fever. The logistical failures of De Soto's expedition have been documented by scholars such as Robert S. Weddle, who offers that "de Soto embarked on his Florida venture with a set of preconceived notions that later proved false and ultimately contributed to his failure."[33] These "preconceived notions," alongside and as part of colonization's ideological project of mapping, which asserts its "scientific" authority over "primitive" Indigenous knowledge, are revealed in Harjo's poem to be a product of a racist Eurowestern epistemology and a "heart [not] big enough / to handle" its own expedition's faulty premise.[34]

Harjo's depiction of De Soto's failed expedition disrupts the claimed legitimacy of Eurowestern itineraries of conquest, including mapping, territorial expansion, and wealth accumulation. De Soto's dismay at finding "earth towns, / not gold" is juxtaposed against the Creeks' consistent knowing (better).[35] They dream of De Soto, intuiting his arrival and communicating about his exploitative tactics. Harjo's poem narrates that Creek peoples understood De Soto's colonial project was itself, in its misunderstanding-laden maps and violent rubrics, shot through with liability and embarrassingly wrong. "He should have stayed home," Harjo's subject remarks, "The Creeks knew it, and drowned him in / the Mississippi River / so he wouldn't have to drown himself."[36] While the predominating Western historical record of De Soto's conquest reflects the narrative of his surviving troops, attributing success to an expedition fraught with violence and miscalculations, Harjo's poem contests this record. Instead, Harjo's critical (re)mapping of the conquistador's attempted conquest exposes the fault lines in the colonial record and asserts Indigenous epistemology as inherent to the geohistorical space comprising present-day New Orleans.

By formalizing Native and specifically Creek historical memory as always already present in the construction of the space and the poem, Harjo "upset[s] a terrain of Western knowledge about Native peoples" that not only subordinates Indigenous epistemology as primitive, but seeks to erase and submerge Indigenous ways of knowing.[37] The composite spatial form I posit theorizes Harjo's layering of history, memory, the colonial narratives that comprise the thoroughgoing historical record, and the Indigenous account which, though "buried in the Mississippi mud," is excavated by

Harjo's poem. Harjo uses the multilayered poetic structure to (re)historicize the De Soto conquest by sharing Creek historical memory: "(Creeks knew of [De Soto] for miles / before he came into town. Dreamed of silver blades / and crosses.)"[38] The parenthetical conveying Creek awareness formalizes Harjo's (re)mapping, what Goeman describes as "Native forms of mapping [. . .] that are too often disavowed, appropriated, or co-opted by the settler state through writing, imagining, law, politics, and terrains of culture."[39] The continuity between the poem's parenthetical and the Indigenous-feminist theoretical politics of the parenthetical "(re)" in (re)mapping, part of a praxis of spatial justice offered by Goeman, is perhaps questionably tidy. However, the parenthetical lines, like the marks of a shovel digging deep into the Mississippi sediment, unearth the layers of cultural knowledge that have been systematically (and in many cases literally) bulldozed by the ravages of colonial land development and subsequent regimes of spatial organizational logic. Precious metal-laden in its imagery—"dreamed of *silver* blades" and "DeSoto thought [his yearning] was [for] *gold*" (emphasis mine)—and striking indentations in the poetic form like in the Mississippi earth, Harjo's poetic structure offers a formal layering that addresses the literal and figurative (re)production of space central to Harjo's Indigenous-feminist praxis and aesthetic.

Harjo enmeshes the image of De Soto "looking for gold cities, for shining streets / of beaten gold to dance on with silk ladies,"[40] with the modern, commodified landscape of New Orleans.[41] What De Soto didn't find in the "earth towns" was built over the top of Indigenous lands. The hope for silk ladies was constructed into the "lace and silk buildings" that line the French Quarter, the "streets of beaten gold" crafted into "beaten silver paths," and the colonial armies that stormed the Indigenous land are (re)spatialized as pleasure boats and trolley cars that go up and down and through the city. The use of historical memory of colonization and modern walking-experience of the commercialized New Orleans city space (re)maps the constitution of public (white) space as layered within a history of settler-colonialism. Colonization efforts were "not only about a movement of bodies off reservations, but also [. . .] about respatializing a consciousness and relationship to the land."[42] Imposing colonial spatial consciousness onto Indigenous land is the context for understanding the contentious terrain comprising modern-day New Orleans, forged from historical and ongoing erasure of not only indigenous peoples but of other racialized, classed, and gendered populations.

The composite enables these colonial histories to be mapped forward to assess the continuity with aesthetic representations of contemporary global capitalist spatial practices. In the case of "New Orleans," this centrally entails representing processes of urbanization and global tourism, with interlocking strategies for controlling space and social movement through space. Deriving the composite from the history of photography, for which double exposure was used to layer photographic images,[43] describing Harjo's poetic as composite indeed conjures the visual (and as such heeds recurrent calls to "make visible" that which has been concealed in the colonial project), but more importantly operates as a dynamic cognitive map, one that is not only historical and material but incorporates the subject's Creek epistemology, including intuition, memory, dreams, and oral communication and narrative. Mapping Native knowledge and history onto the urban map of the contemporary colonial city, "New Orleans" is a geopolitical and spatial response to the "violent ongoing racializing and gendering projects [that] continue to be carried out" in cities across the United States and beyond.[44]

The tourist-oriented landscape that Harjo's subject observes is enmeshed with the colonial logics represented by the figure of De Soto. Harjo's subject "know[s she has] seen" De Soto drinking on Bourbon Street,[45] the New Orleans street known for raucous parties and throbbing nightlife. Superimposing the sixteenth-century conquistador onto the contemporary space of Bourbon Street, De Soto is a figural representation of the specter of coloniality that lives on in the "street [that] is famous for a reason," to borrow language from the city's tourism website.[46] De Soto dances "mad and crazy" with women "as gold / as the river bottom"; he finds in them the gold he, himself, never found. De Soto's dream of enterprising land conquest and wealth is realized on contemporary Bourbon Street. "Coloniality continues to be, in this global domain, an unnamed, unspoken driving force of modernization and the market," Walter Mignolo reminds us.[47] "New Orleans" not only maps a trajectory from De Soto through Indian Removal to the "noisy, raucous, nocturnal" Bourbon Street, but renders the "the colonial horizons of modernity" in the layered poetic form.[48]

Joy Harjo's "New Orleans" reveals a continuity between early settler colonial conquest and a predominating market logic that produces inequalities across differentially constructed and increasingly diverse racial, class, and gender scales. Contemporary New Orleans operates, Kevin Fox Gotham, citing Neil Smith, describes, by a "'global urban strategy' [of] gentrification

[. . .] now 'densely connected to the circuits of global capital and cultural circulation'" that has shaped the "socio-spatial transformation of New Orleans over the past half century."[49] Settler colonial-built, nostalgia-maintained, and with the investment of "large corporate entertainment firms," New Orleans, like many cities across the United States, has become a "space of entertainment and consumption."[50] Indeed, only seven years after the decimation of the ninth ward by Hurricane Katrina, which disproportionately impacted Black residents, Jackson Square was named as one of the ten "2012 Great Public Spaces" in America by the American Planning Association (APA).[51] Awarding the city for its "planning excellence," the APA described Jackson Square, where Jackson's "blue horse" rears in anxious uncertainty, as having "been constantly improved by colonial generals and modern mayors alike, while still preserving its historic features." Against this celebratory gesture and nearing twenty years since the disaster, the lower ninth ward is still recovering from Hurricane Katrina, with local coalitions describing the slow progress as "a result of poverty, the scale of the devastation and local, state and federal government inaction."[52]

The hallowed consumer market that surrounds Jackson Square and, more broadly, the French Quarter, reveals the ways in which civic improvement and preservation by urban administrations are "mad and craz[ed]," continuously calibrating itself in pursuit of surplus value. Engels observes in the *Volkstaat* that "[t]he growth of big modern cities gives the land in certain areas, particularly in those areas which are centrally situated, an artificially and colossally increasing value."[53] And in response to the commercial and social concentration on these areas of urban centrality, such as Jackson Square, Harjo's poem adjures us to consider the spaces and people that are buried under and forgotten by urban investments concentrated in valued sections of the city. For modern urbanists and literary scholars alike, the buried narratives of racialization and marginalization are precisely what Harjo's poem produces. "New Orleans" tours the city—remarking on the concentration of wealth and the nearly inescapable celebration of colonial history in the built space of the city.

As if foreshadowing the critical awareness wrought by post-Katrina New Orleans, Black Lives Matter, and movements to remove colonial monuments, fight back against gentrification, privatization, and land and resource exploitation[54] (to name a few), Harjo's composite poetic offers an Indigenous-feminist aesthetic praxis for (re)engaging space, mapping, and history to envision just futures for sites of diverse cultural meaning like New Orleans. "New Orleans" conjures the interlocking histories of coloniality and indigeneity in literalized and embodied forms, visualizing De Soto's body, his death, and his vampiric continuation in the contemporary space of the city. Occupying a shared terrain, these overlapping histories are descriptively constructed like a composite image doubly exposed—layered, evocatively spectral, and holding the violence and vitality of the colonial project and Indigenous life over the space of the city. What I describe as Harjo's composite poetic in "New Orleans" operates as a transgressive (re)mapping, subverting the violent processes of colonial mapping, from contact through Indian Removal to contemporary global tourism and racial capitalism. From early conquest maps to the constitutive diversity of contemporary global capitalist mapping projects, these itineraries of spatial organization and control continually recalibrate their tactics to impose, in both explicitly and insidiously violent ways, forms of settler-colonial and global capitalist power. Mishuana Goeman, whose work on Indigenous feminist praxis and the works of Joy Harjo continues to be an anchor in thinking about the dialectics of mapping in a contemporary archive of Indigenous women's literature, writes, "Harjo's map does not imply 'real' or 'objective' space that categorizes, contains, or isolates humans by representing homogeneity within its border, regions, and nations implementing policies to force their stableness; rather, she creates a space that converges time, space, and human relationships."[55] Harjo's composite poetic holds the contradictions—the violent rubrics and radical (re)mappings—together, portraying the city for what it has been, but while also imagining what it could be.

Notes

1. Walt Whitman, "Longings for Home," *Leaves of Grass*. Walt Whitman Archive, 1860, whitmanarchive.org/item/ppp.01500_01623.

2. Mishuana Goeman, *Mark My Words: Native Women Mapping Our Nation* (Minneapolis: University of Minnesota Press, 2013), 34.

3. Placing Harjo in conversation with broader multiethnic projects to unsettle settler-colonial epistemology—the maps it makes and the places it encloses—is necessarily outside the purview of this paper, though it forms the heart of my ongoing project "Composite City," which theorizes the composite across twentieth and twenty-first century literature of the city.

4. Due to lingering superstition associated with the number thirteen, many buildings omit a thirteenth floor from elevators and building plans, opting instead for skipping from floors twelve to fourteen or reinventing the thirteenth floor as a "mezzanine," or other such

(Re)mapping the Colonial City: Harjo's "New Orleans"

alternative. In this way, the thirteenth floor is an in-between place, both existing and not existing; the material existence of the thirteenth floor collides with the psychological idea of the thirteenth floor.

5. It is said there is no real "East Chicago," as "east" of the city of Chicago is Lake Michigan.

6. Joy Harjo, "The Woman Hanging from the Thirteenth Floor Window," *How We Became Human: New and Poems: 1975–2001* (New York: W. W. Norton & Company, 2004), 62, lines 1, 4, 29. By locating the subject in other liminal spaces, Harjo's identification of "the Indian side of town" underscores the ways in which Indigenous identity has been racialized and spatially organized through colonial regimes at work in the modern American city.

7. Joy Harjo, "The Woman Hanging from the Thirteenth Floor Window," 14–15.

8. Harjo, "The Path to the Milky Way Leads Through Los Angeles," *How We Became Human*, 141–2, line 3.

9. Harjo, "The Place the Musician Became a Bear," 114–15, line 1.

10. Harjo, "New Orleans," 43–46, line 4.

11. Harjo, "New Orleans," 43–46, lines 1–3.

12. Harjo, "New Orleans," 43–46, line 26 and 59–60.

13. Harjo, "New Orleans," 43–46, line 1

14. Goeman, *Mark My Words*, 6.

15. Whitman, "Longings for Home," lines 1 and 5.

16. Charles Baudelaire, "The Painter of Modern Life," in *Norton Anthology of Theory and Criticism*, ed. Vincent Leitch (London: W. W. Norton, 2001), 795.

17. Rita Felski, *The Gender of Modernity* (Cambridge: Harvard University Press, 1995), 1.

18. Felski, *The Gender of Modernity*, 2.

19. Harjo, "New Orleans," lines 29–30 and line 32.

20. Harjo, "New Orleans," lines 33–35.

21. Harjo, "New Orleans," lines 36 and 59–60.

22. Surbhi Malik, "The provincial Flâneuse: Reimagining provincial space and narratives of womanhood in Bollywood," *South Asian Popular Culture* 19, no. 1 (2021): 33–45.

23. Mimi Sheller, *Mobility Justice: The Politics of Movement in An Age of Extremes* (New York: Verso, 2018).

24. Harjo, "New Orleans," lines 5–6.

25. Harjo, "New Orleans," lines 6–9.

26. Kevin Fox Gotham, "Tourism Gentrification: The Case of New Orleans' Vieux Carre (French Quarter)," *Urban Studies*, 42 no. 7 (2005): 1105. As Gotham's article relays, what later became Jackson Square (adorned dramatically with the statue of former President Jackson rearing his horse into the urban space) was originally a French trading center and, later, after 1762, the Plaza de Armas—the center of the Spanish colonial outpost.

27. The Indian Removal Act of 1830 was signed into law by President Andrew Jackson, ripping tens of thousands of Indigenous peoples from their sovereign lands to new territories west of the Mississippi. The genocide of Indigenous peoples in territories comprising (and extending beyond) the present-day United States was systematically advanced by revoking land rights, mass deaths in forced relocation, ensuant violations to treaty agreements and accompanying wars, the intensification of missionaries along the Mississippi, and centuries worth of necropolitical anti-Indian state policies.

28. Harjo, "New Orleans," lines 22 and 51.

29. Harjo, "New Orleans," line 37.

30. Harjo, "New Orleans," lines 40–41.

31. Allison Margaret Bigelow, "Narrative Circuits of New World Copper," in *Mining Language: Racial Thinking, Indigenous Knowledge, and Colonial Metallurgy in the Early Modern Iberian World* (Durham: University of North Carolina Press, 2020), 167. La Florida represents a Spanish colonial defined region encompassing present-day Florida, Georgia, Alabama, Mississippi, and the Carolinas.

32. Harjo, "New Orleans," line 31.

33. Robert S. Weddle, "Soto's Problems of Orientation: Maps, Navigation, and Instruments in the Florida Expedition," in *The Hernando De Soto Expedition: History, Historiography, and "Discovery" in the Southeast*, ed. Patricia Galloway (Lincoln: University of Nebraska Press, 2005) 220.

34. Harjo, "New Orleans," lines 48–79.

35. Harjo, "New Orleans," lines 51–52.

36. Harjo, "New Orleans," lines 55–57.

37. Goeman, *Mark My Words*, 123.

38. Harjo, "New Orleans," lines 43–46.

39. Goeman, *Mark My Words*, 23.

40. Harjo, "New Orleans," lines 40–41.

41. Harjo, "New Orleans," line 64.

42. Goeman, *Mark My Words*, 97.

43. Allan Sekula, "The Body and the Archive," *October* 39 (1986), 15; Edward Said, *Orientalism* (New York: Pantheon Books, 1978), 3. Developed by Francis Galton in the 1880s, composite photography is rooted in a Western social anxiety to define itself against the "criminal" or "aberrant." Galton, described as the founder of eugenics, used double exposure to layer photographic portraits of different individuals in order to assert the (literally) over-lapping, phenotypic traits of different social types. Early iterations of the project focused on convicted individuals, tuberculosis patients, and Jewish peoples, while later studies focused on "desirable" populations including doctors, scientists, and Royal Engineers, among others. Not only was this method scientifically untenable, attempting to extrapolate a unified and thus predetermined "look" of different social classes, but, as Allan Sekula asserts in *The Body and the Archive*, "the law-abiding body recognized its threatening other in the criminal body, recognized its own acquisitive and aggressive impulses unchecked." Also riffing off Foucault, Sekula's examination of the visual history of the criminal versus abiding social body recalls Said's argument in *Orientalism* that "European culture defined its strength and identity by setting itself off against the Orient as a sort of surrogate and even underground self." Just as Harjo's poem hijacks the bourgeois flâneur-ian model and reconceptualizes mapping praxis towards decolonial ends, so too do I aim to break open the Galtonian composite, which pro-duced the "unwitting caricature of inductive reason" in the symbolic character of the visual image, and instead recuperate the theoretic force of the multiply exposed photographic image in conceptualizing the aesthetics of (re)mapped, decolonized space.

44. Goeman, *Mark My Words*, 138.

45. Harjo, "New Orleans," line 68.

46. "See Bourbon Street, New Orleans," *Visit New Orleans*, 2023, https://www.neworleans.com/plan/streets/bourbon-street/.

47. Walter D. Mignolo, *Local Histories/Global Designs: Coloniality, Subaltern Knowledges, and Border Thinking* (Princeton: Princeton University Press, 2012), 220.

48. "See Bourbon Street, New Orleans," *Visit New Orleans*, 2023; Mignolo, *Local Histories/Global Designs*, 219.

49. Kevin Fox Gotham, "Tourism Gentrification: The Case of New Orleans' Vieux Carre (French Quarter)," *Urban Studies* 42, no. 7 (2005): 1099. Gotham here cites Neil Smith's "New Globalism, New Urbanism: Gentrification as Global Urban Strategy" in *Antipode* 34 (2002): 427–50.

50. Gotham, "Tourism Gentrification," 1100.

51. "American Planning Association Designates Jackson Square as a Top 10 Great Public Space for 2012," *Mayor's Press Release Feed, City of New Orleans*, http://www.nola.gov/mayor/press-releases. Announced in the New Orleans city government press release by Mayor Mitchell J. Landrieu on October 3, 2012, the American Planning Association (APA) designated Jackson Square as one of 10 Great Public Spaces for 2012 under the organization's Great Places in America program.

52. "About," *LowerNine.Org*, 2023, https://lowernine.org/. LowerNine.Org is a nonprofit organization focused on the long-term recovery and reconstruction of the lower ninth ward that was decimated by Hurricane Katrina in 2005. The organization continues to support the rebuild of the ward by constructing affordable housing and addressing systemic inequalities that both predate and extend from the event of Katrina.

53. Frederick Engels, *Der Volkstaat* (1874), quoted in David Harvey, *Rebel Cities: From the Right to the City to the Urban Revolution* (London: Verso, 2012), 17.

54. "Port NOLA," *Port of New Orleans*, https://portnola.com/info/news-media/press-releases/port-of-new-orleans-closes-2021-with-major-milestones-in-all-four-lines-of-business. With regard to land and resource exploitation, environmental activists working to restore and preserve the Mississippi River watershed highlight the negative impact of centuries of commercializing the critical waterway that have led to vanishing wetlands and impact to wetland species. The Port of New Orleans reported moving over 2.4 million short tons of cargo in 2021, an increase of 1.7 million short tons in 2020. The increasing movement of fossil fuels, break bulk, and other commodities along natural corridors like the Mississippi River represents continued investment in extractive spatial practices that, comprise the contemporary turn in supply chain capitalism but are nonetheless part of a longer colonial trajectory. My current research project, *Art of Logistics*, theorizes supply chains in contemporary literature, television, and film.

55. Goeman, *Mark My Words*, 144.

10

A CABDRIVER SINGS THE BLUES
Mem Shannon's Articulation of Urban Life and Working-Class Resistance in Late Twentieth-Century New Orleans

Marcus Charles Tribbett

As Stuart Hall theorized in his influential 1981 essay, "Notes on Deconstructing the 'Popular,'" popular culture in capitalist society is a realm of contradictions, a territory in which the struggle over the meanings of the verbal and visual signs of class, race, and gender is enacted in order to reflect and represent the subject position(s) of various groups and individuals.[1] As such, popular culture is always an arena in which the interests of various classes, races, and genders exist in continual competition, where particular areas (signs) are seized upon by people to represent their group identity, and where, in Graeme Turner's words, "the construction of everyday life may be examined."[2] Songwriter and guitarist Mem Shannon's 1995 album, *A Cabdriver's Blues*,[3] illustrates one such struggle for agency in its assertion of a subjectivity resistant to the racial and social class hegemony of the United States, while also creating space for a gendered stance critical of sexual exploitation and male chauvinism. Shannon's remarkable debut utilizes a unique mixture of songs and spoken *audio verité* recordings to define an everyday, urban, working-class identity in late twentieth-century, pre-Katrina New Orleans. By turns funny and sobering, he celebrates city life while simultaneously critiquing America's late-capitalist consumerism and the exploitation of its marginalized citizens, giving the denizens of his city, New Orleans, their due without sentimentality. In doing so, he voices the potentially radical subjectivity of the urban worker and the cabdriver in particular.

That the blues as a Black cultural form historically have been resistant to white, patriarchal cultural hegemony has been well-observed for more than half a century. Among the first to do so was LeRoi Jones (Amiri Baraka) in his *Blues People*.[4] Ben Sidran and Frank Kofsky both write specifically of jazz as a counterhegemonic musical form, but their observations are also applicable to blues.[5] Lawrence Levine discusses the nature of protest in African American secular music and more explicitly connects the culturally subversive elements of blues and jazz than either Sidran or Kofsky.[6] Ray Boggs and Carl Pratt, George Lipsitz, Paul Garon, and Paul Garon and Beth Garon all deal with the blues form as a site of resistance.[7] William Barlow states that the twentieth-century history of the blues exists "on the cutting edge of African-American cultural resistance to white domination."[8] More recently, Ted Gioia locates the blues within a Black cultural tradition "rich in coded or buried meanings, inside jargon, double entendres, and other ways of communicating secretly while in full view."[9]

George Lipsitz's analysis of Mardi Gras Indians is especially useful for understanding how *A Cabdriver's Blues* specifically represents a resistant racial and class-based subjectivity. Like the Mardi Gras Indian tradition, Shannon's album "gives coded expression to values and beliefs that operate every day in the lives of black workers in New Orleans."[10] His use of the *audio verité* recordings "brings out into the open dimensions of repression that the dominant culture generally tries to render invisible."[11] To use the terminology of anthropologist and cultural theorist James Scott,[12] the *audio verité* recordings are resistant to repression because they present Shannon's simultaneous engagement with the "public transcript" of power while revealing the "hidden transcripts" of both the dominant and the subordinate in his recorded cab conversations. He thus uses the materials of his everyday work life to create a powerful commentary on social inequality, utilizing "the lived experience which breathes life into . . . inanimate objects" to quicken the album's pulse.[13] Although the work is neither a straightforward statement of working-class power nor a feminist or Black nationalist manifesto, it need not be for it to be considered resistant and even potentially radical. As Tony Bennett has argued, the possibility of a class consciousness in popular culture that is radically resistant to hegemony is generally nascent since it necessarily relies on combining various groups who are different in most respects but who are "distinguished from the economically, politically, and culturally powerful groups within society";

however, these groups are "potentially capable of being organised . . . if their separate struggles are connected."[14] Furthermore, Lipsitz notes that "images in negotiation with power are often ambiguous, complicated, and implicated in the crimes they seek to address."[15] Ultimately, in the careful sequencing and juxtapositioning of songs with recorded conversations, Shannon presents an urban scene that is complicated enough to both repel and attract cabbie, resident, tourist, and listeners alike, yet cosmopolitan enough to earn his affection and our admiration.

Populated by prostitutes (and the sexual tourists who seek their services), small time gamblers, armed crooks, average Joes, rich professionals in town for a convention and a good time, and the eponymous cab driver himself, Shannon's fascinating audio cityscape simmers with life. The album opens with an *audio verité* conversation between cabdriver and passenger, an older gent, identified only as the "5th Ward Horseman," who reminisces with his cabbie about how the neighborhood they're driving through has gone downhill and how times were better in the past. When Mem agrees, saying "Po' boy sandwiches don't taste like they used to. . . . I don't know if it was the mayonnaise they was using or . . ." the Fifth Ward Horseman interrupts him: "You know Mem, it's because of this: We'd eat one of them every now and then. . . . It's common now." Even amidst the abundance of consumable goods under late capitalism, there is a sense of loss and a nostalgia for better days past: the block has changed for the worse, the Horseman says, because so many people have been killed there that it just "closed up"; the jobs and businesses are gone. Thus, the album immediately contradicts the logic of neoliberalism, asserting from the beginning that there is a cultural poverty even amidst an abundance of material goods as long as there is no corresponding enrichment of people's lived experience.[16]

The second track and first song extends this critique, establishing both the singer's working class origins and musical *bona fides*. "Play the Guitar, Son" is an exhortation from father to son: Get out of this hard life through your creativity and music:

> Son, please find a better way. /
> I work sixteen long hours in a dirty lumberyard, /
> and when you get grown, boy, /
> I don't want you working that damned hard.

Though Mem sings that he doesn't believe his father cared if he ever became a star, it's clear his father wanted him to have a different life from his own, gifting him with a beat-up old guitar even if that meant only the nurturing of his creative and musical ambitions, a cultural sustenance as vital as the material one provided by a job.

Infused with a critique of consumerism, the album doesn't celebrate mere pecuniary interest, despite being concerned with unemployment and job loss. In fact, Shannon returns to his opening theme in track five, "My Baby's Been Watching TV." Switching from the street and the club scene to the domestic sphere, this song laments the influence of daytime television and home shopping networks on his wife's spending habits: "On my baby's last birthday. I promised her a night out on the town. / I gave her two whole weeks of my pay just to buy a new evening gown. / She said, "baby I know just what I want, 'cause I saw this new thing on TV." / The girl went out and bought Cadillac hubcaps for earrings and a dress lit up like a Christmas tree! / I can see it coming. And it's another battle that I just can't win. / My girl's been watching TV, watching that Oprah Winfrey again."

Although the song's perspective is very conventional and perhaps chauvinist in its depiction of gender roles, it clearly also attacks the mindless consumption offered up as a substitute for genuine cultural creativity by corporate capitalism. Consumer culture as represented by the televised ads for one useless mass-produced item after another has nothing to offer the singer. It's merely a mechanism for eating up his paycheck and only causes him domestic strife: "Now I'm tired of fussing and fighting. / And I've had just about all that I can take. / If she tries one more new thing on me, / I'm throwing the TV sets in the lake!" The next song continues the theme of unrest on the domestic front, as Shannon offers an ode to a night of insomnia. Troubled and restless, he sings: "I've been up all night, me and my bed just had a fight." New York City cabbie Booker Page, from Studs Terkel's classic *Working*, could probably relate: "Oh, I'm so tired. My bottom gets so. . . . Oh, every muscle aches in my body. It's my leg and feet, ankles and so forth. . . . My pedaling the gas and the brake, gas and brake, and so forth."[17] With the added pressure on his marriage from consumer ad culture, there is literally no rest for the weary Mem.

Much of the album focuses on the exploitation of sex workers by the tourists who come to New Orleans for a good time, but the prostitute we actually meet, the "$17.00 Brunette" of track three, is hardly helpless in the face of it, even if she does ask for and Mem agrees to give her a ride, despite her telling him up front that she doesn't have the money for the full fare. A streetwalker who talks about how hard it has been hustling tricks that week, when Mem acts surprised she has made so little despite doctors and lawyers being in town, the $17.00 Brunette tells him: "Them doctors are scared . . . you hear me, they're scared. I made seventeen dollars. You know what I'm saying? . . . I know them doctors are scared. I hate it when them bitches come to town. You know the first thing they holler about? It's AIDS. . . . I'm not worried about fucking 'em anyhow, I want to steal their money. . . . They want to make you drunker than what they are; that way they can take advantage of you. I don't give a fuck how drunk they make me, I'm still pop their money. You heard me? You heard me?"

"I hear you twice," Mem replies. "They could have me fallin' down I'm still gonna try to take their money," she says.

Shannon's compassion in giving her below market or perhaps free cab fare isn't the only marker of his solidarity with working women on the album nor of his distrust of the sex tourists who seek them out. Despite her mercenary attitude toward her johns, Shannon doesn't undercut the $17.00 Brunette's perspective, immediately following up their conversation with the song "You Ain't Nothing Nice." She may not be nice, and she may have the singer "drunk as whiskey" (turning the tables on a potential client perhaps), but she "can make a man sweat when it's thirty below." This song validates the $17.00 brunette for her attractive sexuality and clever machinations with alcohol, rather than condemning her for being only a hustler.

Simultaneously, Shannon uses the album to undercut male chauvinism, not just for its role in the transactional system of prostitution but also in the form that pretends to celebrate women in consensual sexual relationships with men. In track fourteen, another *audio verité* entitled "The Older Broad," we meet a thoroughly friendly but mixed up man, whose casual misogyny is incredibly jarring after the love song that precedes it: even while he's lauding his woman and praising his own good luck at finding a fantastic new love, he can't help but try to connect like an adolescent with his male cabdriver by bragging about how good looking she is for "an older broad" ("This broad like forty-five years old but she only looks thirty-five. I ain't never seen no broad [like that]") and about how she "wants to fuck all damn night . . . and wear me out." He's clearly happy with his new love situation but can't

A Cabdriver Sings the Blues: Shannon's New Orleans

conceptualize it in other than sexist terms. "I caught a good un with that thing. . . . Most of 'em here are dizzy upstairs," he tells Mem who amiably interjects the occasional "yeah" or chuckle.

"Got to Go," which immediately follows the misguided guy in the "Older Broad," resonates with Shannon's pent-up frustration with the city. Relating his bad luck with romance, it directly contradicts the track before as if to say, "How can a guy like that find love but not me?" Ultimately, after a false ending, though, he admits he's not likely to leave New Orleans forever: "I might come back again to see my mama. / I might come back again to see my friends. / I might come back again, but I'll soon have to go. / I might come back again to get some gumbo. / I might come back again, but I won't stay long. / I might come back again, but I'll soon be gone. / I might come back again to feed my dog. / I might come back again just to see Mardi Gras."

Invoking the prime tourist attraction, New Orleans's main event, is no coincidence in an album consumed with presenting and implicitly critiquing the misguided, wealthy, perverse, or downright nasty visitors to the city with whom he shares his cab.

One passenger, Chantelle, obviously a local, even thinks there's nothing worse than being a tourist or being seen as a tourist. Interestingly, Chantelle speaks in the sing-song ethnic caricatured voice of an immigrant cabdriver while mocking both tourists and the unscrupulous drivers who would exploit them. Animated and somewhat threatening, the subtext of her conversation with Mem is that he better not be trying to take advantage of her: "I've been places where I wasn't from there, and I knew I was paying too much for something, but they know I'm a tourist, so they know I don't know no better. But I just tell 'em, 'Look dude, I'm not a fucking tourist, first of all. . . . I know it's not twenty-five dollars. You run that fucking meter and let's see what it'll be.' I told him that you can have a kiss outta my ass. . . . Because the guy was like, 'Why you gettee so upsetee?' "Cause you can kissee my assee. I'm not a fucking tourist, fool.'"

Perhaps trying to reassure her of his own honesty, Shannon replies, "He was trying to rip you off, there's no doubt about that," and the conversation returns to sexual exploitation, as Chantelle tells him: "Well actually he thought he was getting him something tonight. He gotta kiss outta my ass. Hell, I mean, AIDS is running around." "That's what they keep tellin' me," Mem says.

Shannon sharpens his critique of culturally hegemonic forms of gender and sexual exploitation by offering well-timed vignettes of the well-off tourists and conventioneers he picks up on the job. He's especially cautious of those seeking sex for hire in two different *audio verité* tracks, "Ode to Benny Hill" and "Dick Tie Commandos." In the former, British passengers seeking a night of "cabaret" climb into his cab. Half jocular, half serious they ask Mem for recommendations and going rates at the strip clubs, queries he mostly deflects and dodges, before finally asking them: "So what are we doing?" [i.e., Where do you want me to take you?], after which they give him a destination. Although the main speaker of the group is jovial and friendly, his attempts to establish a rapport with the driver are undercut by the serious tone he adopts when asking about the strip clubs: "What's the going rate in there? Complete nude?"

The "Dick Tie Commandos" of track eleven, more sex tourists heading to the Quarter, are perhaps the most insulting of his passengers, even while on the surface much more friendly than the previously introduced "Miserable Bastard" of track nine. Laughingly, they tell Shannon, "We want to buy one of those dick-ties downtown somewhere." Smugly, one of the Commandos speaks about Mem as if he weren't even in the cab. "It seems to me," he says, "that these people down here haven't lost their sense of humor." "No, they still have a sense of humor," a companion replies. This song is also interesting for the way in which it shows a heterosexist comfort with male homosociality but discomfort with homosexuality. Reading the signs they are passing, one Commando says: "Girls, girls, girls, all girls." "Where are the boys?" another asks. "You can let me out here," another chuckles uncomfortably. Even the cabdriver appears to participate in a little mild homophobia: "I want to get out, too." But the overarching feeling of the track is again a kind of disdain for the passengers, and his statement may be as much about present company in general than the specific question about where all the boys are. Shannon may be signifying, in other words, and the two songs that follow offer different versions of love and sexuality than many of his passengers are seeking. While the sex tourists are merely looking for commodities, "The Boogie Man" celebrates sex, but is about being there sexually for his lover as well: "I'm your boogie man," he sings. "Hot-cha hot-cha hot-cha wonder, hot-cha hot-cha hot." And "Maxine" is a plaintive love ballad sung for his longtime woman, asking her to never worry about him leaving.

In the face of men who don't want to pay the streetwalking brunette of track three what she's worth, who want to take advantage of her by getting

A Cabdriver Sings the Blues: Shannon's New Orleans   167

her drunk, Shannon offers a cutting class-based analysis of the wealthy doctors and lawyers who are so stingy with their money in track eight, "Taxicab Driver": "I'm a taxicab driver, / and my luck is bad. / I'm having problems." At the heart of the album is this anthem to his working life, filled with the indignities of the job, and his conviction that "There has got to be a better way, / and if my luck ever changes, / I'm gonna quit this cab business someday." But the late, spoken part of the song shows all the accumulated knowledge he has that keeps him sane and safe in his working environment. As a man whistles and hails his cab, Mem says "I don't believe this. Now it's ninety degrees, three o'clock in the morning, he's got on a long wool overcoat and trying to flag me down in an alley. I wasn't born yesterday if you know what I mean." Simultaneously he critiques the wealthy tourist customers who seek his services, in the same terms he offered the $17.00 Brunette: "We got doctors and lawyers in town this week. Tips won't be that big this week. Boy, boy, boy. What a life. They keep asking me why I'm singing the blues: I'm living the blues, and it's killin' me!" Certainly, this criticism of poor-tipping wealthy people is hardly unique. As another of Terkel's cabdrivers, Chicago's Lucky Miller, observed over fifty years ago, "I can say for sure that the best tippers are not people who live on Lake Shore Drive, or the businessmen. They're generally the blue-collar people I pick up in the neighborhoods."[18] Yet by invoking the blues as both a song tradition and a shared cultural experience of oppression, Shannon isn't simply offering a class-based criticism: he is explicitly relating his work-a-day life to his own racial and musical heritage here as well. The material exploitation is class-based, but the experience is racialized; the oppression he faces racist.

And his concern for personal safety from violence is not misplaced. As Lucky Miller told Terkel, "A person who's driving a cab a number of years tends to become hardened. I hate having to turn somebody down. On the other hand, I think of the reality. I may have [a lot of cash] on me at the end of a good day. The money itself is expendable, but my life isn't. I read of incidents in which drivers have been shot even after surrendering their money."[19] This experientially acquired wariness leads Mem to question his next passenger, "The Miserable Bastard," who seemingly appears out of nowhere: "Where did you come from . . . out of a limo?" The Miserable Bastard instantly responds, "You got a problem with that? . . . I'm not a cop and I don't have a gun." From there, the Bastard gives Mem more of a hard time, insulting him and also deriding the people he sees out the window of the cab.

"You got air conditioner in here?"

"No, sorry, I don't."

"Whatsa matter with it?"

"It's broke and I haven't had time to have it fixed."

"Do I get a discount for that, or what?"

"No, sorry."

"Do I get a discount for your personality or what?"

"Sorry if you don't agree with my personality."

The Bastard laughs, "Give it a rest." After identifying himself as an attorney, he tries to get Mem to speak derisively of shabbily dressed people they are driving by. "Let me ask you a question," he says, "I'm reasonably educated, what do you think about when you see, like, what you see in front of you?"

"I don't think much of it because they're minding their own business. So, you know, it's just another sight to see. I've seen it before."

"Aww, come on now. . . . That's a generic answer. Do you kinda like look at it like that's white trash?"

"No, . . . he could be a lawyer, you don't know. Just because he's got that outfit on and ridin' that bike, you figure he's not worthy. But you don't know what he is." The cabbie refuses to join the Miserable Bastard in his elitism or validate his sense of superiority, and despite politely saying "same here" when the passenger says "it was a pleasure to share a ride with you," it is doubtful that Shannon took much pleasure in his company.[20]

Following the conversation with the elitist jerk of the track before, "One Hot Night," track ten, represents the nadir of the album. Here the singer has been fighting with his woman, obviously about their finances and how hard it is to find a decent job. He admits to the temptation of easy money through criminal activity: "When it's hot outside and the rent is due / and that little bitty baby is dependin' on you, / the wrong thing it sure can cross your mind." His out-of-work friend "down at the bar" talks the singer into driving the getaway car on a robbery, but the job goes sour, and the singer has "been runnin' ever since / . . . [and] still can't feed that little baby child." Despite the desperation of this father turned outlaw, and notwithstanding Chantelle's soon-to-follow reinvocation of the sobering reality of gender harassment and sexually transmitted disease that immediately precedes track seventeen, the last song on the album, "If This Ain't the Blues" is self-deprecating but still truth-telling, the anguish softened by humor but not eliminated. After an operation cures the blindness of his wife and kids, for example, they leave the singer, saying he's "the ugliest man they ever did see." The blues is real, he sings, even as he pokes fun at himself, and it is explicitly couched in economic terms: "I got a permanent layoff from my job. / The boss said 'it's just as well 'cause you're fired anyway.'" Even as we laugh at the jokes, who can blame him when he sings, "I can't take much more"?

But, although Chantelle has spoken harshly of tourists, and Mem himself has sung that he's got to go and can't take much more, the album ends with Shannon's celebration of the cosmopolitanism of his city. Track eighteen, "Food Drink and Music," is an *audio verité* montage. We hear the overwhelming sounds of the cityscape: traffic whistles, screeching tires and brakes, horns blaring, sirens howling as a man exclaims that "the police got a paddy wagon loaded up. . . . [They got] handcuffs on the brothers. No, two paddy wagons!" Shannon begins asking passenger after passenger what country he or she is from and is obviously delighted by the range of responses he receives. Tellingly, he seems to rebuff a woman who asks him, "What time do you get off?" "Whenever," he replies. The album closes with the same phrase repeated four times, "Boy, boy, time for me to go home!" followed by the sound of a car door slamming closed. In the end, despite perverted sex tourists, poor tipping rich men, elitist pricks, foul mouthed women, and a man who doesn't know a better way to compliment the woman he loves except by bragging about her sexual appetite and good looks, Shannon is proud of his city, its residents, and his job; and the range of visitors to New Orleans only validates his opinion. Ultimately, the interplay of voices on his album provides space for Shannon's own, resistant to the grinding inequality that his song persona witnesses and assertive of the value of his urban-created class, race, and gender identity.

More than two decades after the release of his first album, Shannon appears to have been ahead of his time. In the post-Katrina era, the painful economic changes in his city that he saw and lamented in the 1990s have only been magnified. Now, people look back on nineties-era New Orleans as an almost bucolic period and mourn the loss of that city, but that makes *A Cabdriver's Blues* no less prescient. In fact, it makes it more so. The harsh effects of what in that period we knew as late capitalism but now call neoliberalism have grown much worse since the natural and ensuing slow-motion human disaster. In the wake of Katrina, the inequalities described so poignantly by Shannon in 1995 have increased. Naomi Klein began analyzing what she terms "disaster capitalism" almost immediately following the storm.[21] A little more recently, Vincanne Adams has used ethnographic research to outline what she calls "recovery capitalism."[22] In both accounts, we see the consequences of a neoliberal ideology that pushes to privatize relief to disaster victims, while starving governments of funds for recovery aid, and that plunges many survivors deeper into despair as it exacerbates inequalities that are rooted in social class and race. Critical of the Bush administration's response to the tragedy, Klein writes, "When it comes to paying contractors, the sky is the limit; when it comes to financing the basic functions of the state, the coffers are empty."[23]

And not just the state is at risk from this type of economic policy, but any publicly funded entity. Anne Lovell, for example, chronicles the demise of Charity Hospital in particular—despite its lack of severe storm damage— to show how it was allowed to fail because its charitable mission did not fit with business-friendly recovery plans for New Orleans.[24] As just one of many examples of a New Orleans institution that served poor and black New Orleanians that was not rebuilt after Hurricane Katrina, Charity's downfall is a microcosm of the problems wrought by neoliberalism on the city. Not that Charity was viewed uncomplicatedly as a bastion of hope for African American residents of the city prior to the flood. In Shannon's song "Charity," from his 1997 sophomore effort, the hospital is not only the facility where the "baby girl child" and the "baby boy in your mama's arms," whom the song is addressed to, have been born; it is also the place where others like them have come to die before their time: "If these walls could talk / They wouldn't have much good to say. / Young lives ruined and cut short / each and every day. / They just keep on coming. / Will they ever stop this flow / through the doors, through the doors of Charity?"[25]

Still, although his song refuses to romanticize the place (and although the answer to his question is now "yes . . . but perhaps not in the way you might have hoped"), Charity Hospital's importance to the lives of the singer and the community he gives voice to is obvious in these lyrics. Furthermore, Lovell argues that after Katrina a type of "situational identity" with regard to Charity arose in the wake of its closing, an identity influenced by both racial and economically populist readings of the facility: "Generations were born, treated, and died at Charity Hospital, where many African American parents, siblings, and extended kin found lifetime employment."[26] That identity manifested itself most clearly in the moniker adopted by those who led the movement to reopen the hospital, the "Charity Hospital Babies." Both the hospital's closure and the failure of efforts to reopen it have taken their toll on the African American community of the city, particularly on the psyches of those most marginalized: "How people perceive their health today [in New Orleans] remains dramatically split along racial lines, with blacks almost three times as likely as whites to fear health services might not be available to them."[27]

As with public hospitals, neoliberal policies have also seen the demise of public housing in New Orleans after Katrina. One of many commentators on this trend, Thomas Jessen Adams suggests that a public concern for "security" and "defensible spaces" allowed urban planners to demolish housing projects, areas that might have been made more "defensible" with much less costly landscaping alterations, in favor of mixed-income housing units.[28] Adams notes that since "New Orleans has come to embody the ultimate location where a new rot at the core of the United States is being revealed," many people have been willing to eliminate housing projects that were emblematic of inner-city decay in the public mind, though physically and architecturally they did not much resemble the projects of the northeastern and upper midwestern cities that are most associated with urban blight.[29] While Eric Ishiwata, like Adams, has rightfully pointed out that the news coverage of Katrina's impact revealed a persistent US poverty and hopelessness among the city's black underclass that had been largely ignored prior to that time, and that this revelation offered "a conspicuous challenge to the allegedly 'race neutral' policies of the neoliberal state,"[30] Adams further argues that the demands of New Orleans's tourism-based economy required that this disclosure be covered over once more and the "rot" quickly forgotten. What better way to do it than with so-called "mixed-income" housing units, erected in the name of "security" on the demolished ruins of the old projects, even if this process was a simple pretext for gentrification that allowed well-off people to feel good about helping lower-income residents to better accommodations while ridding the city of the danger supposedly represented by public housing? Who cares if the "mixed-income" mandates in the development agreements have sunset provisions that allow the private developers, who used public assets to construct them, to later sell units in these "mixed" developments at full market value? As Adams writes, "this is a process whereby capital . . . is able to latch onto a cultural demand for public safety and the feeling of security and turn it into a vendible commodity"[31] and thus allow investors like Goldman Sachs to turn a profit while ultimately pricing lower-income people out of the very market that was supposed to serve them—or at least some of them—in the first place.

Written and released prior to Katrina but rereleased on his only post-Katrina album, *Live at Tipitina's*, Shannon cuts to the heart of this issue on "Who Are They?": "They say everything is lookin' real real good. / They must have forgot to check my neighborhood. / . . . / I got two little questions I'd love somebody to answer. / Somebody please tell me, / Just who are they and has anybody ever seen 'em?"[32]

Whoever "they" are, they certainly do not seem interested in seeing the seedy side of the city exposed for long. And while Shannon may never have seen "them," it is perhaps worth noting that "they" aren't particularly interested in seeing him, or those who look him, either.

In the tourism industry of the neoliberal economy, service sector employees are to be neither seen nor heard: "Hospitality . . . depends upon the social erasure and invisibility of the workers who produce it and their quotidian labors," particularly workers of color.[33] That includes a former cabby turned entertainer. In fact, in the new "sharing economy," riders are not supposed to be looking for a service from a cabdriver at all, but rather to be arranging a ride with a small businessperson who owns his/her own capital (a car) and who runs his/her own enterprise by subcontracting from a larger ride-sharing service like Uber or Lyft. Cabs and cabbies themselves are disappearing, and if the upshot of this is that an upstart, wealthy Silicon Valley corporate entity no longer has to provide any capital equipment, maintenance costs, benefits, or overtime pay to run its business, well, that is simply more profit for them. And as for everybody else, people can either choose to "share" their cars and their labor to make a living, or they can pay someone who does not resemble a service worker on the surface but rather just another car-owning fellow citizen who is sharing his/her car with them for their apparently mutual benefit.

Journalist and author Steven Hill offers a trenchant assessment of this new business arrangement:

> The idea of a "sharing" economy sounds so groovy—environmentally correct, politically neutral, anti-consumerist and all of it wrapped in the warm, fuzzy vocabulary of "sharing." . . . [Yet] the so-called "new" economy looks an awful lot like the old, pre-New Deal economy—with "jobs" amounting to a series of low-paid micro-gigs and piece work, offering little empowerment for average workers, families or communities."[34]

Describing a culture where "huge swaths of workers are becoming free-lanced, contracted, and temp-ed, and even many regularly employed, fulltime workers are being slowly squeezed," Hill warns of country based on a "1099 economy," a "freelance society" that severs traditional social connections between employer and employee, leaving "millions of Americans . . . to their own devices, stranded on their own island of survival."[35]

And what of the ultimate freelancers, the streetwalkers Shannon chronicles so vividly yet sympathetically in a *Cabdriver's Blues*? How has the post-Katrina neoliberal order treated them? In 2011, Doreen Piano interviewed Women with a Vision (WWAV) executive director Deon Haywood who offers a clue. In the years following the disaster, sex workers were targeted using a two-century-old law designed to prosecute the solicitation of gay sex from male prostitutes: Louisiana Statute 89.2, Solicitation of a Crime Against Nature or SCAN.[36] According to Haywood, the postdisaster enforcement of this law, that had previously rarely been invoked, amounted to a "new Scarlet letter" that dramatically increased the exploitation and incarceration of prostitutes in New Orleans because, not only were the penalties for violating it (or even being suspected of violating it)[37] increased, but also those convicted were required to register as sex offenders for life. Haywood, whose organization has a long, preflood history of outreach and service involving HIV and reproductive health education for people of color in the poorest communities of the city, described the situation succinctly:

> The basic premise is that you can be arrested for . . . oral sex in exchange for money. If you're caught or even suspected of sex work, you are charged with being a sex offender. But many women who were charged pre-Katrina never actually had the law enforced. Now the law is not only being enforced but the number of years for the charge has increased from ten to fifteen. The main concern is not only the penalties and possible incarceration but it becomes an identifying marker. Before Katrina, you could be registered as a "sex offender" by law but you were never charged. Now, post-Katrina, the charge is on your ID or driver's license.
>
> . . . It's totally ridiculous and unfair, especially the amount of time for this conviction.[38]

Poor, often struggling with substance dependency and untreated emotional and psychological trauma from sexual violence, some homeless, these women and transgendered persons faced a much more difficult time improving their lives when their convictions and sex offender statuses denied them the ability to find legitimate work, even at fast food joints, or to go to school. "If I'm a registered sex offender," Haywood said, "I have cards mailed out about me to people in my neighborhood or to schools where their children are. This situation creates serious emotional and mental stress," the last thing addicts needs if they are trying to go straight: "they lose their basic means of transcending their situation."[39]

For all of its survivors, stress was a constant companion in the months and years following the storm. For many of the most vulnerable, "recovery" offered only more misery. Describing the early period following the hurricane, Haywood mentions how the influx of male workers and professionals to the city changed the atmosphere on the streets:

> I really felt like these were not my men. . . . There were guys in a car or walking down the street catcalling. . . . We got many calls from women. . . . A lot of them struggled with sexual violence. But I really felt it was different [from pre-Katrina times] and I've done outreach in the city since I was nineteen or twenty years old, but when I got back, I thought, "Who are these people?"[40]

Some desperate women inevitably turned to prostitution to make ends meet, as one anecdote from Haywood suggests: "We had someone come in our office about a week ago who was forty-one years old, homeless, lost her job, her husband is disabled, and they were struggling. For the first time in her life she started tricking, making a living off of her body."[41] Even for the more fortunate, the storm left a trail of despondence behind. New Orleans journalist Chris Rose's powerful 2007 personal narrative, *1 Dead in the Attic*, shows the psychological and emotional devastation caused by Katrina in its immediate aftermath, leading him to describe himself and his "glassy eyed" and "fidgety" neighbors as inmates of "Mad City."[42] Rose's chronicle of his own (and many of his neighbors') descent into despair and physical disintegration—his depression and weight-loss, the dissolution of his marriage, the emergence of an addiction, the suicides of friends, and his own emotional numbness—won a Pulitzer and is as brutal to read as it is easily recognizable for survivors of profound trauma.

Shannon captures such despair in his incredibly poignant song "All I Have," track five from his 2007 release *Live: A Night at Tipitina's*. Sung from the perspective of a mother who is standing with her daughter among the ruins of their family home, when the girl asks her, "Mama, why do you want to come back to this place? / That hurricane took everything away," she replies: "Baby, I know it looks just like a pile of junk and trash / but it's all, it's all I have." Examining discarded pieces of their lives one by one from among the detritus, the mother straightforwardly describes the origin of each: "Pick up that old baby's bottle over there: / I bought that from K&B drugstore when you were born. / And look at your Daddy's old hardhat: / He worked hard on that river so we could have a home. / And them two dishes laying over there in the dirt: / Part of a set I bought from Krauss department store through the layaway. / And give me that old bible over there: / Your Auntie gave me that when your Daddy passed away. / . . . / Look at my bag of old Zulu beads: / Y'all could hardly wait for Mardi Gras Day. / Before that storm came, we would never ever miss a parade. / And look at that box of old school report cards: / From Booker T., Fortier, Rabouin, and Cohen,[43] / Junior got put out of so many schools, / we could hardly tell where he was going."

Witnessing her loss stated so simply, the effect of the song is heartbreaking. "All my memories are in this pile of junk and trash, it's all I have," mama repeats to daughter. How does someone come back from this? Many of the city's most marginalized former residents have not. According to Gary Rivlin in *Katrina After the Flood*, US Postal Service data indicates that less than a third of the addresses in the Lower Ninth Ward that received mail before the storm do so now, with a growth rate that would require nearly a quarter century more to fully repopulate the area even if it continues.[44]

Yet that isn't the end of the story. Women with a Vision and similar organizations, along with the New Orleans Justice Project and the Center for Constitutional Rights, resisted the harsh new interpretation of the SCAN statute with lawsuits and media outreach, and by June 2013, a settlement had resulted in the removal of the names of all persons convicted of a SCAN violation from the Louisiana Sex Offender Registry.[45] The ongoing mission of social justice for the sexually marginalized in New Orleans has not ended. In July 2016 the Desiree Alliance, a sex-worker led national organization of advocacy groups, held its sixth annual conference, titled "The Sex Worker Rights Movement: Addressing Justice," an event cosponsored by WWAV.[46]

Shannon, too, strikes a resilient pose on the post-Katrina live album. Defiant in the face of hardship, immediately after the mournful "All I Have," he provides a cover of Tom Petty's 1989 rock hit "I Won't Back Down" as the next track, singing: "You can stand me up by the gates of Hell, / I'm gonna stand my ground / and I won't back down. / . . . I'm gonna keep this world from draggin' me down. / I'm gonna stand my ground."

On "Phunkville," the album's closing groove, he sings, "I'm from Phunkville / and we don't allow no standin' still." Interrupted by an out-of-tempo pause, a personal and musical echo of the historical rent left by the disaster in the fabric of New Orleans's history, "Phunkville" gives listeners "a place in my mind / where I fool around with . . . time." Even the lyrics of "All I Have" suggest the possibility of rebirth and rebuilding when the mother tells her daughter, "You're still young and you can start all over again."

Since the release of *A Cabdriver's Blues*, Shannon has continuously returned to themes of inequality and racial and working class empowerment, giving social commentary in such songs as "Wrong People in Charge," "One Thin Dime," and the aforementioned "Charity" on his second album (1997); in "Who Are They?" and "The Last Time I Was Here" on his third, *Spend Some Time with Me* (1999); in his cover of B.B. King's "Why I Sing the Blues" with new verses critical of US politics and our educational system on his fourth, *Memphis in the Morning* (2001); and in "The Reason" and "A Perfect World" on his fifth, *I'm From Phunkville* (2005). Each of these five albums was released before Hurricane Katrina. Only *Live: A Night at Tipitina's* (2007) has been released since. One hopes the despair and loss so powerfully evoked in "All I Have" has not silenced Shannon for good. We need to hear more resistant voices like his, and if the city he both criticized and celebrated in the mid-1990s has largely vanished, replaced by a thin chimera—an even meaner one with an even glitzier tourist economy that has done little to mitigate racial, gender, and social class inequities and sexual exploitation—we can hope to turn back the clock, to fool around, like him, with time. He can help us try. Even in the wake of the flood, his 1995 masterpiece is still very much worth a listen.

Mem Shannon Discography (by release date)

Shannon, Mem. *A Cabdriver's Blues*. Hannibal/Rykodisc HNCD 1387, 1995, compact disc.
Shannon, Mem. *Mem Shannon's 2nd Blues Album*. Hannibal/Rykodisc HNCD 1409, 1997, compact disc.
Shannon, Mem. *Spend Some Time with Me*. Shanachie SHANCD 9013, 1999, compact disc.
Shannon, Mem. *Memphis in the Morning*. Shanachie SHANCD 9031, 2001, compact disc.
Shannon, Mem. *I'm from Phunkville*. Northern Blues Music NBM 0029, 2005, compact disc.
Shannon, Mem. *Live: A Night at Tipitina's*. Northern Blues Music NBM 0041, 2007, compact disc.

Notes

1. Stuart Hall, "Notes on Deconstructing the 'Popular,'" in *People's History and Socialist Theory*, ed. Raphael Samuel (London: Routledge and Kegan Paul, 1981), 227–40.

2. Graeme Turner, *British Cultural Studies: An Introduction*, 3rd ed. (London: Routledge, 2003), 6. For Turner, the examination of popular culture is explicitly political, for it allows us to see "the power relations that constitute this form of everyday life and thus reveal the configurations of interests its construction serves."

3. Mem Shannon, *A Cabdriver's Blues*, Rykodisc HNCD 1387, 1995, compact disc.

4. LeRoi Jones, *Blues People* (New York: William Morrow, 1963).

5. Ben Sidran, *Black Talk*, 2nd ed. (New York: Da Capo, 1981); Frank Kofsky, *Black Nationalism and the Revolution in Music* (New York: Pathfinder, 1970).

6. Lawrence Levine, *Black Culture and Black Consciousness* (Oxford: Oxford University Press, 1977), 239–70 and especially 293–97.

7. Ray Boggs and Carl Pratt, "The Blues Tradition," in *American Media and Mass Culture*, ed. Donald Lazere (Berkeley: University of California Press, 1987), 279–92; George Lipsitz, "Working People's Music," also in *American Media and Mass Culture*, 293–308; Paul Garon, *Blues and the Poetic Spirit* (London: Eddison, 1975; repr., New York: Da Capo, 1979); and Paul Garon and Beth Garon, *Woman With Guitar*, rev. ed. (San Francisco: City Lights Books, 2014).

8. William Barlow, *Looking Up at Down: The Emergence of Blues Culture* (Philadelphia: Temple University Press, 1989), 325.

9. Ted Gioia, *Delta Blues* (New York: Norton, 2008), 24.

10. George Lipsitz, *Time Passages: Collective Memory and Popular Culture* (Minneapolis: University of Minnesota Press, 1990), 235.

11. Lipsitz, *Time Passages*, 238.

12. James Scott, *Domination and the Arts of Resistance: Hidden Transcripts* (New Haven: Yale University Press, 1990).

13. Angela McRobbie, *Postmodernism and Popular Culture* (London: Routledge, 1994), 27.

14. "The Politics of the 'Popular' and Popular Culture," in *Popular Culture and Social Relations*, ed. Tony Bennett, Colin Mercer, and Janet Woollacott (Milton Keynes: Open University Press, 1986), 20. James Smethurst has argued further that popular culture in the United States tends to "use a model of a multiracial community of class interests" and that "people tend to figure class and class identification with the materials at hand," as Shannon certainly does with his in-cab recordings. "Everyday People: Popular Music, Race and the Articulation and Formation of Class Identity in the United States," in *The Resisting Muse: Popular Music and Social Protest*, ed. Ian Peddie (Burlington, VT: Ashgate, 2006), 86.

15. Lipsitz, *Time Passages*, 238.

16. One need not have read David Harvey's *A Brief History of Neoliberalism* (Oxford: Oxford University Press, 2005) or David Graeber's *Debt: The First 5,000 Years* (Brooklyn: Melville House, 2011) to recognize that the relentless push by corporate capitalism over the past half-century to monetize every human relationship, to subject as many human interactions as possible to the forces of "the market," has resulted not only in the collapse of the traditional manufacturing base for labor in this country, but also directly in the valuation of people's worth only in terms of how much money they can command in our economy: their very jobs are defined as worth-less if they are low paying, no matter how essential they may be to the functioning of our culture. By extension, workers themselves are derided and their needs ignored.

17. Studs Terkel, *Working* (New York: Ballantine Books, 1972), 269.

18. Terkel, *Working*, 271.

19. Terkel, *Working*, 272.

20. His parting response to the Bastard is likely rooted in a strategy of deference that Scott warns cannot be read as simple acquiescence or courtesy. See pages 23–28.

21. Naomi Klein, *The Shock Doctrine: The Rise of Disaster Capitalism* (New York: Picador, 2007). In particular, see chapter 20, "Disaster Apartheid: A World of Green Zones and Red Zones," 513–34.

22. Vincanne Adams, *Markets of Sorrow, Labors of Faith: New Orleans in the Wake of Katrina* (Duke University Press, 2013), 112.

23. Klein, *The Shock Doctrine*, 517.

24. Anne Lovell, "Reformers, Preservationists, Patients, and Planners: Embodied Histories and Charitable Populism in the Post-Disaster Controversy over a Public Hospital," in *Hurricane Katrina in Transatlantic Perspective*, ed. Romain Huret and Randy J. Sparks (Baton Rouge: LSU Press, 2014), 100–120.

25. Mem Shannon, *Mem Shannon's 2nd Blues Album*, Hannibal/Rykodisc HNCD 1409, 1997, compact disc.

26. Lovell, "Reformers, Preservationists, Patients, and Planners," 103–4.

27. Lovell, "Reformers, Preservationists, Patients, and Planners," 116.

28. Thomas Jessen Adams, "The Political Economy of Invisibility in 20th-Century New Orleans: Security, Hospitality, and the Post-Disaster City," in Huret and Sparks, *Hurricane Katrina in Transatlantic Perspective*, 127.

29. Thomas Jessen Adams, "The Political Economy of Invisibility," 122.

30. Eric Ishiwata. "'We Are Seeing People We Didn't Know Exist': Katrina and the Neoliberal Erasure of Race," in *The Neoliberal Deluge: Hurricane Katrina, Late Capitalism, and the Remaking of New Orleans*, ed. Cedric Johnson (Minneapolis: University of Minnesota Press, 2011), 33.

31. Thomas Jessen Adams, "The Political Economy of Invisibility," 129.

32. Mem Shannon, *Live: A Night at Tipitina's*, Northern Blues Music NBM 0041, 2007, compact disc. First released as track one on *Spend Some Time with Me*, Shanachie SHANCD 9013, 1999, compact disc.

33. Thomas Jessen Adams, "The Political Economy of Invisibility," 129.

34. Steven Hill, *Raw Deal: How the Uber Economy and Runaway Capitalism Are Screwing American Workers* (New York: St. Martin's Press, 2015), 13.

35. Hill, *Raw Deal*, 38.

36. SCAN is also referred to as "Crime Against Nature by Solicitation" or CANS.

37. Haywood states that some police officers often targeted transgendered persons, whether or not they were caught engaging in solicitation, because of their belief that any African American transgendered person was *ipso facto* a prostitute. See pages 203 and 208.

38. Doreen Piano, "Working the Streets of Post-Katrina New Orleans: An Interview with Deon Haywood, Executive Director, Women with a Vision, Inc," *WSQ: Women Studies Quarterly* 39, nos. 3/4 (Fall/Winter 2011): 208. https://doi-org.ezproxy.library.astate.edu/10.1353/wsq.2011.0061. The introduction to the interview notes that eighty percent of the registrants for sex offender status under the SCAN statute were African American women, compounding its already class-biased enforcement. See pages 202–3.

39. Piano, "Working the Streets," 209.

40. Piano, "Working the Streets," 215.

41. Piano, "Working the Streets," 210.

42. Chris Rose, *1 Dead in Attic: After Katrina* (New York: Simon & Schuster, 2007), 51.

43. This list of former New Orleans educational institutions contains some of the poorest and least effective high schools in the city, ones that served a largely Black student body and that have also been casualties of neoliberal policies applied to K–12 education.

44. Gary Rivlin, *Katrina After the Flood* (New York: Simon and Schuster, 2015), 412.

45. Elisabeth Jandro, "The Regulation of Sex Work and Sex Workers" in *Sex, Sexuality, Law, and (In)justice*, eds. Henry F. Fradella and Jennifer M. Sumner (New York: Routledge, 2016), 234–35. Jandro uses the acronym CANS for the law.

46. Information on both the Desiree Alliance and Women with a Vision, as well as photos from the 2016 conference, could be found at their respective websites and Facebook pages as of August 9, 2016. As of October 2023, WWAV was still led by Deon Haywood. (See wwav-no.org.) However, according to their website (also as of October 2023), the Desiree Alliance has currently suspended its conference activities out of concern these could put its organization and attendees at risk of running afoul of federal FOSTA/SESTA laws passed in 2018. (See desireealliance.org.)

11

SLAVE-BRICKED STREETS AND WOMEN'S WORK
The Practiced Place of Brenda Marie Osbey's New Orleans

Shari Evans

In a 1986 interview with Violet Harrington Bryant, New Orleans poet Brenda Marie Osbey describes her style of writing as "*community of narrative/narrative of community*. The concept I build is a literal community in which people live. I see narrative as [. . .] the talking to and the talking about or through."[1] Osbey's place-based poetry both invokes and practices a "*community of narrative/narrative of community*"[2] that participates in the making of the city through language that creates and calls forth its community. The Poet Laureate of Louisiana from 2005–7, Brenda Marie Osbey has published six collections of poetry centered on her home community of New Orleans. Osbey's poetry is rich with the texture and language of Creole culture, the blended Hoodoo and Catholic religions, and the particularities of the everyday lives and complex histories of the people who inhabit and therefore create her city, and her collections often recreate the "community of narrative/narrative of community"[3] through their structure. For example, Osbey's 1998 collection of poetry, *All Saints*, begins with an "Invocation," a calling into being of the practiced city-space of New Orleans: "The slave ancestors who lie beneath the swamps, inside the / brick of which our / homes, our streets, our churches are made; / who wrought iron into the vèvès that hold together the Old / City and its attachments; / personal gods and ancestors; musicians and street dancers; / Hoodoo saints and their little Catholic cousins . . . / our saints continue to live among us."[4]

The poem that begins the collection invokes and names the slave ancestors, identifies their labor and its manifestation that literally "hold together" the city, and ties them to the personal and cultural practice of religion through individuals, musicians, and street dancers, as well as the worship of gods and ancestors, those Hoodoo and Catholic saints.[5] The reader's voice joins the poem's as they together create a "community of narrative" through Osbey's invocation that calls out layers of interactions: between religions and the collapse of their distinctions as Catholicism is made kin to Hoodooism; between language speakers and their cultures as the French, English, Spanish and Ki-Kongo and Bambara languages together create Creole; and between times as the slave ancestors "beneath the swamps" or "inside the bricks" mingle with the "saints [that] continue to live among us."[6] The slave ancestors' ironwork joins with the invocation and the practice it highlights to collapse the material substance of the city and the continued, daily creation of it together into one community. Thus, both the buildings in the city and narratives about it are equally integral to its continual recreation.

This paper examines Brenda Marie Osbey's narrative poetry through Michel de Certeau's concept of space as a practiced place, suggesting that Osbey's recreated New Orleans is made into a dynamic—and spectral—space through the interplay of women's lived experience and practice, language that is place- and culture-specific and resonant with meaning, and the always-present interaction of history, memory, and legend. Like de Certeau's "walk through the city," Osbey's poetry engages the practice of everyday life "down below"[7] that creates a living space. Crucially, Osbey's language and subject matter engage and remember the intricacies of the traumatic and multilayered past rather than forget or erase it, and thus her writing maintains an ethical practice of place.

Osbey calls forth a New Orleans that is thick with the memory of its layered past and the ghostly spaces left behind. This poetry is decidedly place-bound and space-creating as it grounds multiple layers of history, consciousness, memory, and meaning in such concrete realities as the slave-bricked city streets on which the living and dead walk simultaneously as mythic, historic, and familial figures. As James Baldwin says, language is "the most vivid and crucial key to identity; it reveals the private identity, and connects one with, or divorces one from, the larger, public, or communal identity."[8] Language both carries and transmits history, reveals lived experience, connects to and carries on ritual, and links the personal to the communal as Osbey's invocation links the worship of "personal gods and ancestors" to the everyday practice of "musicians and street dancers."[9] As it details the practices of the everyday, Osbey's poetry also exposes the layers of social, cultural, familial, and individual history that together create a city and make evident the practices that create it—and have been creating it—daily for centuries. The poetry exposes the process of loss and reclamation, of grappling with history and the present, on which every vibrant city-space depends. Osbey's poetry and its practice of an everyday life of the city that joins the present with the past reveals an integrative and communal ethics of place.

In her essay, "Writing Home," Osbey remarks that home is "a set of connections, associations, memories, and sensibilities," marked by kinship between place and people.[10] She says,

> Home, then, is an atlas, a body of maps of constellations of people, and of experiences and relations shared among people, living and dead and yet to be born, with whom one has more in common than can ever adequately be stated. It is an intangible something lodged deep within. It is transmitted through the memory, blood, air, and dust of our people. In the religion, faith, practice, language, history, myth, all converge.[11]

Through "writing home" in her poetry, suffusing it with the practice and experience of religion, faith, language, history, memory, and kinship, Osbey activates these "maps of constellations," joining past to present and future, both transmitting "home" to readers materially and culturally linked to it and ritually creating a bridge for readers distant from it.[12] Her poetry, then, serves as an atlas that connects the maps of the city, its inhabitants, and their experiences through time and place. In particular, by giving voice to the seemingly insignificant or ignored experiences of outsiders and the unacknowledged everyday labor of women, Osbey's poetry remaps the city into a dynamic and multilayered space. Significantly, for Osbey and for this collection, that connection between the past of the slave ancestors and their descendants is active and alive, transmitted through women's work in memory and flesh, and the language and practice of everyday life.

Osbey's city poetry, in its focus on language, history, and lives that have been forgotten or ignored, is positioned as a counter to the cultural amnesia of totalizing nationalist narratives and policies that disenfranchise and dispossess. Critic Minrose Gwin suggests that "cultural memory comes into being through cultural amnesia. [. . .] Such forgetting [of extensive cultural trauma like slavery or genocide] is necessary to the unifying narratives of strong nationalisms. [Yet,] while collective memory is shaped by forgetting, it is also haunted by it."[13] As Gwin notes, there is an ethics of remembering that runs counter to that unifying narrative which depends on forgetting the things that disrupt it. Osbey's narrated city-space, because it holds and remembers trauma, is neither traumatized nor haunted by the forgotten; instead, the past is integrated into and through the present. The readers of Osbey's poetry bump up against this past and must confront their own cultural amnesia in the service of "*community of narrative/narrative of community.*"[14]

Engaging Spectral Space: The "Good Killing Hand"

My term "spectral space" brings together a number of ideas—first, the idea of space articulated by Michel de Certeau, and second, ideas of trauma, memory, and narrative stemming from Toni Morrison's concept of "rememory"[15] and such responses to it as Marianne Hirsch's concept of "postmemory."[16] The city-space of Osbey's New Orleans is spectral because it is activated by living memory, by acknowledged trauma and the practice that ties the living to the dead, by culture that suffuses language and practice, and by an embedded call-and-response that makes each individual, including the reader, both part and whole.

In *The Practice of Everyday Life*, Michel de Certeau argues that lived space eludes the intention, or what architectural theorists call the program, of the built environment. The programmed space of a city, then, is always disrupted by the multiple vantage points of its inhabitants; it is further disrupted by these inhabitants' "ways of operating" in, around, and through built space. The everyday practice of a place, then, can undermine the program of urban planners or the acknowledged narrative of a place.[17] Further, de Certeau makes a distinction between "space" and "place," suggesting that while "place" is a static site with one assigned meaning, space is "a practiced place" in which "vectors of direction, mobility, and time" intersect and rearrange themselves.[18] It is the interplay between enactment and disruption of program that creates the space of a city. Space is dynamic. Further, de Certeau suggests that "A space exists when one takes into consideration vectors of direction, velocities and time variables. Thus space is composed of intersections of mobile elements. It is in a sense actuated by the ensemble of movements deployed within it. . . . [S]*pace is a practiced place.*"[19] This idea of space as a *practiced place,* actuated—carried out in practice—by the intersection of "mobile elements"[20] of time (history, memory, lived and imagined experience) and action (the multiple activities that are located in a particular place), seems particularly potent for such place-based narrative poetry as Osbey's, because while it is always grounded in a particular location, that grounding is activated by the particular lives she describes—the rituals of daily life that make a place a space—and the language she uses. Osbey's use of language echoes the everyday practice of the city and its dwellers she describes.

The space of Osbey's city includes the continued movement between past and present, from the invocation that calls out to slave ancestors, saints and gods, and public performers alike. Its active space includes not only the practice of everyday life but also the traumatic experience of the past. Importantly, while acknowledging the trauma inherent in a city built upon lives and cultures upended by slavery, Osbey's poetry suggests that it is through the everyday practice that connects history to the present that trauma is, if not healed, not forgotten either. Taken in a larger context of African American literary responses to such historic trauma, the spectral space Osbey enacts offers a vivid alternative.

Even though the history and experiences Osbey recounts call forth the collective, historic, and individual traumas of the past, the active remembering that takes place in Osbey's poems is not, for example, the frightening and overpowering traumatic counter to "rememory"[21] that Sethe envisions in Toni Morrison's *Beloved*, in which the traumatic past threatens always to come back and claim new victims, to force them to reexperience a horror which has been experienced already. For Sethe, rememory is something that happens to her, something outside of her own agency, and it is something she attempts to protect her daughter Denver from by isolating and enclosing her in their house, 124. In defining rememory, Sethe tells Denver that the things she experienced exist both in her mind, her "rememory," and "out there in the world"; because of that, at any moment, she might "bump into a rememory that belongs to somebody else" and be changed by it. Sethe warns Denver that "Where I was before I came here, that place is real. It's never going away. . . . The picture is still there and what's more, if you go there—you who never was there—if you go there and stand in the place where it was, it will happen again; it will be there for you, waiting for you."[22] Transmitted through these images, the traumatic "thought pictures" that are held in and bound to a place, rememory is dangerous; it lies in wait, threatening to mark Sethe's daughter as she has herself been marked by the horrors of slavery. Uncontained and unattached, rememory threatens to reenact trauma, perhaps because it has been left behind, intentionally forgotten, but never processed or integrated into the self or the communal identity. As Marianne Hirsch suggests, "rememory" is both "a noun and a verb, a thing and an action. Communicable, shared and permanent, because it is spatial and material; tactile, it underscores the deadly risks of intergenerational transmission."[23] The trauma that Sethe experienced at Sweet Home, that her mother experienced at "the place before that,"[24] is the individual representation of the communal trauma of slavery; it is "not a story to pass on,"[25] and the place(s) in which this harm took place has a tenuous but threatening *hold* on that experience. Yet silence becomes an echo chamber in which trauma reverberates. Trauma is the repetition of experience without understanding, without change—what Trinh T. Minh-ha calls repetition without difference. Sethe's and her mother's silences before hers are attempts to protect their children from the harm of knowing, but the silences themselves create another trauma, the trauma of forgetting, the loss of the past. As Morrison's fiction attests and trauma theory supports, repression or active forgetting does not prevent trauma from reasserting itself, from returning; yet Osbey's poetry counters that the language and stories of her living culture provide space for the remembrance and integration of traumatic experience and history.

Hirsch notes a difference between "what Morrison has called 'rememory' and what [Hirsch] [has] termed 'postmemory'—between, on the one hand, a memory that, communicated through bodily symptoms, becomes a form of repetition and reenactment, and, on the other hand, one that works through indirection and multiple mediation."[26] For Hirsch, postmemory indicates an experience of images that draw out second-generational responses to trauma that are necessarily "mediated not through recollection but through projection, investment, and creation."[27] I would suggest that Osbey provides a space—because it contains both living culture and a ritualized connection to place and the past—in which we can move between the materiality of the places of traumatic reenactment in "rememory" and the "indirection and multiple mediation" of Hirsch's secondary "postmemory."[28] This is a *spectral space* because it is haunting, although not necessarily for the characters within the narratives, who live with and honor their dead; rather, it bears the trace of the unexamined past denied by the larger American culture. In Osbey's poetry, trauma, although also embedded in flesh and transmitted over time, does not threaten to overtake individuals or communities because the practice of the everyday life of the city is also the practice of remembering and honoring the dead and their experiences, a practice which is carried out in the present through women's daily labor of recognizing their ancestor's work.

Osbey summons and takes account of the storied past and its uncomfortable, messy truths through such poems as "The Head of Louis Congo Speaks," in which the severed staked head of Louis Congo (a free Kongo plantation owner and slave-executioner) successively "cries out for water," "weeps," "calls for his medicine," "confesses his sin," "has his little say," and "begs a favor" of the people who have enacted justice.[29] As they bump into a past that many have collectively forgotten, readers are both brought back into it and reminded of their own agency in re-membering the past as a way of enacting the future. Because the past is made up of the messy lives of people, it contains the full range of human experience and emotion, and especially the contradictory impulses and actions that make up individual lives. Louis Congo, in this way, encompasses the messiness of that history; as a free Black slave owner and executioner he is a Judas to other Blacks, driven by his own greed and desire for power and disconnected from and disinterested in the people he enslaves and executes until he is himself executed. Louis Congo, or his head, calls forth the specific identities of the people who have enacted revenge; not slaves, but: "congo, tiamca, colango, matinga / bambara, negro / senegal, creole."[30] This list, repeated in whole and parts throughout the poem, becomes an invocation that replaces Louis Congo in the community he betrayed, a community that was created through common experience with the slave trade. Louis Congo's head calls on commonality as he pleads to be buried whole, with his medicine bag "burne[ed] with [his] ashes,"[31] as well as for understanding: "and it is a good thing to be hated and feared— / is it not— / in a strange man's land."[32] He calls on common religion—an understanding of the significance of his "medicine bag" and its part in making him whole—as well as a common understanding of power and its demands. The poem reminds the reader of the complicated, messy, and horrifying history of slavery as it played out through individual lives and cultures; it pleads with the reader for recognition as Louis Congo pleads for a glass of water, for recognition of his "good killing hand,"[33] of his translation of cultural ideals warped in their transplanting in a new place. The language and narration of Osbey's poetry is this new space—the practice of the past, but with a difference. The story of Louis Congo disrupts national narratives of slavery as a neat dichotomy of passive victim and active oppressor, of Black and white, that doesn't take into account the complexity of either culture or human experience.

Speaking the "Mobile Elements" of the City: Poet as Damballah

For Osbey, the language of New Orleans, itself a mixture of multiple ethnicities and cultures, ties its inhabitants to their common past; further, it creates a community that is distinct, that carries its own history, and, most importantly, that remembers its past. Osbey tells us that "the two greatest sins [she] can think of are forgetting and self-denial";[34] losing language would be both, because language holds the key to the communal and personal past. Poetic language, then, is conscious practice, the activation of an ethical city-space. For Osbey, and New Orleans, this connection between language and culture is even more significant because New Orleans Creole culture is made up of multiple languages, each suggestive of a particular history, worldview, and people. Important to this remembering, then, is the glossary that Osbey's books include, in which she details the place- and culture-specific meanings of terms, individuals, places, and things. Through the interplay between the glossary and the poems, Osbey provides additional layers of meaning for outsider-readers. Osbey's "slave bricks," for example, evoke the physical labor of slaves who manufactured the bricks that line the streets and buildings of the city, but also the magical properties those bricks—because of their ties to the ancestors   hold: her glossary tells us that as "the handiwork of slave ancestors, the bricks are believed to possess spiritual power and are used most frequently to bless and purify the homes of the faithful."[35] Like Louis Congo's head, the forgotten or repressed labor of the slave ancestors speaks in her poetry. These two words, "slave bricks," reverberate with meaning, calling forth remembrance of ancestors, of the slave system that brought them here and set them to work in the brick factory, and of practitioners of a Creole religion that use the bricks to "bless and purify."[36] The "slave . . . bricks"[37] also serve as an invocation, as an act in which the reader is asked to participate, the blessing and purifying of the text, the remembrance of ancestors and their agency. The reader must act in order to know; the glossary and its engagement of the cultural specificity of language, place, and people identify and bridge a distance that can finally make the unfamiliar familiar.

The glossary puts the reader into the position of choosing to know or not know the layered meaning of Osbey's language, to either engage with the dynamic history of language in Osbey's glossary or to ignore it. The reader is made to recognize his/her difference, if the language or its meaning is new, but also invited in as the glossary itself provides a bridge to make the unfamiliar familiar and to engage the reader in acts of remembrance that act like the ironwork that holds the city together. Osbey identifies her "ideal [. . .] audience" as "black, New Orleans, and working-class, because many of [her] characters are exactly that." She explains, "to those people I don't have to explain that language."[38] Yet, the glossary allows Osbey to "explain that language" to her outsider-readers. It not only allows the reader to join with Osbey in creating this space of New Orleans through the practice involved in engaging language, but also bumps against and comes to re-member the communal memory that Osbey has invoked.

Without the glossary, the reader, if not Osbey's "ideal" audience, would only understand one layer of meaning. With the glossary, the evocative language in "slave-bricked," "bamboula," and "misbelieve," and names like "Banganga des Mystères," "Mbempa," and "Papa Legba" takes on the practice of cultural memory.[39] By integrating words that are place-bound in New Orleans, and that recall the specific cultures that created them, Osbey creates layers of narrative, both in each individual poem and in the context of the grouping together of poems in this collection. As spectral space, these layers reveal meaning that is found in the relationship between words, between tellings, in the contact between linguistic units, in the gap between times, in "all the stuff surrounding the stories."[40] The glossary also recognizes language as practice, and practice as choice. In practicing the book, the reader has multiple possibilities: read it through, then refer back to the glossary; search the glossary every time you come up against a name or unfamiliar word; memorize the glossary first, before reading the book. It echoes, then, our relationship to a city through its maps or its written or oral history, or through an intentional not-knowing, a flattening of the city or language to a particular moment in time and one individual's experience. But the reader, like the city-dweller or visitor, must recognize that s/he has made a choice.

Reading *All Saints*, we experience a living language, a creole whose unique identity emerges through the integration of bits and pieces of the multiple languages and cultures it employs. Osbey intersperses words that originated in French, like "mòn" or "pòn" (mother or father, "familiar or contemptuous usage, depending on the context"),[41] "avocat," and "sortilège" ("literally, 'sorcery, magic' [but] in traditional Hoodoo, the ritual of tying knots, symbolizing the binding or sealing of a situation or condition");[42] Spanish and Portuguese, like "aguardiente" ("*agua + ardiente*, literally, 'burning water' [—] cane liquor; . . . manufactured and drunk by the slaves of Louisiana, the Caribbean, Latin America; used also as spiritual offering or libation");[43] Ki-Kongo, like "Banganga des Mystères" ("pl. of *nganga*, ritual expert + Haitian Creole *Mystère*, spirit deity [—] loosely, priests, priestesses, diviners; the Banganga heal with roots, herbs, and charms and venerate the most ancient and highest ranking among the dead") and "Damballah"; and Creole, like "chamy bag" or "paquet d'medecin." [44] The glossary transforms these words into passageways—the "mobile elements"[45] of the Creole city-space Osbey is writing. This is an invocation we choose to understand, or not, but we practice it as we read the words, speak the language. We can traverse the layers of meanings (and cultures) embedded in each word; or we can choose to not know, to instead guess at meanings, to passingly note how "colorful" her language is, and gauge our own understanding by rejecting the offering. The glossary is Osbey's offering to her reader—it is her way of acting as a "Damballah," "that deity who mediates between the worlds of the living and the dead"[46]—navigating the spectral space both between the living and the dead, through her re-membrance and memory, and between insiders and outsiders, those inside and outside of her community.

But the reader has to choose to cross that bridge, to move beyond a sort of limbo of understanding, into a new community. Here is the practice of reading, where readers, too, have to work, have to create a space for a text to move within, have to guess at meanings and understand how words resonate in their own worlds. The practice of reading blurs with Osbey's practice of language as, through her language choice and her glossary, she allows her readers insight into the specificity of cultural and historic meaning and the practice of place. The reader does not become a permanent member of this community, but does get a chance to live within it, to practice it, for a moment, closer to the way its members might, and be reminded of the complexity and multiple meanings that are embedded in everyday words, the meaning that haunts if it is not acknowledged.

The Faubourg as Practiced Place: "Most Anything Can Be Done"

The city and its history loom large in Osbey's poems through intimate portrayals of daily practice. For Osbey, this city space draws on the "the memory, blood, air, and dust of our people. In the religion, faith, practice, language, history, myth" that "all converge" in the transmission of a culture through its practice.[47] In a series of poems about the Old City, the Faubourg or neighborhood, Osbey identifies the multilayered practices of the city space that make it uniquely itself. For example, in the poem "Faubourg," Osbey describes the "city within the larger city" by the activities of its occupants, the women who "walk in pairs and clusters / moving along the slave-bricked streets," women for whom "there is always work to be done."[48] These women have children to be "scolded and sung to," "blues to be sung or heard," and most importantly, "the dead must be mourned and sung over," as they are "chanted or marched" to the tombs that must then be "tended" and "slave bricks crushed and scrubbed across doorways."[49] As the women walk, as they "shift" a "burden" "from an arm to a hip / from the hip to the head" they occupy the past, present, and future of the city-space in the labor they have completed, are engaged in, or will enact.[50] The women of the Faubourg activate and create it through their labor from cradle to grave and beyond. They are active and passive, nurturing and exacting, feel love and loss, and maintain connection across and through generations. The women buy and sell women's labor and its product as well, as they "call out" for wares "to sell or buy or search for at market. / and along the narrow banquettes leading there— / a cook / a seamstress / a day's-work-woman to find or be found."[51] That is, women occupy all space, all spheres. All of this activity illustrates that "most anything can be done in the faubourg," because the women there in fact *do* "most anything"; their rituals and activities of daily life create its space.[52] The layering of past, present, and future activities and meanings are the practice that turns the Faubourg, and the poem, into a space (in de Certeaux's terms), an atlas (in Osbey's). It is a space haunted by the blues that are "sung or heard / above the trees and rooftops / all hours of the day and night" and by the dead who are "mourned and sung over," by the "love to be made / conju to be worked"—that is, by a world that is both spirit and flesh, past and present, simultaneously.[53] And the Faubourg exists because of black women's work, work that has been most often forgotten, suppressed in the name of the gendered narrative of prosperity, and that therefore most needs to be recovered and remembered.

The practice that makes a space occurs over time, and it is the forward and backward movement implied by this temporal component that Osbey's work engages. In the same way de Certeau points out that the practice of a place "on the ground" can be at odds with or elide its intended use, Osbey's "Faubourg" is inscribed by its inhabitants' daily activity which is also connected to and in conversation with the activities of those who came before: What *is* practiced, what *has been* practiced and what *will be* practiced reciprocally link the dead to the living in this and other Osbey poems. The city-space, activated by this practice that links vectors of time, is what they make it. Rather than carrying an ideology into practice, Osbey's poems transform place into space through memory by actuating the city's historical, communal, and individual memory, location, and experience.

The city is the space in which its members link past to present through rituals of mourning and practices of remembering. "Faubourg" describes living women walking, working, and loving and their communal commerce with the recent and ancestral dead. The rituals Osbey calls up, of mourning, singing, and praying "the dead" to "the other side" as well as "chant[ing] and march[ing] [them] to their tombs," indicate the layering of time: both living and dead occupy this space.[54] As Osbey notes in her essay "Writing Home," "[T]radition and faithfulness require that we acknowledge Our Dead in our day-to-day lives. [T]hey remain among us through our own active reverence and remembrance [i.e., ritual]."[55] Mourning and active re-membering, the practice of integrating "Our Dead" into daily life, then, create this particular space. Without them, the Faubourg would be reduced to a static place, its history relegated to the past, its present flattened. Without their labor, the past is lost. By recognizing women's work in remembering, maintaining, and perpetuating, Osbey's Faubourg recenters the city and its culture as women's space maintained by women's labor.

The space of the Faubourg, as in all of Osbey's poems, involves an active re-membering of the past that is always connected to the present and to the future. Osbey carries with her the sense of "home, history, rootedness. [. . .] Nobody who possessed such history could reject it out of hand,"[56] and her poetry bears witness to and participates in this active re-membering that creates the city. In calling forth the women who communally care for both living and dead through the daily rituals of their lives, Osbey pieces together familial, cultural, and personal pasts and futures.

The Urgency of Ethical Practice in "Alberta": "She Cannot Speak to Me Further"

Osbey's poems move us between a sense of the city as a space made up of the intersections of individuals, actions, and history, and a sense of the way the city and its structures are internalized and played out in the lives of individual women and over generations. The city as Osbey envisions it is made up of multiple individuals that hold and practice a specific history and culture, and promise a particular future. As the poem "Faubourg" outlined and invoked the daily practice and work of the women who make the city, the poem "Alberta (Factory Poem / Variation 2)"[57] provides a more intimate look at women's experience of that labor. In "Alberta," the creative work of reimagining/re-membering is doubly evident. The poem, divided into four sections, serves to bear witness to the speaker's grandmother's life, but also to position that life within reverberating communities—with the women with whom Alberta labors, with their men and their children (both those they care for and those they cannot keep), and within a larger society demarcated by the "white mannequins / who would not say *thank you* / for the any number of needles sewn through flesh."[58] Each community leaves its mark on Alberta and the other women, as does the needle "sewn through flesh," and the absent "thank you"; but the women simultaneously leave their mark as well, not only in the garments they sew, but also in the way their "bottoms bore into the long wooden benches / where they squatted gap-kneed more than sat" or "stood all day / wiping the oil from [their] finger[s] / into the blackened wood / of [their] upright atlas machines."[59] The wood bears the trace of the women, reverberates with the lives they've led, regardless of whether or not the "white mannequins" notice. These women "stand and stitch together / collars and lapels / welt pockets to decorate"[60] those mannequins; the clothing itself now reverberates with meaning, bearing silent witness to the lives of the women who made it.

Osbey testifies to both a personal history, represented in the speaker's grandmother Alberta, and a communal history, as Alberta is positioned within a community of similar women, and it also reveals the mark of larger society and its structures in the "white mannequin" who owns, wears, and buys the women's labor as well as in the gendered structure of the factory itself, where the men "worked the mezzanine / the cutting floor above / looked out across the vast crowded floor of women."[61] The men's work above is "men's labor. / calling for a certain daring precision. / and higher paying / affording short breaks [. . .] to take time to look across the crowded floor of women / on the ground floor / manufacturing blues."[62] While the men watch, Alberta works "alongside /women / who stood to stitch men's suits [. . .] to put food on the table / to keep children in school / or a husband home / to avoid the indignity of government 'relief' / to protect a mother or a father / from the old folks' home."[63] The physical labor of their bodies—both the unpaid gendered experiences of menstruation, pregnancy, abortion, and birth; the caretaking of children, spouses, and parents; and their paid labor in the factory—holds the joy and sorrow of their multiple roles and their endurance. They "stood together," "worked together" and "cussed old man solomon" as well as the "cloth [they] stitched" and "the lives it cost [them] to stitch it."[64] Importantly, their suffering is shared and communally expressed.

In their roles as mothers, spouses, daughters, and proud individuals, the multiple lives and intentions woven into the narrative suggest the dynamism of space when these roles are practiced ethically. The place of the factory becomes the space of the poem with descriptions of women eating "bread dry-long-so" from their pockets "because they were given no time for lunch" and "women bleeding through triple-layered toweling" or "standing guard against the door" as another brought on a "quick, violent abortion."[65] While the women labor as workers and as women, the men watch from the floor above in Solomon's factory, a real place that can be called back into presence through Osbey's poetic language. These are the traces of lives stitched into fabric, and worn into wood, and now remembered through the granddaughter's retelling.

At the end of the third of four stanzas in the first section, Alberta speaks: "*all kinds of things i saw and did* she said / *working in a factory of women*."[66] Offsetting the narrative that describes "when my grandmother Alberta was a girl"[67] are Alberta's words that indicate the silences and gaps the narrator is filling in. Like the "most anything" that can be done in the faubourg, or echoing question "what good is any woman's name?" from the poem "Faubourg,"[68] Alberta draws attention to the spectral space of what is left out of the narrative or what can be practiced outside of it and so, like the slave bricks which become sacred powder, can claim the space to remember. It is in the italicized words of Alberta that the reader recognizes the speaker's role in the narrative, as witness, called to imagine, recreate, and honor these silenced women's lives because they are otherwise unremembered, unknown. The factory of women and the women's labor that Alberta participated in are silent and invisible, except in the traces they leave behind in stitch and cloth, in wood, and in story.

The last stanza of Section 1 describes the call-and-response of the women on the factory floor "singing across to one another / lyrics spun out above the hum of motors and needles," who as they sew "tossed out a line / and it would come back / stretched by the heavier voice / of some woman who stood all day. . . ."[69] The call-and-response pattern is repeated as Alberta tosses out a line that the speaker returns, as the poem tosses a line for the reader to return. The stanza ends with Alberta's words: "*is it any wonder* she asks / as if i were to answer / *is it any wonder we sang like that?*" The interspersion of narrative description and Alberta's sparse words is repeated again in the next stanza, with words "offered at a lower register" for no one to hear.[70] Yet the narrator does hear, as the poem itself testifies.

The final section begins with a quote that returns us to Alberta, but also echoes what came before, situating her within the practice of this space of women "manufacturing the blues / for all we were worth." The quotation, however, rather than indicating Alberta's self-narration, instead calls attention to its "manufacture" as well. The women create the blues, the fabric used as they stitch together men's clothes; the women also sing the blues, the narrative of their experience of struggle, loss, endurance, and sensuality that is also a testament to the creative impulse that structures it. Underlying each is the power of the women's labor, their work, and their creativity that structures everything else they do whether or not it is recognized. The last stanza begins, "these are the last words / the words my grandmother alberta / did not say to me."[71] The narrative of Alberta's life has been recreated, reimagined by the speaker (and the poet) in the space of what was unsaid. The active sewing back together of Alberta's lived experience, its manufacture, which the speaker has imagined, is layered with the lives and experiences of her community, and so transforms and integrates the trauma of that experience. It is both *registered* and remembered here, but with a difference.

Yet the poem doesn't end here. Instead, it returns to the images of sewing and marked flesh, the women's work with which it began. Alberta, we are told, "is dead / she cannot speak to me further / of her youth among these women."[72] Alberta can no longer tell her own story, yet the story remains, transmitted to and through the granddaughter, and the reader. Alberta "can no longer hold up at eye level / her slightly yellowed middle finger / sewn through the nail / the smooth even split / where the machine tore flesh and nail."[73] The "smooth even split" in Alberta's nail, the traumatic mark of history and labor on Alberta's flesh, remained as a physical mark of memory while she lived, but more importantly, now that she "is dead and buried / and reduced to ash" what remains is *not* the traumatic mark, or its silence, but the narrator herself, Alberta's "last remaining evidence / the smooth / straight / seam."[74] The traumatic mark, the nail split apart by the stitching together of cloth, is now fully woven into the granddaughter's narrative. The "smooth / straight / seam" that links granddaughter to grandmother stitches together cultural and familial history through Osbey's *community of narrative/narrative of community.*[75]

From the individual and generational perspective of Alberta and her granddaughter to the everyday work of the women of the Faubourg, and through the language and history of the city, Brenda Marie Osbey's New Orleans women, activate and generate a spectral city-space. Osbey invites readers in and engages them through imagery and incantation, while mapping their way through the thickness of language whose meanings are examined in her glossary. In the practice of Osbey's spectral space, the speaker enlivens Alberta's unspoken life through her practices of piecing it back together and continuing it forward. At the end of the poem, the speaker continues the call-and-response ritual, answering her grandmother's last imagined words, connecting back and outward to the women who left their mark in fabric, wood, and relationships. The poem joins together living and dead, past and future, as the poem, too, "toss[es] out a line" "stretched to endurance" to the reader. It is up to the reader—as it was to the speaker, to the poet—to throw the line back.[76]

Notes

1. Violet Harrington Bryan, "An Interview with Brenda Marie Osbey," *Mississippi Quarterly: The Journal of Southern Culture* 40, no. 1 (Winter 1986–87): 43.

2. Bryan, "An Interview with Brenda Marie Osbey," 43.

3. Bryan, "An Interview with Brenda Marie Osbey," 43.

4. Brenda Marie Osbey, *All Saints* (Baton Rouge and London: LSU Press, 1997), ix.

5. Osbey, *All Saints*, ix.

6. Osbey, *All Saints*, ix.

7. Michel de Certeau, *The Practice of Everyday Life*, trans. Steven Rendall (London: University of California Press, 1984), 93.

8. James Baldwin, "If Black English Isn't a Language, Then Tell Me, What Is?" in *The Price of the Ticket: Collected Nonfiction* (New York: St. Martin's Press, 1985), 650.

9. Osbey, *All Saints*, ix.

10. Brenda Marie Osbey, "Writing Home" in *Southern Literary Journal* 50, no. 2 (Spring 2008): 36.

11. Osbey, "Writing Home," 37.

12. Osbey, "Writing Home," 37.

13. Minrose Gwin, "Introduction: Reading History, Memory, and Forgetting" in *Southern Literary Journal* 40, no. 2 (Spring 2008): 6.

14. Bryan, "An Interview with Brenda Marie Osbey," 43.

15. Toni Morrison, *Beloved* (New York: Vintage, 1987), 43.

16. Marianne Hirsch, "Marked by Memory: Feminist Reflections on Trauma and Transmission," in *Extremities: Trauma, Testimony, and Community*, eds. Nancy K. Miller and Jason Tougaw, (Chicago: University of Illinois Press, 2002), 74.

17. de Certeau, *The Practice of Everyday Life*, xiv.

18. de Certeau, *The Practice of Everyday Life*, 117.

19. de Certeau, *The Practice of Everyday Life*, 117.

20. de Certeau, *The Practice of Everyday Life*, 117.

21. Morrison, *Beloved*, 43.

22. Morrison, *Beloved*, 43.

23. Hirsch, "Marked by Memory," 74.

24. Morrison, *Beloved*, 43.

25. Morrison, *Beloved*, 323–24.

26. Hirsch, "Marked by Memory," 73.

27. Hirsch, "Marked by Memory," 8.

28. Hirsch, "Marked by Memory," 8.

29. Osbey, *All Saints*, 98–103.

30. Osbey, *All Saints*, 98.

31. Osbey, *All Saints*, 103.

32. Osbey, *All Saints*, 102.

33. Osbey, *All Saints*, 102.

34. John Lowe, "An Interview with Brenda Marie Osbey," *Southern Review* 30, no. 4 (Autumn 1994):103.

35. Osbey, *All Saints*, 126.

36. Osbey, *All Saints*, 126.

37. Osbey, *All Saints*, 126.

38. Lowe, "An Interview with Brenda Marie Osbey," 96.

39. Osbey, *All Saints*, 123–27.

40. Lowe, "An Interview with Brenda Marie Osbey," 110.

41. Osbey, *All Saints*, 125–26.

42. Osbey, *All Saints*, 126.

43. Osbey, *All Saints*, 123.

44. Osbey, *All Saints*, 123.

45. de Certeau, *The Practice of Everyday Life*, xiv.
46. de Certeau, *The Practice of Everyday Life*, 37, 124.
47. Osbey, "Writing Home," 37.
48. Osbey, *All Saints*, 37–38.
49. Osbey, *All Saints*, 37–38.
50. Osbey, *All Saints*, 37.
51. Osbey, *All Saints*, 37.
52. Osbey, *All Saints*, 38.
53. Osbey, *All Saints*, 37.
54. Osbey, *All Saints*, 37.
55. Osbey, "Writing Home," 37.
56. Osbey, "Writing Home," 41.
57. Osbey, *All Saints*, 15–19.
58. Osbey, *All Saints*, 15.
59. Osbey, *All Saints*, 16.
60. Osbey, *All Saints*, 16.
61. Osbey, *All Saints*, 18.
62. Osbey, *All Saints*, 18.
63. Osbey, *All Saints*, 15.
64. Osbey, *All Saints*, 18.
65. Osbey, *All Saints*, 15–16.
66. Osbey, *All Saints*, 16.
67. Osbey, *All Saints*, 15.
68. Osbey, *All Saints*, 38.
69. Osbey, *All Saints*, 16–17.
70. Osbey, *All Saints*, 18.
71. Osbey, *All Saints*, 19.
72. Osbey, *All Saints*, 19.
73. Osbey, *All Saints*, 19.
74. Osbey, *All Saints*, 19.
75. Bryan, "An Interview with Brenda Marie Osbey," 43.
76. Osbey, *All Saints*, 16–17.

12

DEMYTHOLOGIZING THE
NEW ORLEANS "OCTOROON"
Natasha Trethewey's *Bellocq's Ophelia*

Mary C. Carruth

To my colleague, Joan Wylie Hall

In a 2004 interview, Natasha Trethewey describes the creative process that inspired her ekphrastic poems about E. J. Bellocq's photographs of mixed-race sex workers in Storyville, New Orleans's legal red-light district from 1897 to 1917. Bordered by Basin, Customhouse, Robertson, and St. Louis Streets, Storyville commodified and reproduced the image of New Orleans as "the great Southern Babylon" during the city's transition from what Alecia Long calls "the nation's largest slave market and most permissive port" to "a tourist destination that . . . facilitated indulgence, especially in prostitution and sex across the color line."[1] Trethewey first saw the photographs by E. J. Bellocq, an unconventional commercial photographer who lived in his French Creole family's home not far from Storyville,[2] in a graduate seminar on American material culture. His work depicted the sex-workers as ordinary women, some dressed, some partially clothed or naked, during their leisure time and in domestic spaces. Trethewey felt "immediately struck by the power of the images," recalling: "They were stunning, they were compelling, they were filled with the 'punctums' that Roland Barthes talks about—those little things within a photograph that often will draw you out of the immediate action of the photograph to contemplate all that is behind it or outside it."[3] Although at the time, Trethewey was in search of a poetic persona through whom she could explore her own biracialism, she assumed that the light-skinned women in the photographs were "white."[4] Not until her subsequent research informed her that Bellocq took photographs in many brothels, including Mahogany Hall, a house of "octoroons" or "quadroons," ("whites" with "one-eighth" or "one-fourth" African ancestry, respectively), did Trethewey realize that the subjects in the pictures were not "white" but could pass as "white," as she herself did, sometimes intentionally, sometimes not.[5] Her research had identified the faded plush wallpaper in some of these photographs as that of Mahogany Hall, increasing the likelihood that these women were mixed race.[6] As Trethewey explains, "That is the sort of luminous detail I latched on to and said, 'Ah, this is a way to investigate that liminal space of appearing to be one thing to people on the outside and having an inside that's different, something that people can't see.'"[7]

Trethewey's experience of this "liminal space" is the effect of socially constructed binaries that uphold color, class, and gendered hierarchies in American cultures—of presumed contradictions between identity and appearance, "blackness" and "whiteness," "harlotry" and "ladyhood." As historian Jessica Adams observes, the gendered binaries defining "good" or "bad women" were beginning to be tested in turn-of-the-twentieth-century New Orleans when "the growing resemblance between the appearance and behavior of prostitutes [who accompanied men to fashionable events] and that of respectable women was alarming."[8] Thus Adams suggests that Bellocq's photographs "both acknowledged a connection between prostitutes and 'normal women' and revalenced it."[9]

At the same time that Bellocq's photographs call into question these fictions of gender, they also unmask the fictions of race. The racial classifications prominent in the early twentieth-century US South, which defined a person having one African American ancestor as "colored," emerged from the social processes of slavery, colonization, and immigration.[10] These taxonomies, as Natasha Trethewey indicates, were "a form of knowledge production that subjugated peoples," and part of her cultural work is to understand how they still influence the perceptions and treatment of peoples globally.[11] One of the US promulgators of this essentialist, pseudoscientific notion of race is Thomas Jefferson, who had a lifelong relationship with his "octoroon" slave, Sally Hemings, (the much younger half-sister of his wife, Martha), with whom he fathered six children.[12] In a letter to Francis Gray on March 4, 1815, Jefferson includes a "calculus of color, a "tidy mathematical formula to define the race and the place of the quadroon."[13] As Emily Clark observes, "the complicated, messy identity and status of Sally Hemings were tamed by the comforting discipline of symbolic logic."[14] Yet Jefferson's algebra was not only a psychological defense against the incongruities in his personal life but also "one of a range of symbolic strategies Americans deployed in response to racial anxieties magnified by the Haitian Revolution," which threatened a racial reordering of the Atlantic world.[15] Besides his abstract formula, the social construction of the American quadroon served a similar role in allaying racial fears: "Both were equally fanciful reductions of a complex reality."[16]

In the US South in the late 1800s, as Grace Elizabeth Hale suggests, "the figure of the mulatto became much more threatening" to white southerners in an "increasingly anonymous world," made possible by modern transportation, such as railways; as a result, "visible cues [clothing and speech] became increasingly important as markers of identity, as ways to categorize others."[17] Thus, "segregation made racial identity visible in a rational and systematic way," for it "replaced the need to know others personally in order to categorize them."[18] Not coincidentally, one year before the creation of Storyville in New Orleans, the Supreme Court had decided the *Plessy v. Ferguson* case, upholding Louisiana's 1890 Separate Car Act and setting precedents for the Jim Crow policy of "separate but equal." In fact, Homer Plessy's act of civil disobedience—his successful passing as "white" in a rail car of the East Louisiana Railway until he identified himself as "colored" to the conductor—undermined the notion of stable racial categories that Justice Henry Billings Brown assumed in his decision. As Emily Epstein Landau speculates, "the notion of 'invisible' blackness presented a frightening specter of race despoliation to whites" and to defend against fears, observers assumed that "blood 'would out'"—that they could detect someone with African ancestry, no matter how inscrutable.[19] Natasha Trethewey dramatizes this specular basis of "race" and its dehumanizing effects in a poem titled "August 1911" in *Bellocq's Ophelia*. Trethewey's fictional narrator, Ophelia (named after Shakespeare's character), describes how customers turn her and other sex workers into a "spectacle: black women / with white skin, exotic curiosities."[20] As if such mixed-race women did not exist in the North, Ophelia notes that "We are no surprise to the locals, though / visitors from the North make a great fuss."[21] When a man with a monocle inspects Ophelia's face "to find the hint/that would betray [her], make [her] worth / the fee," she "look[s] away from [her] reflection—small distorted—in his lens."[22] In the context of sex work in Storyville,

Landau explains, "the marketing of miscegenation . . . relied on the notion that blood would out through sex at the appropriate moment, fueling the special attraction toward so-called octoroons."[23] As Malin Pereira points out, the social construction of the "octoroon" embodied "the two most highly prized qualities in a woman of that time and place, white aesthetic norms of beauty and black exotic sexuality."[24] This patriarchal ideal developed from an antebellum racialized sexual morality that allowed the master to satisfy his desires with a presumably licentious "black" slave while his "white" wife remained on a pedestal as a passionless "true woman."

One of Bellocq's photographs—of a naked woman lying on a wicker divan, surrounded by flowers on a pillow and the carpet—reminded Trethewey of Millais's Pre-Raphaelite painting of the drowning Ophelia. After her seminar ended, she rushed to the library, found the collection of Bellocq's photographs[25] and inspired, began to draft the title poem of *Bellocq's Ophelia*:

> At the time, I think I had been searching for a way to write about my own experience growing up biracial in the Deep South, the experience of often being looked at a lot when I was a child, and being asked over and over what are you, and always feeling under the gaze of some scrutiny. And so . . . when I saw the woman in the photograph and learned . . . that there were these Octoroon Houses where the exotic curiosities of women who looked very white were more valuable to customers because they weren't, it seemed to me a perfect voice through whom to contemplate my own experience growing up biracial.[26]

While Bellocq's photographs served as the genesis of *Bellocq's Ophelia*, Trethewey explains she could not have developed her persona without immersing herself in a sensory experience of New Orleans, her mother's birthplace and a city she visited often in her childhood because her father, the late poet Eric Trethewey, lived there. In reply to interviewer Ana-Maurine Lara's observation about "how our bodies carry memories," Trethewey reflects: "Well, I knew I had to create Ophelia as if I was remembering. As much as I used photographs in that project . . . , I spent a lot of time in New Orleans. . . . growing up, so it felt like a landscape that was part of my development. But I went back to be in it in a different way, to take notice of things that I might not have taken note of with as much intent, and it was only that way that I could begin to imagine a persona: Ophelia."[27]

As Trethewey's reflections reveal, her invention of Ophelia coincided with the growth of her poetic voice and her continual negotiation of the cultural objectification of her own mixed-race identity and body. Born of a white Canadian father, Eric Trethewey, and an African American mother, Gwendolyn Ann Turnbough, in 1966, a year before the Supreme Court's dismissal of state "miscegenation" laws in *Loving v. Virginia*, Trethewey feels a sense of "psychological exile." She attributes this alienation to "the duality of the mixed-race body and. . . . the laws of the state of Mississippi, the laws of the US that rendered a person like [her] illegitimate, and . . . [her] parents as lawbreakers."[28] Part of Trethewey's individual and cultural work is "to reclaim this place that [she] had been constantly exiled from . . . through language."[29] In *Bellocq's Ophelia*, Trethewey exposes and interrogates the nostalgic myth of the New Orleans "octoroon," which served to fulfill the post–Civil War fantasies of "white" men longing to regain—or gain for the first time—mastery of mixed-race women's bodies. Contrary to the myth's claims, taboo interracial sex and race-mixing were not just localized to New Orleans, marking its supposed exceptionality as a foreign city, but existed in all parts of the United States and indeed the Americas.

Trethewey's techniques for revisioning the Storyville photographs include foregrounding the gazes and animating the still bodies of the subjects; and collapsing oppositions between reader and poem, spectator and image, the present and the past, and spatial boundaries. Most central strategy is the activation of Ophelia's voice, subjectivity, and gaze. Through Ophelia's self-consciousness and ironic tone, Trethewey denaturalizes the raced, classed, and gendered meanings ascribed to the "octoroon." By deconstructing the image of the "octoroon," she strips away at an enduring metaphor of New Orleans, one that turned the city into "a perpetual colonial space in the national imagination" so that America could deny its own "interracial population and practices."[30]

The title poem of *Bellocq's Ophelia* develops the contrast between Shakespeare's passive Ophelia in *Hamlet* and Trethewey's Ophelia, introducing the theme of self-discovery and its central metaphors of gaining a gaze and coming to voice. This poem also introduces Trethewey's interest in the act of framing and directing the reader's and viewer's gaze to knowledge outside the frame. In Millais's painting, Trethewey says, Ophelia "dies face-up, / eyes and mouth open as if caught in the gasp / of her last word or breath. . . ." Her "final gaze aims skyward, her palms curling open / as if she's just said, *Take me*."[31] In contrast, the "other Ophelia, nameless inmate in Storyville" poses naked for Bellocq, "there for the taking / But in her face, a dare": "Staring into the camera, she seems to pull / all movement from her slender limbs / and hold it in her heavy-lidded eyes. / Her body limp as dead Ophelia's, / her lips poised to open, to speak."[32]

This other Ophelia's daring gaze back at the camera suggests the reversal of the gendered and raced-looking relations in early twentieth-century Storyville, the possibility of the silent sexualized object becoming a speaking and mobile subject—across the time and space that divide Bellocq and early twentieth-century viewers from contemporary readers and viewers.

In less skilled hands than Trethewey's, poetic representations of Storyville, itself a nostalgic replica of antebellum racialized sexual mores, might inadvertently reinscribe the very nostalgia they intend to critique. Jessica Adams notes the literal translation of the word "nostalgia" is "wounds of returning."[33] While "nostalgia" has evolved to denote "a longing to return to a past that probably never existed and to places that have changed irrevocably," its literal meaning suggests "that the past itself may return, inflicting new wounds."[34] Such a potentially harmful return of the past materialized at the end of the nineteenth century when "the southern plantation was being renewed as myth" in popular and consumer culture.[35] As Adams concludes, "the dynamics of ownership associated with and summed up by the plantation financed . . . the successes of Storyville's octoroon brothels."[36] To enter imaginatively this nostalgic myth without reinscribing it, Trethewey practices a politics of black feminist location, theorized by bell hooks. Trethewey's remembering is not "nostalgia, that longing for something to be as it once was, a kind of useless act" but "a politicization of memory," which "serves to illuminate and transform the present."[37] As William M. Ramsey expresses it, Trethewey's "historical inquiry is "an excavation of pliable materials [like Bellocq's photos] for revised narratives."[38]

Trethewey explains her technique of animating the subjects in photographs as it relates to her first collection, *Domestic Work* (2000). The opening poem, "Gesture of A Woman In-Process," is based on a 1902 picture by white photographer Clifton Johnson, which shows one of two African American launderers refusing to stay still for the shoot. One of her hands makes a motion with her apron, turning it into "a swirl of white in the center of the photograph"; her gesture conveys to Trethewey "the way people will not simply be confined to the frames into which we might put them, historically or in memory, and that, indeed, her gesture of continual movement enables her to resist being trapped in that particular historical framework."[39] Trethewey uses similar techniques in "Photograph of a Bawd Drinking Raleigh Rye," the last poem in Part II of *Bellocq's Ophelia* and one of the three poems in the book written in Trethewey's voice. The sex-worker's glass of rye resists stasis as she appears to invite the reader to become implicated as viewer in the gaze: "The glass in her hand is the only thing moving— / too fast for the camera—caught in a blur of motion. / She raises it toasting, perhaps, the viewer you become / taking her in—. . . ."[40]

The woman's "twirling her shot glass," as Trethewey points out, is one of Barthes's punctums because "she refuse[s] to hold still and thus the blur that occurs . . . reminds us that this is not simply a moment that can be frozen and captured but that it is representative of an ongoing sequence of events. The photograph's just one frame, like in a film."[41] Such subjects of photography exert their agency, and as Trethewey explains, "insist on inserting themselves into our contemporary imagination."[42] The woman's toast appears intended for Bellocq and the viewer; by extension, her lifted glass invites Trethewey's reader into voyeurism. Addressing this reader/viewer as "you," Trethewey then traces the gaze taking in the woman's image: "your eyes starting low, at her feet, and following those striped stockings like roads, / traveling the length of her calves and thighs."[43] The spectacle widens to include commodified images of women: "Even the bottle of rye is a woman's slender torso and round hips."[44] In short, the scene reiterates the idea of woman as product to be consumed. In the last lines, the poet directly confronts the contemporary reader/voyeur in a Whitmanesque gesture, dissolving both temporal and spatial boundaries: "—And there on the surface of it all, a thumb— / print—perhaps yours? It's easy to see this is all about desire, / how it recurs—each time you look, it's the same moment, / the hands of the clock still locked at high noon."[45]

Up until the last three lines, this poem could be misread as a nostalgic playful portrait of a Storyville prostitute. However, Trethewey's direct address of contemporary readers politicizes memory in order to illuminate and transform the present moment. She compels them to acknowledge their own implication in the objectification of biracial women as eroticized others and as Katherine Henninger says, "their continuance of voyeuristic traditions that represent these women."[46]

The most prominent technique Trethewey implements for preventing a nostalgic reinscription of the myth of the "octoroon" is creating an interiority

Demythologizing the "Octoroon": Trethewey's *Bellocq's Ophelia*   205

in her persona. Ophelia uses wit and irony to unveil the arbitrariness of racial definitions even as she commodifies her mixed-race body to increase her "swelling purse."[47] What Trethewey calls the "format of [Ophelia's] self-discovery"[48] is in the form of the narrator's letters and diaries, private genres enabling her to test her voice and inscribe her growing identity. Interpreting *Bellocq's Ophelia* as a mixed-race identity project, Malin Pereira suggests that a "kunstlerroman," or "artist-novel plot" overtakes a Pygmalion plot in these poems. In the former, "the biracial woman's complex interiority develops and finds expression as she becomes an artist of her own making, and lives"; in the latter, "the biracial woman is rendered by [a] white male master as an aesthetic object, white outside and black inside, which culminates in her literal or figurative death."[49]

Part I features a single poem, "Letter Poem," which Ophelia addresses to her beloved teacher, Constance Wright, in Oakvale, Mississippi. She recounts her migration to New Orleans and her travails in trying to pass as "white" in order to secure respectable employment commensurate with her hard-earned literacy. Donning class markers, she hides her brown hands in "lace gloves," crocheted by Constance and speaks "plain English."[50] As segregation is solidifying during this period, her racial identity, however, is defined not by her performance, but by the intrusive gaze of the white dominant culture: ". . . I walk these streets / a white woman, or so I think, until I catch the eyes / of some stranger upon me and I must lower mine, *a negress* again."[51] Ophelia's look down exemplifies how, according to Trethewey, "we are enthralled to the language that seeks to name us; thus "mulatto," "quadroon," "octoroon," "sambo," "albino"[52]—the dehumanizing categories that the poet seeks to deconstruct. Finally, Ophelia discloses to Constance that—hungry and evicted from her hotel—she is recruited by an "elegant businesswoman," Countess P—,[53] a character based on the historical "octoroon" Countess Willie V. Piazza, proprietor of a Basin street brothel.

Part II then opens with "Countess P—'s Advice for Girls," a lightly satirical dramatic monologue. Trethewey exposes the entrepreneurship and capitalistic motives behind Countess P's nostalgic recreation of the myth of the "octoroon." The madam exploits the burgeoning mass culture of the time to replicate a "high-class" mansion and teaches novices like Ophelia the art of appealing to her presumably higher-class clients. The madam admonishes: "Look, this is a high-class house—polished / mahogany, potted ferns, rugs two inches thick. / The mirrored parlor multiplies everything—"[54]

The poet structures the monologue as a series of tercets containing Countess P—'s imperatives to her "new girls": "Empty your thoughts—think, if you do, only of your swelling purse"; "hold still as if you sit for a painting"; "see yourself in his eyes"; "wait to be asked to speak"; "become what you must" and "let him see whatever he needs"; "train yourself not to look back."[55]

Part II includes fourteen Storyville letters in free verse. These, as Trethewey explains, are "an attempt to show [Ophelia's] constantly changing self because they are written in different stanzas and lines and the forms are different."[56] Ophelia's first letter from Storyville details her being auctioned off "as a new-comer / to the house—as yet untouched," though the Countess knows of her past sexual harassment and assault in Mississippi.[57] A parody of the pre–Civil War "octoroon" balls in New Orleans,[58] the cultural vestiges of slavery, Ophelia's performance includes her recitation of poetry and her posing in a *Tableau vivant*, a "living picture," where she remains silent and motionless, according to the Countess's cues. Her presumed cultivation implies "a more dignified / birth and thus a tragic occasion for [her] arrival / at [the] house,"[59] caricaturing the stock figure of the tragic mulatta. In the last two stanzas, Trethewey gives Ophelia a self-reflexivity, unmasking the fictions of race in her character's sarcasm toward the charade in which she participates. In this initiation rite, the Countess renames Ophelia: ". . . She calls me Violet now— / a common name here in Storyville—except / that I am the *African Violet* for the promise / of that wild continent hidden beneath my white skin. . . ."[60]

Trethewey again highlights her persona's self-awareness and wit in "February 1911." Ophelia describes fellow sex-workers like herself, "of a country sort, kindly / and plain," who "like, too, / the perfumed soaps and fine silk gowns we wear in the evenings."[61] Yet, perhaps fooled by the very illusion she impersonates, she criticizes them for not wearing their "silk wrappers" during the day but "their underclothes about the house,"[62] in other words, for not passing as higher class during their off hours. Admitting to her own class aspirations, she recalls telling them harshly, "*You are what you look like.*" In this ironic line, Trethewey complicates the gaze, including class as a category with gender and race in looking-relations. As Ophelia realizes that her accusation is false in terms of the women's presumed essential "race," though true in terms of class markers of respectability, she exposes the absurdity of gender and racial classifications: "—I bit down hard on my tongue at the sight / of their faces—fair as magnolias, pale as wax— / though all of us bawds in this fancy *colored* house."[63]

Trethewey's play on the word "fancy" suggests the social fabrication of the categories "colored" and "octoroon" as well as the consumer cultural construction of the Storyville brothels. Similarly, her use of the gendered, classed, and raced clichés "fair as magnolias, pale as wax" suggests the constructed nature of "whiteness."

The poem dated "March 1911" first describes Bellocq, who purchases time only to photograph Ophelia. His camera delineates her white skin, making her a "reversed silhouette / against the black backdrop. . . ."[64] As she "suffer[s] the distant eye he trains on [her]," she recalls picking-time in Mississippi where as an African American field hand, she would "sink and disappear" in "a sea of cotton, / white as oblivion."[65] Escaped from this anonymous labor and ready for self-definition, albeit through Bellocq's eye, she concludes: ". . . Now I face the camera, wait / for the photograph to show me who I am."[66]

Not until she purchases a Kodak and becomes Bellocq's apprentice, however, does Ophelia begin to feel the power of her own gaze—to direct the lens at "a dream of her own making."[67] As Ophelia assumes agency, her inner "blackness" becomes more visible to her than her outer "whiteness," turning around "the whole world." In the description of Ophelia's skin color, Trethewey plays on the word "pitch," an allusion to the coal-based paste that minstrels painted on their white faces and bodies. This image of the "inside out" underscores the performativity of Ophelia's mixed race and her discovery of her own agency and ability to control the gaze: ". . . In the negative / the whole world reverses, my black dress turned / white, my skin blackened to pitch. *Inside out,* / I said, thinking of what I've tried to hide."[68]

She discovers "the way the camera can "dissect / the body, render it reflecting light / or gathering darkness—"[69] The dominant white gaze cannot define the body's colors and shadings, but an individual's vision, realized by a still new, magical invention. The camera "can also make flesh glow / as if the soul's been caught / shimmering just beneath the skin."[70] Ophelia's "recognition of her artistic destiny—the heart of the *kunstlerroman* plot"—occurs, as Malin Pereira points out, "in her seeking to use [the camera] to express the soul just beneath the skin, just beneath the specular basis of racial categorization."[71] For the subject of her own photography, Ophelia realizes she is "drawn to what shines"; her camera offers her "the glittering hope of alchemy."[72] Yet, the camera cannot always truly capture an image. When Ophelia tries to "capture" a red bird, it refuses entrapment in time and space, "lifting in flight, a vivid blur,"[73] like the sex worker's moving glass in "Photograph of a Bawd

Drinking Raleigh Rye." Perhaps the bird foreshadows Ophelia's own eventual escape from restrictive frames.

By the end of Part II, the poem, "—Postcard, en route westward," marks Ophelia's progress toward imminent transformation. The poem is a renga, a series of linked haiku stanzas capturing Ophelia's and the speaker's trip westward. Anticipating spring, the now mobile speaker describes her own metaphoric shedding of skins in the upcoming change in seasons: we are "shedding / our coats, the gray husk / of winter," and she feels "what trees must—budding, green sheaths splitting—skin/that no longer fits."[74]

After this transitional poem, Part III presents Ophelia's diary entries, ten unrhymed sonnets. Here Trethewey tells the same story again, subverting her own inclination to be linear, so that the narrative of Ophelia's year and a half in the brothel circles back in on itself.[75] Trethewey chose the form of "very uniform fourteen lines" to suggest the beginning of a stable sense of self, but not "a grand authentic self," since in a postmodern way, she believes Ophelia is "constantly changing."[76] In the sonnet "(Self) Portrait," photographer Ophelia is waiting to get the best shot of a train departing from a station as she herself waits to leave. Disrupting her concentration is her memory of leaving her mother: "The first time I tried this shot / I thought of my mother shrinking against / the horizon—so distracted, I looked into / a capped lens, saw only my own clear eye."[77]

Because Ophelia leaves the lens's cover on, what she sees when she looks into the camera is the reflection of her own eye, what Trethewey says is "a metaphor for the eye being turned inward to the self."[78] At this moment, Trethewey explains, "Ophelia begins to have a little more sense of herself so that she can look inward and not always through someone else."[79] That the word "self" is in parentheses in this sonnet suggests the randomness of Ophelia's arrival at a sense of self, and the self's tentativeness. This parenthetical self disallows the idea of an essential, core, or "authentic" identity in favor of an open-ended and postmodern notion of self. As Malin Pereira adds: "Such an emphasis on an in-process, never stagnant or fixed self should remind us of mixed-race identity, which . . . is fluid and context-specific, breaking previous frames of racial categorization through being in-process."[80]

Trethewey forestalls a sense of resolution at this point. Ophelia possesses only the potential for creating an alternative vision, just as in the title poem, her lips are only "poised to open, to speak."[81] As Katherine Henninger concludes, Trethewey emphasizes Ophelia's "creative initiative" more than any

Demythologizing the "Octoroon": Trethewey's *Bellocq's Ophelia*

"truth" her art might capture; the new reality presented in *Bellocq's Ophelia* is a "postsouthern one . . . in consciousness."[82]

The final poem, "Vignette," is written in the poet's voice and ends with Ophelia's leave-taking. Ophelia is posing for Bellocq outside the brothel. Sitting in a chair in front of Bellocq's "black scrim," she "wears / white, a rhinestone choker, fur, / her dark crown of hair—an elegant image, / one she might send to her mother."[83] Bellocq waits "for the right moment, a look on her face / to keep in a gilded frame, the ornate box / he'll put her in."[84] As she poses, a fetish, the woman stops listening to Bellocq's chatter about a circus coming to town and even forgets he is present. Instead she becomes absorbed in a childhood memory of a contortionist in a sideshow, whose strained and aching body reminds her of her own: ". . . This is how / Bellocq takes her, her brow furrowed / as she looks out to the left, past all of them. / Imagine her a moment later—after / the flash, blinded—stepping out / of the frame, wide-eyed, into her life."[85]

Here Trethewey engages multiple gazes—Bellocq's, Ophelia's, and the reader's. Then she ends *Bellocq's Ophelia* with a command to the reader "to imagine" Ophelia stepping out of Bellocq's and her book's frames. Ophelia rejects stasis and entrapment by the camera and the poem, like the red bird she tried to photograph. She leaves behind the fantasy of the "octoroon" and enters her life, by implication, in contemporary time and space. "Vignette" is the only other poem, besides "Photograph of a Bawd Drinking Raleigh," in which Trethewey directly addresses the reader. In "Photograph" she holds the reader accountable for voyeurism and the continued erotic othering of mixed-race women. In "Vignette" she inspires the reader to visualize Ophelia's departure—in other words, to imagine a different set of schemas from the racial, class, and gender ideologies that undergird fixed power- and looking-relations. Like Bellocq, Ophelia, and Trethewey herself, the reader may become a creator of a new reality.

Notes

1. Long, Alecia P. *The Great Southern Babylon: Sex, Race, and Respectability in New Orleans: 1865–1920* (Baton Rouge: LSU Press, 2004), 1.

2. See Rex Rose, "The Last Days of Ernest J. Bellocq," *Exquisite Corpse: A Journal of Letters and Life* no. 10 (Fall/Winter 2001–2002), http://www.corpse.org/archives/issue_10/gallery/bellocq/index.htm.

3. Charles Rowell, "Inscriptive Restorations: An Interview with Natasha Trethewey." *Callaloo* 27, no. 4 (Fall 2004): 1028. DOI: 10. 1353CAL.2004.3181.

4. David Haney, "A Conversation with Natasha Trethewey," *Cold Mountain Review* 33, no.1 (Fall 2004): 19–34. Rpt. In *Conversations with Natasha Trethewey*, ed. Joan Wylie Hall (Jackson: University Press of Mississippi, 2013), 22.

5. Haney, "A Conversation," 22.

6. Jessica Adams, *Wounds of Returning: Race, Memory, and Property on the Postslavery Plantation* (Chapel Hill: University of North Carolina Press, 2007): 52.

7. Adams, *Wounds of Returning*, 52.

8. Adams, *Wounds of Returning*, 51–52.

9. Adams, *Wounds of Returning*, 51–52.

10. See Michael Omi and Howard Winant, *Racial Formation in the United States*, 3rd ed. (New York: Routledge, 2015).

11. Daniel Cross Turner, "Southern Crossings: An Interview with Natasha Trethewey," *Waccamaw: A Journal of Contemporary Literature*, no. 12 (Fall 2013): 10. http://archived.waccamawjournal.com/pages.php?x=324.

12. See Annette Gordon-Reed, *The Hemingses of Monticello: An American Family*, 2nd ed. (New York: W. W. Norton, 2009).

13. Emily Clark, *The Strange History of the American Quadroon*, (Chapel Hill: University of North Carolina Press, 2013), 2.

14. Clark, *The Strange History of the American Quadroon*, 2.

15. Clark, *The Strange History of the American Quadroon*, 5.

16. Clark, *The Strange History of the American Quadroon*, 5.

17. Grace Elizabeth Hale, *Making Whiteness: the Culture of Segregation in the South, 1890–1940* (New York: Vintage Books, 1998), 128–29.

18. Hale, *Making Whiteness*, 130.

19. Emily Epstein Landau, *Spectacular Wickedness: Sex, Race, and Memory in Storyville, New Orleans* (Baton Rouge: LSU Press, 2013), 138.

20. Natasha Trethewey, *Bellocq's Ophelia*, (St. Paul, MN: Graywolf Press, 2002), 26.

21. Trethewey, *Bellocq's Ophelia*, 26.

22. Trethewey, *Bellocq's Ophelia*, 26.

23. Landau, *Spectacular Wickedness*, 138.

24. Malin Pereira, "Re-reading Natasha Trethewey through Mixed Race Studies," *The Southern Quarterly* 50, no. 4 (Summer 2013): 1043. *ProQuest*. https://www.proquest.com /scholarly-journals/re-reading-trethewey-through-mixed-race-studies/docview/1464666751 /se-2.

25. See Lee Friedlander and John Szarkowski, *Storyville Portraits: Photographs from the New Orleans Red-Light District, Circa 1912, E.J. Bellocq* (New York: Museum of Modern Art, 1970).

26. Steve Everett, Natasha Trethewey, and Rosemarie McGee, "Emory University Creativity Conversations," 4. http://creativity.emory.edu/documents/creativity-convo -transcripts/2008/Everett_Trethewey_transcript.pdf.

27. Ana-Marine Lara, "Interview with Natasha Trethewey," in *Conversations with Natasha Trethewey*, ed. Joan Wylie Hall (Jackson: University Press of Mississippi, 2013), 126–35.

28. Lara, "Interview," 132.

29. Lara, "Interview," 133.

30. Clark, *The Strange History*, 9.

31. Trethewey, *Bellocq's Ophelia*, 3.

32. Trethewey, *Bellocq's Ophelia*, 3.

Demythologizing the "Octoroon": Trethewey's *Bellocq's Ophelia*

33. Adams, *Wounds of Returning*, 5.

34. Adams, *Wounds of Returning*, 5.

35. Adams, *Wounds of Returning*, 21.

36. Adams, *Wounds of Returning*, 10.

37. bell hooks, *Yearning: Race, Gender, and Cultural Politics* (Boston, MA: South End Press, 1990), 205. Thadious M. Davis connects hooks's theory to Trethewey's remembering in *Southscapes: Geographies of Race, Region, and Literature* (Chapel Hill: University of North Carolina Press, 2011), 60.

38. William M. Ramsey, "Terrance Hayes and Natasha Trethewey: Contemporary Black Chroniclers of the Imagined South," *Southern Literary Journal* 44, no. 2 (Spring 2012): 123. https://doi.org/10.1353/slj.2012.0009.

39. Rowell, "Inscriptive Restorations," 1024.

40. Trethewey, *Bellocq's Ophelia*, 34.

41. Haney, "A Conversation," 19.

42. Haney, "A Conversation," 20.

43. Trethewey, *Bellocq's Ophelia*, 34.

44. Trethewey, *Bellocq's Ophelia*, 34.

45. Trethewey, *Bellocq's Ophelia*, 34.

46. Katherine Henninger, *Ordering the Façade: Photography and Contemporary Southern Women's Writing* (Chapel Hill: University of North Carolina Press, 2007), 171.

47. Trethewey, *Bellocq's Ophelia*. 11.

48. Everett, "Emory University," 4.

49. Pereira, "Re-reading Natasha Trethewey," 139.

50. Trethewey, *Bellocq's Ophelia*, 7.

51. Trethewey, *Bellocq's Ophelia*, 7.

52. Lisa Devries, "Because of Blood: Natasha Trethewey's Historical Memory," in *Conversations with Natasha Trethewey*, ed. Joan Wylie Hall (Jackson: University Press of Mississippi, 2013), 106–12.

53. Trethewey, *Bellocq's Ophelia*, 11.

54. Trethewey, *Bellocq's Ophelia*, 11.

55. Trethewey, *Bellocq's Ophelia*, 11.

56. Haney, "A Conversation," 23.

57. Trethewey, *Bellocq's Ophelia*, 11.

58. See Clark, *The Strange History*, 97–131.

59. Trethewey, *Bellocq's Ophelia*, 11.

60. Trethewey, *Bellocq's Ophelia*, 11.

61. Trethewey, *Bellocq's Ophelia*, 17.

62. Trethewey, *Bellocq's Ophelia*, 17.

63. Trethewey, *Bellocq's Ophelia*, 17.

64. Trethewey, *Bellocq's Ophelia*, 21.

65. Trethewey, *Bellocq's Ophelia*, 21.

66. Trethewey, *Bellocq's Ophelia*, 21.

67. Trethewey, *Bellocq's Ophelia*, 44.

68. Trethewey, *Bellocq's Ophelia*, 43.

69. Trethewey, *Bellocq's Ophelia*, 27.

70. Trethewey, 2 *Bellocq's Ophelia*, 7.

71. Pereira, "Re-reading Natasha Trethewey," 123.

72. Trethewey, *Bellocq's Ophelia*, 27.

73. Trethewey, *Bellocq's Ophelia*, 44.

74. Trethewey, *Bellocq's Ophelia*, 33.

75. Marc McKee, "A Conversation with Natasha Trethewey," in *Conversations with Natasha Trethewey*, ed. Joan Wylie Hall (Jackson: University Press of Mississippi, 2013), 138.

76. Haney, "A Conversation," 23.

77. Trethewey, *Bellocq's Ophelia*, 46.

78. Haney, "A Conversation," in *Conversations*, 23.

79. Haney, "A Conversation," 23.

80. Pereira, "Re-reading Natasha Trethewey," 136.

81. Trethewey, *Bellocq's Ophelia*, 3.

82. Henninger, *Ordering the Façade*, 172.

83. Trethewey, *Bellocq's Ophelia*, 47.

84. Trethewey, *Bellocq's Ophelia*, 47.

85. Trethewey, *Bellocq's Ophelia*, 47.

13

"BECAUSE WE NEED TO HURT IN PUBLIC"
Embodying the Spectacle of Hurricane Katrina's Black Suffering in Patricia Smith's *Blood Dazzler*

Shanna M. Salinas

The chaos of Hurricane Katrina is perfectly captured in Patricia Smith's poem "Up on the Roof," which depicts the familiar image of residents stranded atop their homes awaiting rescue: "*Up on the roof, stumbling slickstep, you wave all your sheets and your blouses, / Towels, bandannas, and denims, and etch what you ask on the morning: / When are they coming to save us? Cause sinking is all that you're feeling. / Blades spin so close to your breathing. Their noise, crazy roar, eats invective, / blotting out words as you scream them. They turn your beseeching into vapor.*"[1] The "noise, crazy roar" of the helicopters overhead subsumes the voices of those screaming for help: "blotting out words as you scream them."[2] Those helicopters are a mixture of rescue helicopters and media, with the latter framing the Black body in distress as the center of the spectacle: "Cameras obsess with your chaos. Now think of how America sees you: / Gold in your molars and earlobes. Your naps knotted, craving a brushing."[3] This "chaos" isn't simply the localized disaster created by Katrina; it's a personal chaos experienced by the poetic speaker who understands her body is being witnessed—and broadcast—at its most vulnerable. However, in this instance, hers isn't only a singular, individuated body, but transformed as site and *sight* for the projected representative visual for all Black bodies in distress: "Then mud cracks its script on your forearm, / each word a misspelled agenda."[4] The media coverage of Katrina's Black bodies in distress is likened to a script marked upon the body itself; or, in other words, a "misspelled agenda" that represents the way in which the Black body is seen, considered, and produced in accordance with an existing national construct.

In this paper, I explore the tension between the individuated Black body in despair and the conceptual Black body as abandoned by the national body politic, informed by Harvey Young's theorization as to how "spectacular events" conscript and inform an understanding of Blackness. Thusly, Hurricane Katrina is understood as one such spectacular event, or what Nicole Fleetwood refers to as a "weather media event" predominantly comprised by "images of suffering, emoting, and abandoned Black bodies in the floodwaters of New Orleans."[5] Within this framework, I analyze Patricia Smith's presentation of Black embodiment as contingent upon the spectacle of public suffering. Her persona poems in *Blood Dazzler*, wherein otherwise non-corporeal entities like New Orleans, Hurricane Betsy, Hurricane Katrina, and the Superdome are given voice and become embodied presences, aid Smith's emphasis on the sociohistorical constructs that determine the particular valences of visibility projected onto Black bodies. I examine Smith's representation of bodies—the victims and the survivors of Katrina's "chaos"—and embodiment—Katrina's "eye"/I as one that sees the destruction she wreaks upon New Orleans and its inhabitants—as both sites, and sights, of visible suffering. The crux of my argument centers Young's notion of "compulsory visibility" via the way Smith depicts the sensationalizing spectacle of the media's coverage, and ultimately how she attempts to redirect the reader and/or listener's gaze beyond the spectacle itself, to the way that Black bodies are compelled to perform discursive Blackness.

Smith, a four-time National Poetry Slam champion and National Book Award Finalist for *Blood Dazzler*, writes poems that are "written to be spoken and performed."[6] As a spoken-word poet, or in delivering her work at poetry readings, she uses her voice and body to enliven her poems and poetic speakers. In "Performing the Poet, Reading (to) the Audience," Julia Novak extends Anthony Howell's analysis of a performance artist's "performance self," or the projection of a created persona through the performer's body, to what she terms the "poet-performer's" delivery of a poem.[7] For Novak, poets use their bodies in a way similar to actors or performance artists, in that meaning is created through the poet's delivery, voice inflection, and enacted embodiment as much as through the content of the poem. In analyzing Smith's reading of "Skinhead," a poem not included in *Blood Dazzler*, Novak states that Smith "draws on the incongruity and tension between her own ethnic identity and that of her poem's self-righteous speaker, as well as on the effect of authentification produced by her presence in the performance."[8] The striking contrast between the poetic speaker (white male) and Smith (Black female) forces the audience to focus on Smith's Black body while she inhabits the "I" of the white supremacist's perspective. This move adds heightened resonance to the racial slurs used in the poem, and likewise compels the audience, in turn, to contend with Smith's racialized body accordingly. Extending this framework to *Blood Dazzler*, the irrefutability of Black embodiment becomes crucial to the performative reconstitution of the people and bodies she depicts in her persona poems; she forces us to consider how the spectacle of the racialized Black body was constructed by the media's representation of abandoned Black residents during their Katrina coverage.

The impetus for what would eventually become *Blood Dazzler* initially began with one poem, "34," a series of thirty-four brief, sequentially numbered persona poems told from the perspective of the thirty-four elderly residents found dead in an assisted living facility after they were abandoned by employees. These individual poetic speakers give voice to their respective experiences, as well as to a collective experience of abandonment and fear during and after Hurricane Katrina touched down in New Orleans: "They left us. Me. Him. Our crinkled hands. / They left our hard histories, our gone children and storytells."[9] These poems present a wide gamut of emotions, as each resident confronts the horror of abandonment on an individualized experiential level. In the fifth poem, the unnamed poetic speaker reflects on the family that never visits: "See what they have done, / how hard and sweet they done dropped me here?"[10] This emotional devastation is echoed by Resident 7, this time in relation to the abandonment felt across various vectors of "home"—St. Rita's Nursing Home, New Orleans, and the United States—all of which decree the nursing home residents as not worth saving: "We knew we had been bred for sacrifice, / . . . / We are prepared. / We are wrapped in white."[11] Some residents are defiant: "I ain't scared of no wet, no wave. I done seen more than this."[12] Others, like in poem 18, are silenced, left completely blank, presumably because this resident has already drowned. These bodies are so plentiful that they become a force within the water, as one resident's only line relays: "A sudden ocean of everyone's shoulders."[13] Smith attempts to reproduce the sensations and emotions to which we, as a viewing audience, were not privy, in spite of the fact that St. Rita's flooding was one of the most prominent news stories during the Katrina coverage.

By capturing the immediacy of the moment, Smith presents Katrina, specifically the innumerable issues that both produced and were produced from the "weather media event," as firmly rooted in the present.

During interviews, Smith regularly discusses how audiences at poetry readings would respond to "34," specifically citing a conversation she had with a woman firmly invested in the then-current media narrative of post-Katrina recovery:

> "Well . . . uh . . . they just had Mardi Gras, didn't they? Things are better now. I mean, I saw some pictures on CNN." It was at that moment that I realized that not everyone felt it necessary to process the horrors of Hurricane Katrina. For some it remained a pesky, persistent scar, wrecking the sleek American landscape. Time had passed. This story was best filed away. Since New Orleans and the surrounding devastated region were seldom in the news anymore, people who felt that way were no longer forced to look closely at what had happened, at what was still happening. They refused to hear poor people, tossed out of cramped trailers, begging their country to notice. They no longer chose to notice anything outside the sad, manufactured gaiety of the French Quarter. They didn't want to be reminded of our country's gross ineptitude, or listen again to the mumbled apologies of a clueless leader. There were those who refused to acknowledge a stark reality—an era, indeed, an entire culture, had been sacrificed to the water. That's when I decided to keep writing.[14]

In the time that had elapsed, the media had moved on: New Orleans was no longer submerged in water, but there were still people abandoned and in distress. The media shifted from centering the spectacle of Black suffering to an erasure of the residual materiality of that suffering. The so-deemed "post-Katrina" New Orleans was seen as a space of recovery due to the news focus on Mardi Gras and the careful avoidance of the devastation that exists outside the route perimeter. However, the images of Black bodies in distress are not only the absent presence undergirding this coverage, but a wholly necessary lingering specter, for it is the trace of these images that sustain the image of New Orleans as a newfound site of recovery. It is within this juxtaposition of the seen and the unseen that Smith's poems work to reconstitute visibility and to reconstruct the media spectacle.

In an interview with *The Writers' Block*, Smith acknowledges that the media coverage of Katrina was the primary, centralized way most people, herself

Hurricane Katrina's Black Suffering in Smith's *Blood Dazzler*

included, were able to access information about what was happening in the Gulf region, saying, "the majority of people experienced Katrina exactly the way I did: in front of their computers, in front of their television sets, through newspapers."[15] The fact that many of Smith's poems were borne from the discarded details and images produced by field reporters in New Orleans whose stories were deemed "too graphic" for publication (her husband was an Associated Press editor at the time), position *Blood Dazzler* as mediated through mainstream news coverage, but not fully operational within its representation.[16] The space in which Smith's poems operate—simultaneously informed by media coverage while representing the seen and *unseen* aspects of specularized Katrina—speaks to the need to resee what has been presented, the way in which images of Black bodies in distress have become synonymous with Hurricane Katrina. Fleetwood's "weather media event," which can be understood as a "media process of production and as a discursive tool by which particular narratives are naturalized and certain bodies made vulnerable," underscores the way in which media function discursively, as both products and producers, to reify dominant national investments around race and class.[17] Katrina's discursivity is locatable through Fleetwood's turn to Michael Ignatieff's analysis of the New Orleans Convention Center, which he describes as a "dumping ground for housing a group of displaced subjects, or 'body objects.'"[18] New Orleans's citizens, whose abandonment and suffering were on full display to the viewing public, became part and parcel of the storm's aftermath: the surviving remnants amidst the devastation, yet discarded by the body politic. These "body objects" are within and without the US, undeniably marked as a disposable populace, but ultimately necessary to a national disaster narrative that requires destruction and despair. As such, the entirety of New Orleans becomes an extension of the convention center, an expansive site of body objects, most notably centered on, and through, the Lower Ninth Ward, which likewise becomes sign and symbol for Katrina itself.

The concentrated media attention on devastation and suffering situates the predominantly black and at-risk Lower Ninth Ward as the locus for their coverage. Primarily oscillating between the submerged Lower Ninth Ward, the horrors of the Superdome and convention center, and those stranded on Interstate 10, Katrina is rendered by and constituted through these suffering Black residents, or, more precisely, through the discursive power of the Black body in despair that is projected nationally. In *Embodying Black Experience: Stillness, Critical Memory, and the Black Body*, Harvey Young turns to performance theory in order to delineate the racialization of Blackness within historically formative, and *performative*, moments, contending that the "black body appears as a discursive practice employed within a particular setting or situation."[19] Young contends that such Blackness is staged through "spectacular events," wherein the "black body, whether on the auction block, the American plantation, hanged from a lightpole as part of a lynching ritual, attacked by police dogs within the civil rights era, or staged as a 'criminal body' by contemporary law enforcement and judicial systems, is a body that has been forced into the public spotlight and given a compulsory visibility. *It has been made to be given to be seen.*"[20] The spectacular event, in this case, the broadcasting of Hurricane Katrina and its impact on Black residents in New Orleans, scripts and *conscripts* Blackness as a "compulsory visibility" in accordance with the overriding gaze of Blackness-in-despair. While there is a distinction between actual, individuated bodies and the conceptual Black body, these are, ultimately, mutually constitutive entities, relying on one another for solvency and meaning. In other words, debased conceptual Blackness is attenuated through individuated suffering by Black bodies, the visibility of which becomes suffused across Black bodies on a national scale. In turn, the media coverage of Katrina represents not only Blackness at a particular location (the Lower Ninth Ward) and within a particular geographical territory (New Orleans), but by and within the national imaginary itself: a directed gaze that suspends and animates Blackness as universally monolithic and applicable, but made manifest by individuated bodies.

The ubiquity of the spectacle of suffering associated with the coverage of Katrina has led some critics to accuse Smith of participating within this discursive representative practice in depicting Katrina's impact on New Orleans and its residents. In "A Poetics of Disaster: Katrina in Poetry, Poetry After Katrina," Brad Richard characterizes Smith's *Blood Dazzler*, specifically stanza 15 in her most celebrated poem, "34," as participating in the exploitative spectacle of suffering: "Instead of evoking the horror of this scene, as she beautifully did with the corpse in 'Give Me My Name,' Smith exploits it in order to call attention to the poem's performance of emotion. It's what she does through most of the book: she carpetbags our grief."[21] That Richard references carpetbaggers—an allusion to the view held by southerners during the post–Civil War Reconstruction era that northerners were moving South, encroaching in this now-Union territory, in order to rob southerners of what little wealth and power remained—in his assessment of Smith, a

Chicago-born poet, writing first-person poetry from the perspective of New Orleaners, in effect, suggests that Smith is an interloper who exploits New Orleans for her own personal advancement. Richard furthers this assessment by claiming Smith "also carpetbags the very idea of New Orleans" through a "tourist's experience of the city" that "sentimentally satirizes a certain kind of French Quarter experience [and] gives us something akin to 'Poets Gone Wild: New Orleans.'"[22] While not discounting a particular entitlement by Richard to stake territorial claim over New Orleans as a native resident, or to the trauma and grief he and other residents experienced, the entirety of his critique seems to be centered on Smith's status as an outsider who repackages clichés about New Orleans as "nothing but a party town where you can do any dumb drunken thing you want—laissez le bon temps and all that. That's not just unimaginative, it's insulting"; however, he fails to consider that perhaps Smith uses this tourist cliché as a purposeful entry point for her narrative strategy precisely because she's *not* a native. In this poem, "Why New Orleans Is," we enter the city as tourists, with our expected preconceptions about the space. Smith represents New Orleans as the majority of nonnatives view the city: based upon how it has been constructed and marketed as a site for tourists, and in which New Orleans fully contributes in securing. As Kris Macomber, Christine Mallinson, and Elizabeth Seale detail in "'Katrina That Bitch' Hegemonic Representations of Women's Sexuality on Hurricane Katrina Souvenir T-Shirts," Decatur Street stores offered mementos emblazoned with slogans like "Katrina Gave Me a Blow Job I'll Never Forget" and "Girls Gone Wild" with hurricane radar images, labeled Katrina and Rita respectively, and "positioned like breasts on the front of the t-shirt" a mere seven months after Katrina hit the city.[23] In effect, these souvenirs play up New Orleans as the "Big Easy" and emphasize Mardi Gras's "hedonistic party scene" reputation for profit as a component of its post-Katrina recovery narrative.

To this end, I argue that Smith appeals to the readers' overriding knowledge of New Orleans as a seductive party-destination in order to stress the stark contrast between this image and the dominant discourses constructed by the media specularization of Katrina. She, like others, exposes what isn't visible within the overriding construct of visibility. In "'We Know This Place': Neoliberal Racial Regimes and the Katrina Circumstance," Jordan T. Camp analyzes the "mass mediated cultural outlets [that create] manufactured images, narratives, and imaginaries of the Black poor as either hapless victims or the source of the social problems they endured."[24] The post-Katrina response was one of recollection and recovery, not only in terms of material conditions and psychological recuperation, but in representation as well: "In New Orleans, artists, activists, and theorists at the grassroots draw on collective memories of past social conflicts to challenge the hypervisibility of racialized and gendered poverty, violence, and misery."[25] As such, Smith draws upon the collective memory of those who witnessed Katrina through the media, as she states in an interview: "I wanted something that was as accessible as possible to everyone who experienced it." By using what she termed "touch-points" of recognition from media coverage, Smith tries "to put the reader or listener in the midst of the experience instead of sitting back and being like a casual observer."[26] As viewers, we, the national and international audience, are all participants, not merely observers. Smith implicates us, her audience, as complicit with how Katrina was viewed, because we were its viewers. It is from this position that Smith compels us to interrogate what we have seen.

From this vantage point—a revisitation of the "weather media event" through recollection, or re-collection—Smith begins the spectacle anew, but this time she firmly places the reader or listener in a position to be a reobserver through a very purposefully constructed narrative arc anchored, initially, through updates from news forecasts that frame Hurricane Katrina's emergence. In "5 p.m., Tuesday, August 23, 2005," Smith presents the weather predictions—with an epigraph from National Hurricane Center—prior to the introduction of Katrina as a poetic speaker. This introduction centers the formation of the weather center as a vocal counterpoint to Katrina's consciousness. In this poem, Smith introduces us to the time, date, and point of origin of the storm, "over southeastern Bahamas [which] has become organized enough to be classified as a tropical depression twelve" to stage Katrina's concurrent development: "A muted thread of gray light, hovering ocean, / becomes throat, pulls in wriggle, anemone, kelp, / widens with the want of it. I become / a mouth, thrashing hair, an overdone eye."[27] Smith continues this approach in the opening four poems to trace Katrina's growing strength and force—from "tropical depression," to "tropical storm," to "Hurricane Katrina"—which finds the eye of the storm moving closer to New Orleans, in "5 p.m., Thursday, August 25, 2005": "My eye takes in so much— / what it craves, what I never hoped to see."[28] The "eye" of Katrina compels her closer to landfall, where her vision of the scene is positioned as compulsory: "the eye / pushes my rumbling bulk forward, / urges me to see

/ what it sees."[29] The center force of the storm, the "eye" becomes the seeing mechanism through which she witnesses her own increasing power. By "8 a.m., Sunday, August 28, 2005," Katrina is at her strongest, a category 5, and has already struck Florida; she is "[n]ow officially a bitch," who is ready for the notoriety of her status and spreading fear: "So I huff a huge sulk, thrust out my chest, / open wide my solo swallowing eye."[30] By positioning the storm through Katrina's "eye"/ "I," Smith "urges [us] to see" with Katrina's gaze instead of solely our own.

Katrina's "solo swallowing eye" finally leads her to New Orleans in "She Sees What It Sees," which likewise introduces the point of destruction in the first lines of the poem: "And the levees crackled, / and baptism rushed through the ward."[31] That poem is juxtaposed with the one that follows, "What Was the First Sound," which signals the "sound" as the clamoring break of the sky and the levees, "heaven's seam splitting."[32] Once again, Smith's consideration is viewed through Katrina's eye, or "gaze": "Under August drape, / Miss Katrina's swollen gaze / Considered bodies. / Consider bodies, / Already filled with water / but secure in bone."[33] Smith's nonce form in this poem relies on tercets, with the last line of the stanza repeated as the first line in the next stanza. While it bears similarities to a villanelle and a pantoum, it conforms to neither. Moreover, Smith breaks her form in the last stanza, which expands by incorporating modified versions of previous lines: "To the first plops of rain, / add the sound of purple, / shitted bricks losing bone, / the seam splitting and finally spilling / bodies / already filled with water."[34] This stanza form duplicates the content: expansion to the point of rupture, with the fourth line serving as a stand-in for the now too-full levee. Much like the levee breaks and spills flood waters into New Orleans, similarly, the stanza's break ushers in death, with this initial spillage of bodies at the end of the poem seeping into the resulting poems.

While Smith initially portrays Katrina as the centralized cause of the death and destruction, Smith shifts focus to the culpability of media and governmental failures. Katrina may represent the force of that destruction, but she isn't the cause of suffering. In "Man on the TV Say," residents of New Orleans watch the evacuation orders: "On the wall behind him, there's a moving picture / of the sky dripping something worse than rain. / *Go*, he say. Pick up y'all black asses and run."[35] The difficulty of movement out of New Orleans is presented as a call-and-response between the voice of the news anchor and the counter-response to the invective "Go" by the poetic speaker: "*Go*. Uh-huh.

Like our bodies got wheels and gas."[36] The biggest criticisms of governmental agencies in the aftermath of the storm involved the procedural measures in place for evacuation, rescue, and triage. While mandatory, the evacuation failed to consider those not in a position to leave without assistance, whether medical or financial. The difficulty of leaving is beyond the economic disadvantages of those without a car, or those physically unable to leave, but also includes the psychological struggle involved in leaving the only home some residents have ever known: "*Get on out.* Can't he see that our bodies / are just our bodies, tied to what we know?"[37] These residents' bodies are linked to their homes and the city proper: anchored to a place through history. Smith emphasizes this fact by pairing this poem with "Only Everything I Own," where the house takes on synonymous properties with its owner: "This is my house. / This was my grandfather's house. This is my thin wood, spidered pane. / These are my cobwebs, my four walls, my silverfish, my bold roaches."[38] This image of being tethered to a place is further reinforced in the series of poems about Luther B., a dog left behind, tied to a cypress tree, as his family evacuates with the intent to return after Katrina passes.

These predicaments of these residents is further underscored through the contrast of the usage of the word "go" in "Inconvenient," which is told from the perspective and positionality of those with the means of mobility, for whom the passing storm is an inconvenient interruption to their financially-stable, able-bodies lives: "Go / What, again? What nuisance, this back and forth."[39] Their location in the city places them outside the urgency of peril; for them, Katrina's impending arrival means "missed manicures," "dull dinners / of canned soup," and nothing more serious than "wet drumming / in the flower beds, stretched nerves, maybe a hint of mold."[40] Their desire to remain in New Orleans stands in stark contrast to those depicted in the previous poems, which Smith emphasizes in the scathing critique of her closing lines, as an unnamed wife and husband depart the city: "After he slides his pampered girth behind the wheel, / we point the car toward rumored sun, scan the sky / for signs. Again, we run. Left to me, I wouldn't budge. / Up here the dollar sings. We pay for this boredom."[41] Through a comparison of those who left New Orleans versus those who decided or were forced to remain, Smith reveals a very complicated decades-long narrative of belonging and mobility, one that explains how certain residents—predominantly Black, poor, and other residents of color occupying the most at-risk areas of the city—were placed in a position of disposability.

Smith furthers her criticism by targeting those most responsible for this disparity in mobility and safety. In "What to Tweak," "Michael Brown," and "The President Flies Over," she portrays the distance of governmental officials from those in New Orleans. In "What to Tweak," Smith intersperses e-mail excerpts from Marty Bahamonde, an employee of Federal Emergency Management Agency on site in New Orleans, to his boss, Michael Brown, the head of FEMA, whose only response appears at the end of the poem: "Thanks for the update. Anything specific I need to do / or tweak?"[42] Brown, in the poem that bears his name, is described through a first-person persona poem: "I am not much / beyond button cuff."[43] Smith closes the poem with Brown stating, "I am a man, a stacker of clean paper. / Tiny storms inhale my hours."[44] After, Smith shifts her attention to President George W. Bush, who flies overhead in Air Force One, "[a]loft between heaven and them," to survey the damage. He is depicted as an entitled inheritor of the country below him: "This is my / country as it was gifted to me—victimless, vast."[45] By ending the poem with "I understand that somewhere it has rained," Smith transforms the president from entitled owner, one who reigns over—quite literally—*his* country, into an utterly clueless leader whose lack of understanding for and separation from the community-at-large makes him directly responsible for the conditions that have rained down upon its citizens.

The culpability of President Bush, and other governmental officials and agencies, are placed in conjunction with other persona poems, specifically in "Superdome," when the building, a governmentally-assigned space of triage, shelter, and support for evacuees, becomes sentient and deflects all blame for the conditions within its sanctuary: "I did not demand they wade through the overflow from toilets, / chew their own nails bloody in place of a meal."[46] Smith aligns the worried and fearful bodies inside, those not being supplied meals by FEMA, with the bodies of the government and the Superdome: "Glittering and monstrous, I was defined by man's hand, / my tight musculature coiled beneath plaster and glass. / I was never their church, although I disguised myself as shelter / and relentlessly tested their faith."[47] "Defined by man's hand" as a sporting arena, but marked as a place of safety and "shelter" by New Orleans, the Superdome's own bodily "musculature" cannot function as such. Instead, it becomes a reinforcing site that underscores any notion of enduring "faith" in the government has been misplaced, a point further reinforced in "Gettin' His Twang On," where Smith depicts Bush playing guitar with country singer Mark Willis in front of the media. Bush plays guitar for the crowd and performs for the "flashing bulbs, [. . .] in the Ninth, [as] a choking woman wails / *Look like this country done left us for dead*."[48] Cameras focus on the President while the woman's wailing becomes the unheard "soundtrack" to the media scene: "He plucks strings. We sing."[49] Smith's juxtaposition can be better understood through what Henry A. Giroux terms the "biopolitics of disposability," where he builds upon Michel Foucault's concept of biopower in an age of "hyper-neoliberalism": "The Bush administration was not simply unprepared for Hurricane Katrina as it denied the federal government alone had the resources to address catastrophic events; it actually felt no responsibility for the lives of poor blacks and others marginalized by poverty and relegated to the outskirts of society."[50] Giroux contends that, within this system, "the poor, especially people of color, have to fend for themselves in the face of life's tragedies but are also supposed to do it without being seen."[51] Smith's depiction echoes this structure: Bush as far removed from the Lower Ninth Ward, while he and all his onlookers fail to see the abandoned wailing woman. However, in this instance, I argue that neglect and disposability of Black bodies are contingent upon being seen, or to return to Harvey Young's theorization, "staged" as such.

To this end, Smith immediately contrasts the media scene with President Bush with the rescue effort of the stranded resident that serves as the focal point for the next poem, "Up on the Roof." Interestingly, this poem marks a point of departure from the persona poems that dominate *Blood Dazzler*. The use of second-person instead of first-person further emphasizes the distance the speaker has from her own body, which has become a stand-in for all Black bodies within this system: "Water the dark hue of anger now laps at the feet you can't stand on. / Cameras obsesses with your chaos."[52] It may be a particular individual experience, but it is a more general state of condition, according to Fleetwood: "Those desperate figures on rooftops, streets, and huddled in the Superdome and convention center were the subject(s) of death. Their morbidity and expendability circulated through the ultra-flexible portable imagine and informational technologies available to media outlets."[53] These "subject(s) of death" are put prominently on display in "Don't Drink the Water," wherein dead bodies serve as residual debris from the storm: "Some mama's body, gaseous, a dimming star splayed / and so gently spinning, threatens its own soft seams, / collides sloppily with mattresses, power lines, / shards of four-doors / On the soft / bark of an oak, H-E-L-*p*, knifed in fever. / The water's black teeth reach for the helpless vowel. / Networks deftly edit and craft this sexy glint / of sudden ocean, wait for mama's bobbing bulk / to sweetly swirl into view, framed—*now!*—by the word."[54]

In this poem, Smith depicts the media's "deftly edit[ed]" staging of this postmortem scene as calculated and strategic.[55] Unlike previous instances where residents are represented on the *verge* of death but are still able to call for assistance, the "bobbing bulk" is framed next to a plea for help as symbolic irony: this woman's helplessness is doubly imbued through the unheeded distress call carved into the tree. Smith's characterization of the sensationalistic coverage further reinforces the notion of the discursive connectivity between disposability and compulsory visibility since this dead woman has no agency whatsoever and her body is completely controlled by the flowing water in tandem with the manner in which the cameras capture and present her body to viewers. In contrast to the muddy, misspelled script marked upon the forearm of the rescued resident in "Up on the Roof," this message was presumably written either by the woman herself, or more likely by another resident. However, through editing, the media superimposes the message onto the dead woman, who is now beyond help. Smith forces our eye, quite literally, to the construct of the media's exploitation of Black bodies as a means to represent the storm's most devastating destruction; in this case, we see the tactical staging behind the most tragic aired images, where "[s]ome mama's body"—drifting alongside the mattress, downed power lines, and other wreckage and debris from the storm—is used for gravitas and viewership.[56]

The media's sensationalistic exploitation of Black bodies as equitable symbology for Katrina's destruction is even more prominently visible once the immediacy of the storm, and therefore the live disaster footage, has subsided. As a result, networks are forced to rely on replaying previous footage, through which they reproduce a narrative of disposability via a highlight reel filled with the most horrifying images: "After days of nonstop coverage of flooded New Orleans, television news organizations turned to recycling several familiar images of black suffering and survival. New media selected specific images and clips from their disaster coverage to stand in for a range of black pathos. For example, there was the repeated image of a dead elderly woman at the convention center, left in a wheelchair, covered by a plaid blanket."[57] This "dead elderly woman" was Ethel Freeman, perhaps the most enduring symbolic image of the tragedy, and to whom Smith writes and dedicates two poems, "Ethel's Sestina" and "Didn't Need No Music, Neither." Freeman and her son, Herbert, waited days for transportation in the worst of conditions; when buses finally arrived, Freeman had already died, and her son was forced to leave his mother's body behind, where it remained unmoved and unattended to for several days outside the New Orleans Convention Center. Her story was played on a veritable loop on every channel; her abandoned body was used as undeniable proof of Katrina's impact on New Orleans, as well as irrefutable evidence of the federal government's abandonment of its citizens.

Smith attempts to give Ethel Freeman her voice back, to reclaim an "I" through these persona poems, so that she isn't simply a symbol for Katrina—the "dead elderly woman" in the wheelchair—or the recycled imagistic stand-in for all Black suffering: "*Look there*, I tell my son. / He don't hear. I'm 'bout to get out this chair, / but the ghost in my legs tells me to wait, / wait for the salvation that's sho to come. / I see my savior's face 'longside that sun. / Nobody sees me running toward the sun. / Lawd, they think I done gone and fell asleep. / They don't hear *Come*."[58] Through Ethel's eyes, through her "I," Smith redirects our view away from Ethel's abandoned body in the chair. The "sun" that signals the end of the storm—and her "salvation"—isn't the bus that was supposed to take her away from the convention center, or the "son" that was forced to abandon her body for the purposes of his own survival, but Ethel's transition from her media constructed body into spirit. Smith's depiction reinscribes Ethel's body as one that can move on its own accord, from her perspective rather than a mediated image.

In effect, this move encapsulates Smith's undertaking in *Blood Dazzler*: she attempts to return a voice and an identity to the unheard and unseen. She disentangles them from the specular media control that presents them solely as disposable bodies in distress; hers is a project of recovery and reinstantiation, which is seen most definitively at work in "Give Me My Name": "A paper tag was pinned to her T-shirt / The blue blurring must have been her name. / She had died next to someone who wanted / her whole and known in the world. / Now her fingerprints slide away with the skin / of her fingers. Five days in the putrid water / have doubled her, slapped the brown light / from her body. She could be anyone now, / pudged, eyeless, oddly gray."[59] Smith literalizes this recovery project via the arduous task of identifying the dead. To most, this unnamed woman would simply represent another victim of the storm, one among the many corpses left behind after the water receded. She, like Ethel Freeman, or "[s]ome mama's body" in "Don't Drink the Water," was someone's mother, wife, or sister. Her individual importance is established by the care someone took to ensure she was "known in the world," through the name they wrote and affixed to her body. Her name, however, is made illegible by the water, seemingly reducing her to "anyone." While the name tag fails to serve its purpose, it isn't meaningless, as seen through the reaction and care extended to her by these recovery workers at the end of the poem: "No one removes her tag, its careful letters / now just flat blue smashes of spiral and line. / This is all the breath there is in the room. / It is the only thing not saying / *give her back to the water.* / It is the only thing not saying dead."[60]

A name is a declaration of identity and humanity. With no means of identification remaining after her name and fingerprints have blurred and ceased to be reliable, her body could very easily be reduced to a nameless corpse: her decaying body as indistinguishable from any of the other bodies left to fester and to rot in the water for days. Yet, there was a life before her death, which Smith underscores through the title of this poem: "Give Me My Name" is a demand, not a request, to be made "whole" again. Her unreadable name, or the "only thing not saying dead," demands that this body be recognized as living. Smith's postmortem reinstantiation of the unnamed woman's body occurs in the subtle dialogue between the poem's title and its content. The title is the only time the pronoun "my" is deployed; the entirety of the poem is focused on the third-person usage of "her." In effect, Smith recontextualizes Fleetwood's concept of the "living dead," or the state-sanctioned "annihilation" of poor communities of color, further reinforced and reinscribed through the specular framing of debasement and disposability during Hurricane Katrina.[61] Smith's living dead are those she positions as refusing to be trapped within the gaze constructed by and through Katrina's "weather media event." They are the embodied ghosts that demand to be heard and seen. They come alive again in each invocation of the "I" in Smith's performances, where her body and voice become vessel and conduit for their previously subsumed ones. Smith's dance-theater collaboration of *Blood Dazzler* with Paloma McGregor in 2010 furthers this project by using bodies and dance to perform select poems from the collection.[62] These performances resurrect these "living dead" by illustrating how their bodies are constructed and known in order for them to be reconstituted and brought to life through the dancers' bodies.

From the outside, *Blood Dazzler* immediately plays up the sensory chaos of Hurricane Katrina as evoked by the word "dazzler" in the title of her collection. Katrina, the announced "dazzler," was, in fact, a confusing, overwhelming visual spectacle of destruction and tragedy. The collection's title derives from a line in "Siblings," a modified abecedarius, in which each line of the poem begins with the name of a previous hurricane, in alphabetical order: "Arlene learned to dance backwards in heels that were too high. / Bret prayed for a shaggy mustache made of mud and hair. / Cindy just couldn't keep her windy legs together."[63] Katrina is absented until the end, when she is presented as intentionally removed by her siblings: "None of them talked about Katrina. / She was their odd sister, / the blood dazzler."[64] Smith's characterization of familial denial lends additional significance to the local and national turn to absent association with and responsibility for what happened to New Orleans and its residents both during and after the storm. Smith's title likewise extends to the multivalent associations imbued in the name Katrina as a cultural signifier, at once representative of the storm's dizzying force and upheaval as well as the unimaginably frenetic aftermath that followed. Through the trajectory of her collection, Smith attempts to slow down the dazzling chaos Katrina reaped on New Orleans, Louisiana, by emphasizing a developmental growth from the storm's inception, through the horrifying destruction it wreaked, and up to the initial poststorm recovery. This slowing-down process is crucial because it renders Katrina truly visible, via a simultaneous array of factors and perspectives. Smith denies any opportunity for the reader-listener to linger in the sites and sights of the disaster alone. She refuses to allow the fetishization of destruction, of which Black bodies have become part and parcel, to be centered. As a result, Smith guides us, the visiting tourist, through New Orleans, in order to disrupt the gaze that fixes suffering and reifies Black disposability.

Notes

1. Patricia Smith, *Blood Dazzler* (Minneapolis: Coffee House Press, 2008), 23.

2. Smith, *Blood Dazzler*, 23.

3. Smith, *Blood Dazzler*, 23.

4. Smith, *Blood Dazzler*, 23.

5. Nicole R. Fleetwood, "Failing Narratives, Initiating Technologies: Hurricane Katrina and the Production of a Weather Media Event," *American Quarterly* 58, no. 3 (September 2006): 767–89.

6. "Patricia Smith: Exploring Life Through the Poetry of Personas," *National Writing Project Resource Hub.* https://teach.nwp.org/patricia-smith-exploring-life-through-the-poetry-of-personas/

7. Julia Novak, "Performing the Poet, Reading (to) the Audience: Some Thoughts on Live Poetry as Literary Communication, *Journal of Literary Theory* 6, no. 2 (2012): 366.

8. Novak, "Performing the Poet," 369.

9. Smith, *Blood Dazzler*, 57.

10. Smith, *Blood Dazzler*, 51.

11. Smith, *Blood Dazzler*, 51–52.

12. Smith, *Blood Dazzler*, 53.

13. Smith, *Blood Dazzler*, 56.

14. David Medaris, "Wisconsin Book Festival: Patricia Smith Speaks," *Isthmus*, October 13, 2008. https://isthmus.com/arts/books/wisconsin-book-festival-2008-patricia-smith-speaks/.

15. "The Writer's Block: An Interview with Patricia Smith." YouTube, uploaded by City of Asylum, October 1, 2012, https://www.youtube.com/watch?v=odjUt1LKyxQ.

16. "The Writers' Block," City of Asylum.

17. Fleetwood, "Failing Narratives," 768.

18. Fleetwood, 769.

19. Harvey Young, *Embodying Black Experience: Stillness, Critical Memory, and the Black Body* (Ann Arbor: University of Michigan Press, 2010), 8.

20. Young, *Embodying Black Experience*, 12.

21. Brad Richard, "A Poetics of Disaster: Katrina in Poetry, Poetry after Katrina," *New Orleans Review* 36 no. 2 (2010): 177–78.

22. Richard, "Poetics of Disaster," 178.

23. Kris Macomber, Christine Mallinson, and Elizabeth Seale, "'Katrina That Bitch!' Hegemonic Representations of Women's Sexuality on Hurricane Katrina Souvenir T-Shirts," *Journal of Popular Culture* 44, no. 3 (2011): 533.

24. Jordan T. Camp, "'We Know This Place': Neoliberal Racial Regimes and the Katrina Circumstance," *American Quarterly* 61, no. 3 (September 2009): 693–94.

25. Camp, "Neoliberal Racial Regimes," 694.

26. "The Writer's Block," City of Asylum.

27. Smith, *Blood Dazzler*, 4.

28. Smith, *Blood Dazzler*, 4.

29. Smith, *Blood Dazzler*, 4.

30. Smith, *Blood Dazzler*, 11.

31. Smith, *Blood Dazzler*, 18.

32. Smith, *Blood Dazzler*, 19.

33. Smith, *Blood Dazzler*, 19.

34. Smith, *Blood Dazzler*, 20.

35. Smith, *Blood Dazzler*, 7.

36. Smith, *Blood Dazzler*, 7.

37. Smith, *Blood Dazzler*, 7.

38. Smith, *Blood Dazzler*, 8.

39. Smith, *Blood Dazzler*, 13.

40. Smith, *Blood Dazzler*, 13.

41. Smith, *Blood Dazzler*, 13.

42. Smith, *Blood Dazzler*, 28.

43. Smith, *Blood Dazzler*, 29.

44. Smith, *Blood Dazzler*, 29.

45. Smith, *Blood Dazzler*, 36.

46. Smith, *Blood Dazzler*, 40.

47. Smith, *Blood Dazzler*, 40.

48. Smith, *Blood Dazzler*, 22.

49. Smith, *Blood Dazzler*, 22.

50. Henry A. Giroux, "Reading Hurricane Katrina: Race, Class, and the Biopolitics of Disposability," *College Literature* 33, no. 3 (2006): 175.

51. Giroux, "Reading Hurricane Katrina," 175.

52. Smith, *Blood Dazzler*, 23.

53. Fleetwood, "Failing Narratives, Initiating Technologies," 781.

54. Smith, *Blood Dazzler*, 33–34.

55. Smith, *Blood Dazzler*, 34.

56. Smith, *Blood Dazzler*, 23.

57. Fleetwood, "Failing Narratives, Initiating Technologies," 775.

58. Smith, *Blood Dazzler*, 46.

59. Smith, *Blood Dazzler*, 74.

60. Smith, *Blood Dazzler*, 74.

61. Fleetwood, "Failing Narratives, Initiating Technologies," 770.

62. "Blood Dazzler @ Harlem Stage." YouTube, uploaded by Harlem Stage, December 3, 2010, https://www.youtube.com/watch?v=luWEmr_F6rE.

63. Smith, *Blood Dazzler*, 75.

64. Smith, *Blood Dazzler*, 75.

ABOUT THE CONTRIBUTORS

Ruth R. Caillouet is the Innovative Assessment Coordinator at the Louisiana Department of Education. After twenty years teaching secondary English in Louisiana public schools, she taught university English courses and trained future teachers. Her research varies from the novels of Toni Morrison, YA and LGBTQI literature, to *Buffy the Vampire Slayer*.

Originally from New Orleans, **Mary C. Carruth** is an associate professor of English at Southern University and A&M College in Baton Rouge, LA. Before returning to her original discipline, English, she served as the assistant director of women's studies at the University of Georgia and then as the director of the Sarah Isom Center for Women and Gender Studies at the University of Mississippi. In 2006, she edited a critical collection, *Feminist Interventions in Early American Studies* (UP of Alabama), which includes her essay on Mary Rowlandson's representation of the body. More recently, she has published articles or presented papers on Anne Bradstreet, Anne Hutchinson, Kenneth Burke, Frank X Walker, and Suzan-Lori Parks. Her interests include life-writings, American and women's literatures, feminist theories, critical pedagogy, and women's and gender studies.

Coeditor and contributor **Nancy Dixon** is an associate professor and chair of English at Dillard University, where she teaches all levels writing and literature courses, including New Orleans, American, and African American literature. She is the editor of the 2013 collection: *N.O. Lit.: 200 Years of New Orleans Literature*, published by Lavender Ink, and more recently of the city's official Tricentennial Anthology, *New Orleans & the World*, published by the Louisiana Endowment for the Humanities in 2017. She has been writing and publishing books and articles on New Orleans and Louisiana writers and literature for over twenty-five years.

Kathleen Downes is a visiting assistant professor at Misericordia University in Dallas, Pennsylvania. Her research and teaching interests focus on medical rhetoric in nineteenth-century American literature and the interdisciplinary study of medicine and the humanities.

Edward J. Dupuy has published several critical articles and reviews, and some poetry. He is the author of *Autobiography in Walker Percy: Repetition, Recovery, and Redemption*. He held various executive positions at a variety of colleges before he retired in 2018 to follow his spouse, Jan Fluitt-Dupuy, to Abu Dhabi, UAE, where they lived for four years. He writes, reads, and cohosts, with Gene Beyt, the podcast *Studio Aesculapius*.

Shari Evans is associate professor of English at the University of Massachusetts Dartmouth. Her work focuses on trauma, memory, and strategies of forgetting and remembering in multiethnic contemporary women's writing; space, gender, ethics, and feminist concepts of "home"; and pedagogy.

Carina Evans Hoffpauir, current Dean of English at American River College, focuses on the complexities of race, gender, and power in literature. Her scholarship, informed by her time as faculty at American River College and Southwestern University, delves into African American literature and representations of American slavery, unearthing hidden narratives and their enduring impact. Beyond the classroom, she also has held roles in writing center administration and has advocated for equity-minded writing program development.

Paul Fess is an associate professor of English at LaGuardia Community College (City University of New York). He specializes in nineteenth-century American literature and African American literature. He is currently working on a book project that examines how music structured the politics and literature of race, enslavement, and citizenship from the US abolitionist movement of the 1840s and 1850s to the end of the Civil War. He has served as a faculty fellow with the Center for Place, Culture, and Politics at the Graduate Center and as ACLS/Mellon Community College Fellow.

About the Contributors

Leslie Petty, coeditor of *Voices and Visions*, is professor of English and T. K. Young Chair of English Literature at Rhodes College in Memphis, Tennessee. She is also the Executive Coordinator for the American Literature Association. Her research primarily focuses on the intersection of first wave feminism and late nineteenth and early twentieth century American literature. Her recent work appears in journals such as *Legacy* and *Studies in the American Short Story*.

Heidi Podlasli-Labrenz is senior lecturer of American Studies. She has taught at Ball State University in Indiana, USA, and the University of Bremen, Germany. Her research interests include Black American women's literature, the short fiction of Canadian writer Alice Munro, and, primarily, the literary work of Kate Chopin. A member of the Kate Chopin International Society, she is responsible for the German bibliography on the website of the organization. Her book-length study which investigates the impact of nineteenth-century German women writers on Chopin's work and her contribution to a compendium which focuses on the global perspectives in Chopin's writings will be published by Bloomsbury.

Tierney S. Powell (she/her) is W. Ann and Rachel Reynolds Fellow and PhD candidate in theDepartment of English at University of Illinois Chicago.

Shanna M. Salinas is an associate professor of English and cochair of Critical Ethnic Studies at Kalamazoo College, where she teaches nineteenth-, twentieth-, and twenty-first century US literature, with an emphasis on race and ethnicity and a specialization in Chicana/o/x literature. Her work can be read in *Transnational Chicanx Perspectives on Ana Castillo*, *Studies in American Fiction*, and *Critical Insights: Virginia Woolf and 20th Century Women Writers*.

Matthew Teutsch is the director of the Lillian E. Smith Center at Piedmont University. He is the editor of *Rediscovering Frank Yerby: Critical Essays* (UPM 2020), and he maintains *Interminable Rambling*, a blog of literature, culture, and pedagogy.

Marcus Charles Tribbett is general editor of the *Arkansas Review: A Journal of Delta Studies*, an academic and creative materials journal in the humanities and social sciences that is focused on the seven states of the Mississippi River Delta region. He is associate professor of English at Arkansas State University, where he also teaches for the interdisciplinary Heritage Studies doctoral program. He has published scholarly work on blues performers, on a nineteenth-century slave narrative, and most recently on contemporary novels by Jesmyn Ward and Tupelo Hassman. Formerly a working musician, he lives with his family in Jonesboro, Arkansas, and enjoys listening to and playing music avocationally.

INDEX

abolitionism, 17–21, 23, 28, 34, 68, 140; in Martin R. Delany's activism and writings, 13–15, 17, 20–25, 28, 30–31, 34

acclimatization, 39, 41–46, 48–49, 52–53

activism, 32–33, 159n54, 220; and Martin Delany's work, 13–16, 20–25, 31–33

Adams, Jessica, 199, 203

Adams, John Quincy, 30

Adams, Thomas Jessen, 171

Adams, Vincanne, 170

African Methodist Episcopal church, 34

agency, 10, 98, 160, 164, 184, 186–87, 225; female, 9, 50–53, 56, 65–69, 73, 75–86, 87n29, 204, 207; racial, 9, 17, 19–21, 24–27, 31, 33–34, 56, 65–69, 160–61

Algiers, 108

Allen, William Rodney, 132n8

American Literature Association, 3

American Planning Association, 155, 159n51

Ammons, Elizabeth, 58, 59

Anderson, Sherwood, 127–28

Anglo-African Magazine, 15, 34n1

annexation, 21–24

audio verité, 8, 160–69

Bahamonde, Marty, 223

Baldwin, James, 181

Barlow, William, 161

Baronne Street, 28

Barthes, Roland, 198, 204

Basin Street, 198, 205

Battle of New Orleans, 30, 150

Baudelaire, Charles, 148

Bay, Mia, 91

Bayou St. John, 110

Beer, Janet, 72, 78, 83–85

Bell, Caryn Cossé, 29

Belle Isle, 122

Belleville Court, 110

Bellocq, E. J., 9, 198–99, 201–4, 207, 209

Bennett, Tony, 161

Béranger, Pierre-Jean de, 138

betweenness. *See* "in between"

Beyoncé, 5, 56–57, 69

Bibb, Henry, 19

"bifurcation of the self," 7, 120–21, 131. *See also* "in between"

biracialism, 9, 62, 91–102, 129–31, 137–44, 199–209. *See also* octoroons; quadroons

Birnbaum, Michelle, 58

Black Lives Matter, 4, 155

Blanc, Antoine, 139–40

blues, 8, 160–70, 172–76, 190, 194

Boas, Franz, 91, 107

Boggs, Ray, 161

Boise, Jean, 137

Boise, Louis, 137

Bonaparte, Napoleon, 38, 140

Bonner, Thomas, 72

Bourbon Street, 115, 119, 154

Boyd, Valerie, 106, 111

Brown, Henry Billings, 200

Brown, Michael, 223

Bryant, Violet Harrington, 180

Buchanan, James, 23
Bush, George W., 170, 223–24
Byerman, Keith, 98–99

Cabildo, 110
Cable, George Washington, 5–6, 39, 47–49, 53, 54n21, 90–99, 101–2
Camp, Jordan T., 219
Canal Street, 78, 84
Carondelet Street, 126
Carrollton, 33
caste, 52, 60; race as, 6, 91–102
Catholicism, 3, 7, 41, 82, 122, 129, 139–44, 180–81
Center for Constitutional Rights, 175
Charity Hospital, 170–71
Charleston, 23, 26, 127
Chartres Street, 27, 79
Cheever, John, 121
Chesnut, Mary Boykin, 68
Chesnutt, Charles, 6, 90–93, 96–102
Chicago, 123, 126, 128, 130, 147, 157n5, 167, 219
Chiles, Katy, 21
Chopin, Kate, 5–6, 56–65, 68–69, 72–86, 105–6
Chopin, Oscar, 80, 105
Civil War, 7, 30, 33–34, 47, 57, 59, 67
Clark, Emily, 200
Coles, Robert, 132n8
Collins, Carvel, 116
colonialism, 7–8, 40, 146–56, 156n3, 157n6, 157n26, 158n31, 158n43, 199, 202
Colophon, 96
Comité de Citoyens, 59
"community of narrative/narrative of community," 180–81, 183, 195
Congo, Louis, 186–87
consumerism, 8, 120, 123–24, 131, 160, 163, 172, 203, 207
contagion, 39; moral, 5, 39, 41–47, 49, 51–53; viral, 39–45
Conti Street, 147, 150–51
Covington, 7, 119–21, 127–28, 131, 132n7
Creek Nation, 7–8, 146, 148–49, 151–54. *See also* Muscogee Nation
Creoles, 4, 9, 47, 60, 91–92, 110, 122, 137–38, 145n28, 198; as authors, 7, 137–44; as depicted in literature, 7, 27, 30, 39, 42–53, 57, 60–62, 91, 94–102, 138–44, 180–81, 186–89

Critchley, Simon, 120, 125
Cuba, 13–15, 17, 21–26, 32–33, 35n6, 151
Customhouse Street (now Iberville Street), 198

Dalcour, Pierre, 137
Dauphin, Desormes, 137
Davis, Mollie Evelyn Moore, 5, 39, 47, 49–53
Davis, Thadious, 90
Davis, Thomas E., 49
Decatur, Stephen, 150
Decatur Street, 147, 150, 219
de Certeau, Michel, 16, 27, 181, 183, 190–91
Delany, Martin R., 4, 13–18, 20–34, 34n1, 35n6, 35n17, 37n64
Desbrosses, Nelson, 137
Desiree Alliance, 175, 179n46
Desmond, John, 132n8
De Soto, Hernando, 8, 151–54, 156
Dillard University, 111
disease, 4–5, 39. *See also* contagion: viral; yellow fever
Doolen, Andy, 15
Douglass, Frederick, 15, 18–20, 35n17
Downey, Arthur T., 36n48
Duffy, John, 41, 43
Dumas, Alexandre, 139
Dyer, Joyce, 58

1854 National Emigration Convention, 20, 34
Elysian Fields Avenue, 130
Emerson, Ken, 37n64
Engels, Frederick, 155
English, Daylanne K., 100
Esplanade Street, 84, 119, 130
Esquire, 121
Ewell, Barbara, 78
exploitation, 43–45, 47, 129, 150–52, 155, 159n54, 160, 165–67, 173, 218–19, 225–26; racial, 9–10, 129, 143–44, 147, 218–19, 225–26; sexual, 8, 129, 143, 160, 163–66, 169, 176. *See also* colonialism; prostitution; slavery

Faubourg, 8, 16, 27, 190–93, 195
Faulkner, William, 105, 122–23
Felski, Rita, 148–49
Ferguson, SallyAnn, 96
flâneur, 86, 146, 148–49, 158n43

Fleetwood, Nicole, 214, 217, 224, 227
Foote, Stephanie, 91
Fort Pierce Chronicle, 112
Foster, Stephen, 30–31, 37n64
Foucault, Michel, 158n43, 224
Fox-Genovese, Elizabeth, 66–68
Frederick Douglass's Paper, 28
Freedmen's Bureau, 34
Freehling, William, 22
Freeman, Ethel, 225–26
Freeman, Herbert, Jr., 226
French Market, 78–79
French Quarter, 3, 108, 110, 150, 155, 166, 216, 219; as depicted in literature, 50, 79, 81, 119, 128, 140, 147, 150, 153
Frizzly Rooster, 109, 112
Fugitive Slave Act, 18–19, 21
fugitive slaves, 4, 13–14, 19

Galatoire's, 7, 112, 114–15, 117
Galton, Francis, 158n43
Garden District, 119, 127
Garon, Beth, 161
Garon, Paul, 161
Garrison, William Lloyd, 18
gender, 4, 8–9, 82, 86, 154–55, 176, 199, 215, 220; in *The Awakening*, 57–58, 65, 68; in Brenda Marie Osbey's poetry, 190–94; in *A Cabdriver's Blues*, 160, 163, 165, 168–69, 174; in Joy Harjo's poetry, 148–49, 153; in Natasha Tretheway's work, 199, 202–4, 206–7, 209; and *The Queen's Garden*, 49–53; and violence, 146, 154, 193. *See also* agency: female
gens de couleur libres, 91–92, 95, 143–44
Gentilly, 119, 123, 127
German Revolution of 1848, 5, 72, 74–76, 82, 86, 87n4
Gilroy, Paul, 20, 22
Gioia, Ted, 161
Giroux, Henry A., 224
Goeman, Mishuana, 147–48, 153, 156
Gotham, Kevin Fox, 154, 157n26
Graeber, David, 177n16
Grand Isle, 57, 59, 61, 63, 81
Gray, Francis, 199
Gunning, Sandra, 58
Gwin, Minrose, 65, 182–83

Haddox, Thomas F., 142, 144
Hahn-Hahn, Ida, 87n29
Haiti, 38, 108, 111, 138–39, 189, 200
Hale, Grace Elizabeth, 200
Hall, Stuart, 160
Harjo, Joy, 7–8, 146–56, 156n3, 157n6, 158n43
Harlem Renaissance, 90, 100, 100, 102, 107
Harper's Magazine, 128
Harvey, David, 177n16
Haywood, Deon, 173–74, 178n37, 179n46
Hearn, Lafcadio, 41–42
Heidegger, Martin, 123, 125
Hemings, Sally, 199–200
Hemingway, Ernest, 127
Henninger, Katherine, 204, 208
Hill, Steven, 172–73
Hirsch, Arnold R., 141
Hirsch, Marianne, 183, 185
Holloway, Karla F. C., 93
hoodoo, 6–7, 106–12, 117, 180–81, 189
hooks, bell, 203
Howard Association, 45
Howell, Anthony, 214
Hughes, Langston, 106–7
"Hunters of Kentucky," 29–30
Hurricane Katrina, 3, 4, 8, 69, 128, 130, 155, 159n52, 160, 169–76; in Patricia Smith's poetry, 10, 213–28
Hurston, Zora Neale, 6–7, 105–12, 114, 117

Ignatieff, Michael, 217
immigrants, 5, 18, 20–21, 41, 43, 46, 73, 99, 138; and New Orleans, 4–5, 39, 41–43, 46–49, 60, 92–97, 165, 199
"in between," 7, 119–31, 156n4
Incan peoples, 151
Indian Removal Act of 1830, 154, 156, 157n27
Indigenous peoples, 4, 7–8, 99, 146–56, 157n6, 157n27, 161. *See also individual groups*
Ishiwata, Eric, 171

Jackson, 106, 112–13
Jackson, Andrew, 8, 30, 150, 155, 157nn26–27
Jackson, Cassandra, 95
Jackson Square, 8, 150, 155, 157n26, 159n51
Jacobs, Harriet, 20
jazz, 56, 113, 129, 161
Jefferson, Martha, 199

238   Index

Jefferson, Thomas, 199
Jim Crow. *See* segregation
Johnson, Clifton, 203
Johnson, James Weldon, 102
Johnson, Lyndon B., 128
Jolivétte, Andrew J., 60
Jones, LeRoi (Amiri Baraka), 161
Journal of American Folklore, 109

Katrina. *See* Hurricane Katrina
Kennedy, Bobby, 128
Ketner, Kenneth Laine, 132n23
Kierkegaard, Søren, 124–25
King, B.B., 176
King, Martin Luther, Jr., 128
Klein, Naomi, 169–70
Kofsky, Frank, 161
Kolbenheyer, Frederick, 73

Lake Pontchartrain, 110, 119
L'Album Littéraire, Journal des Jeunes Gens, Amateurs de Littérature, 137, 140
Landau, Emily Epstein, 200–201
Landrieu, Mitchell J., 159n51
Lanusse, Armand, 137–44, 144n7
Lanusse, Numa, 137
Lara, Ana-Maurine, 201
La Revue des Colonies, 140
Larsen, Nella, 102
Laveau, Marie, 106, 108, 110
Lazo, Rodrigo, 35n6
Leclerc, Victor-Emmanuel Charles, 38
Lépouzé, Constant, 138
Les Cenelles, 7, 137–44
Levine, Lawrence, 161
Levine, Robert, 35n17
Lewald, Fanny, 77, 87n29
Lewis, Cudjo, 107
Liberator, The, 28
Lincoln, Abraham, 34
Liotau, Mirtil-Ferdinand, 137, 139
Lipsitz, George, 161–62
Logsdon, Joseph, 29, 141
Long, Alecia, 198
López, Narciso, 23–24
Lott, Eric, 31
Louisiana Native Guard, 34

Louisiana Purchase, 21, 38–41, 47, 91
Louisiana Staats-Zeitung, 5, 43
L'Ouverture, Toussaint, 38
Lovell, Anne, 170
Loving v. Virginia, 202
Lower Ninth Ward, 155, 159n52, 175, 217–18, 224
Luschei, Martin, 132n8
lynching, 60, 218

Macomber, Kris, 219
Mahogany Hall, 199
Mallinson, Christine, 219
Mammy figures, 67–68
Mardi Gras, 7, 25, 113–14, 161, 165, 175, 216, 219; as depicted in literature, 14, 25–26, 31–32, 130
Marrs, Suzanne, 112
Martine's Hand-Book of Etiquette, and Guide to True Politeness, 77
Mason, Charlotte Osgood, 106–7
"Massa's in de Cold Ground," 31
Mattox, Jake, 23
Mayhaws, The. See *Les Cenelles*
McGregor, Paloma, 227
McHaney, Pearl Amelia, 114, 116
McWilliams, Dean, 98
memory, cultural, 147–54, 175, 181–92, 194–95, 203–4, 220
Memphis, 113, 122
Meysenbug, Malwida von, 5–6, 72–78, 80–86
"middle way." *See* "in between"
Mignolo, Walter, 154
Millais, John Everett, 201–2
Miller, Floyd J., 20, 34n1
Miller, Lucky, 167
Mills, Charles, 150
Minh-ha, Trinh T., 185
Mississippi River, 13, 22, 27, 30–31, 50, 152–53, 159n54
mistress-maid dynamic, 57, 65–68, 75
Mitchell, Margaret, 67–68
Mobile, 30, 107, 127
Möhrmann, Renate, 87n29
Monteith, Sharon, 68–69
Monteleone Hotel, 3, 113

moral contagion. *See* contagion: moral
Morris, Wesley, 56
Morrison, Toni, 56, 58–59, 183–85
Muscogee Nation, 146, 149–50. *See also* Creek Nation

Nagel, James, 92
National Era, 28
neoliberalism, 8, 162, 169–73, 179n43, 224
New Orleans Convention Center, 217, 224–26
New Orleans Crescent, 28
New Orleans Justice Project, 175
New Orleans Times, 49
New Orleans University. *See* Dillard University
New York, 19–20, 100, 106–7, 113, 147, 163
New York Daily Times, 28, 33
New Yorker, 114
New York Times, 56
Nicaragua, 23
Nietzsche, Friedrich, 72–73
nihilism, 7, 120, 131, 132n8
Nolan, Elizabeth, 78
Northup, Solomon, 19, 65–66
North Star, 24, 28
Novak, Julia, 214

O'Connor, Flannery, 122–23
octoroons, 139, 141, 199, 201–7, 209
O'Flaherty, Katherine, 73
"Old Folks at Home," 30
Olmsted, Frederick Law, 28
Omi, Michael, 61
Osbey, Brenda Marie, 8–9, 180–95
Ostend Manifesto, 23

Page, Booker, 163
Paris, 72, 121, 127, 138–40
Pat O'Brien's, 112
Patterson, Orlando, 26
Peirce, Charles Sanders, 132n23
Percy, Mary Bernice Townsend ("Bunt"), 125
Percy, Walker, 7, 119–31, 132nn7–8, 132n23, 133n31, 133n45
Percy, William Alexander, 123, 125
Perdido Street, 28

Pereira, Malin, 201, 205, 207–8
Petty, Tom, 175
Piano, Doreen, 173, 178n38
Piazza, Willie V., 205
Picayune, The, 49
Pizarro, Francisco, 151
plaçage, 17, 137–44
Plácido, 14, 35n6
Plessy, Homer, 200
Plessy v. Ferguson, 59–61, 200
Populus, August, 137
postmemory, 183, 185
Poydras Street, 28
practiced place, 181, 183
Pratt, Carl, 161
Preservation Hall, 113
prostitution, 3, 42, 44, 141, 173–75, 178nn37–38; and *Bellocq's Ophelia*, 9, 198–209; in *A Cabdriver's Blues*, 8, 162–67
Protestantism, 34, 41, 92, 122

quadroons, 91–92, 110, 141, 199–200; in literature, 27, 62, 64, 92, 94, 98–101, 141–42, 205
Questi, Joanni, 137
Quitman, John, 23

race, 5, 8, 17–19, 105–6, 128–30, 147–48, 151–52, 157, 160–61, 167, 172, 178nn37–38, 186, 199–200, 202; as analyzed in George Washington Cable and Charles Chesnutt's works, 6, 47–49, 54n21, 90–102; *The Awakening's* treatment and erasure of, 5, 57–65, 68–69; in Brenda Marie Osbey's poetry, 8–9, 188, 190, 192–93; as caste, 6, 91–102; as explored in Patricia Smith's poetry, 10, 213–28; as important in Martin R. Delany's activism and writings, 4, 14–18, 23–34; in Joy Harjo's "New Orleans," 7–8, 146–56; in Natasha Trethewey's life and work, 9, 198–209; in New Orleans, 3–10, 27–34, 42, 68, 90–99, 129–31, 137–44, 145n28, 147–56, 161, 169–73, 176, 179n43, 198–200, 202, 213–28; and violence, 4, 7, 60, 95, 128–29, 146, 154, 157n27, 218; and Walker Percy, 7, 128–31; in Eudora Welty's work,

112, 114–16. *See also* biracialism; *gens de couleur libres*; Indigenous peoples; octoroons; quadroons; segregation; slavery
racism, 5, 7, 20, 26, 58, 69, 139, 144, 152, 167; as analyzed in George Washington Cable and Charles Chesnutt's works, 90–102. *See also* exploitation: racial; white supremacy
Ramsey, William M., 203
rebellions, 28–29, 32–33, 38, 73, 87n4, 138; in literary contexts, 13–14, 16, 25–33. *See also* revolutions
Reed, Walter, 40
Reizenstein, Baron Ludwig von, 5, 39, 43–47
religion, 4, 17, 32, 41, 64, 67, 82, 122, 129, 133n45, 182, 186–90. *See also* African Methodist Episcopal church; Catholicism; hoodoo; Protestantism
rememory, 183–85
revolts. *See* rebellions
revolutions, 5, 22, 38, 72, 74–76, 82, 86, 87n4, 101, 200. *See also* rebellions
Richard, Brad, 218–19
Riley, Win, 132n8
Riquet, Nicol, 137
Rivlin, Gary, 175
Roach, Joseph, 34n1
Robertson Street, 198
Rose, Chris, 174
Rosicrucians, 130
Royal Street, 114, 119, 147, 150–51

Said, Edward, 158n43
Saint-Pierre, Michel, 137, 139
Sandler, Matt, 16
Sartre, Jean-Paul, 121
Schurz, Carl, 73
scientism, 120, 123–24, 131, 132n23
Scott, James, 161, 178n20
Seale, Elizabeth, 219
segregation, 57, 59–61, 63, 65, 68–69, 90–91, 97, 131, 200, 205
Séjour, Victor, 137, 139–40
Sekula, Allan, 158n43
Seneca Nation, 147
Separate Car Act, 200
sexism, 3, 5, 160, 163–66, 169

sexuality, 10, 122, 166, 201; female, 50–53, 57, 149, 164
Seyersted, Per, 73
Shannon, Mem, 8, 160–70, 172–76, 177n14
Sheller, Mimi, 149
Sicilian Lynchings of 1891, 60
Sidran, Ben, 161
Silva Gruesz, Kirsten, 21
slavery, 4, 17–24, 30, 33, 35n6, 36n48, 38, 43–44, 93, 184–87, 199, 206; in *The Awakening*, 57–59, 61–65, 68–69; in Brenda Marie Osbey's poetry, 180–84, 186–87, 190; in Charles Chesnutt's writings, 96–97, 99, 101; in *The Grandissimes*, 47–48, 94–95; as important in Martin R. Delany's activism and writings, 13–18, 20–34; and New Orleans, 3–5, 8–10, 13–22, 24–34, 42–43, 57, 91, 101, 129, 138–39, 180–84, 187, 190, 198. *See also* abolitionism
Smethurst, James, 177n14
Smith, Neil, 154
Smith, Patricia, 10, 213–28
Somers, Dale A., 60
Southern Living, 128
spectral space, 181, 183–85, 188–89, 193, 195
St. Ann Street, 110
St. Claude, 110
St. Louis, 73, 105
St. Louis Cathedral, 3, 27, 139–40, 142
St. Louis Post Dispatch, 73
St. Louis Street, 198
Storyville, 9, 198, 200–207
Stowe, Harriet Beecher, 17–18, 35n17
St. Rita's Nursing Home, 215
Sublette, Ned, 21, 38
suffering, 42, 45–46, 193; racial, 10, 65–68, 97, 102, 213–28. *See also* trauma
Sundquist, Eric, 21
Superdome, 214, 217, 223–24
Sylva, Manuel, 137

Taylor, Helen, 80, 82–83, 85, 86
Terkel, Studs, 163, 167
Thierry, Camille, 137, 139
Third Treaty of San Ildefonso, 41
Times-Picayune, 49, 60
Tolson, Jay, 132n8

tourists, 8, 146–47, 151, 154–56, 162–72, 176, 198, 219
Trask, Benjamin, 42
trauma, 8–10, 64, 151, 173–74, 181–86, 194–95, 219. *See also* suffering
Treaty of Fontainebleau, 41
Tregle, Joseph, Jr., 41
Tremé, 110
Tretheway, Eric, 201–2
Tretheway, Natasha, 9, 198–209
Tucker, Susan, 69
Turnbough, Gwendolyn Ann, 202
Turner, Graeme, 160, 177n2
Turner, Luke, 108, 110–11
Twain, Mark, 105
Twomey, Louis, 129

"Uncle Ned," 31
University of Mississippi, 93
Urquhart Street, 110

Valcour B., 137–38
Vidal, Gore, 127
Victoria, Queen, 110
Vieux Carré. *See* French Quarter
violence, 87, 95, 130, 173–74, 206; and gender, 146, 154, 193; and race, 4, 7, 60, 95, 128–29, 146, 154, 157n27, 218; spatial, 147–56, 157n27
voodoo. *See* hoodoo

"Wade in the Water," 63
Wald, Priscilla, 38
Waldron, Ann, 112–13
Walker, William, 23–24
Walker's Appeal, 138
Wallace-Sanders, Kimberly, 67
Warren, Robert Penn, 122–23
Watts riots, 128
Weddle, Robert S., 152
Weekly Anglo-African, 33, 34n1
Welty, Eudora, 6–7, 105–6, 112–17, 122–23
white supremacy, 58, 60–61, 68, 214–15. *See also* racism
Whitman, Walt, 146, 148
Williams, Tennessee, 3, 105
Willis, Mark, 223

Wilson, Matthew, 90, 97
Winant, Howard, 61
Winters, Lisa Ze, 19
Women with a Vision (WWAV), 173, 175, 179n46
Woods, Clyde, 17
Works Progress Administration, 105–6, 111, 113

yellow fever, 5, 38–53
Young, Harvey, 214, 217–18, 224
Young, Robert, 61–62

Printed in the United States
by Baker & Taylor Publisher Services